Palgrave Studies in the History of Subcultures and Popular Music

Series Editors
Keith Gildart
University of Wolverhampton
Wolverhampton, UK

Anna Gough-Yates
University of Roehampton, London, UK

Sian Lincoln
Liverpool John Moores University, Liverpool, UK

Bill Osgerby
London Metropolitan University, London, UK

Lucy Robinson
University of Sussex, Brighton, UK

John Street
University of East Anglia, Norwich, UK

Peter Webb
University of the West of England
Bristol, UK

Matthew Worley
University of Reading, Reading, UK

From 1940s zoot-suiters and hepcats through 1950s rock 'n'rollers, beat-niks and Teddy boys; 1960s surfers,rude boys, mods, hippies and bikers; 1970s skinheads, soul boys, rastas, glam rockers, funksters and punks; on to the heavy metal, hip-hop, casual, goth, rave and clubber styles of the 1980s, 90 s, noughties and beyond, distinctive blends of fashion and music have become a defining feature of the cultural landscape. The Subcultures Network series is international in scope and designed to explore the social and political implications of subcultural forms. Youth and subcultures will be located in their historical, socio-economic and cultural context; the motivations and meanings applied to the aesthetics, actions and manifestations of youth and subculture will be assessed. The objective is to facilitate a genuinely cross-disciplinary and transnational outlet for a burgeoning area of academic study.

More information about this series at
http://www.springer.com/series/14579

Keith Gildart • Anna Gough-Yates • Sian Lincoln • Bill Osgerby •
Lucy Robinson • John Street • Peter Webb • Matthew Worley
Editors

Youth Culture and Social Change

Making a Difference by Making a Noise

palgrave
macmillan

Editors
Keith Gildart
University of Wolverhampton
Wolverhampton, UK

Anna Gough-Yates
University of Roehampton
London, UK

Sian Lincoln
Liverpool John Moores University
Liverpool, UK

Bill Osgerby
London Metropolitan University
London, UK

Lucy Robinson
University of Sussex
Brighton, UK

John Street
University of East Anglia
Norwich, UK

Peter Webb
University of the West of England
Bristol, UK

Matthew Worley
University of Reading
Reading, UK

Edited by the Subcultures Network

Palgrave Studies in the History of Subcultures and Popular Music
ISBN 978-1-137-52910-7   ISBN 978-1-137-52911-4 (eBook)
DOI 10.1057/978-1-137-52911-4

Library of Congress Control Number: 2017952705

This Palgrave Macmillan imprint is published by Springer Nature
The registered company is Macmillan Publishers Ltd.
The registered company address is: The Campus, 4 Crinan Street, London, N1 9XW, United Kingdom

For the Network by the Network

ACKNOWLEDGEMENTS

Our thanks go to the AHRC for funding the Network seminar series (2013–15) from which this book emerged. The funding allowed the Interdisciplinary Network for the Study of Subcultures, Popular Music and Social Change to extend its cross-disciplinary dialogue, engage with academic and public partners, and facilitate new research. Equally, our thanks go to all those who have joined and participated in the Network, especially those who attended the AHRC-funded events and helped put this book together.

The steering committee that oversaw the AHRC project comprised: Jon Garland, Keith Gildart, Anna Gough-Yates, Paul Hodkinson, Sian Lincoln, Bill Osgerby, Lucy Robinson, John Street, Peter Webb and Matthew Worley.

ACKNOWLEDGMENTS

CONTENTS

LIST OF FIGURES

CHAPTER 1

Introduction: Making a Difference by Making a Noise

Lucy Robinson, Keith Gildart, Anna Gough-Yates, Sian Lincoln, Bill Osgerby, John Street, Peter Webb and Matthew Worley

L. Robinson (✉)
University of Sussex, Brighton, UK, e-mail: l.robinson@sussex.ac.uk

K. Gildart
University of Wolverhampton, Wolverhampton, UK
e-mail: keith.gildart@wlv.ac.uk

A. Gough-Yates
University of Roehampton, London, UK,
e-mail: anna.gough-yates@roehampton.ac.uk

S. Lincoln
Liverpool John Moores University, Liverpool, UK, e-mail: s.lincoln@ljmu.ac.uk

B. Osgerby
London Metropolitan University, London, UK e-mail: bill@osgerby.co.uk

J. Street
University of East Anglia, Norwich, UK, e-mail: j.street@uea.ac.uk

P. Webb
University of the West of England, Bristol, UK, e-mail: Peter.Webb@uwe.ac.uk

M. Worley
University of Reading, Reading, UK, e-mail: m.worley@reading.ac.uk

© The Author(s) 2017
K. Gildart et al. (eds.), *Youth Culture and Social Change*,
Palgrave Studies in the History of Subcultures and Popular Music,
DOI 10.1057/978-1-137-52911-4_1

1

Youth Culture and Social Change maps out new ways to historicise two overlapping political responses to economic and social change: public unrest and popular culture. Throughout the 1980s young people took to the streets, whether in formal marches organised by trade unions, political groups like the Campaign for Nuclear Disarmament (CND) or Reclaim the Night, or in spontaneous, collective outbursts of disorder. Wherever young people were present in forms of protest there, too, was music. The riots of the 1980s have their own soundtrack that has formed part of the collective memory of the decade. People rocked against racism, sexism, 'the bomb' and the fragmentation of working-class communities. The popular music charts recognised the voices of protest in singers like Pauline Black, Billy Bragg, Elvis Costello, Morrissey and Paul Weller, whose songs of resistance gained both commercial and critical success.

In this book we go further than documenting the sounds of dissent. We explore how music worked as a way of making a difference. The subcultures, networks, tribes and gangs that grew around popular music provided the structures, shapes and styles needed for resistance, resilience and in some cases conformity. The chapters capture the variety of ways that we can research music as a form of protest and as a 'community' that goes beyond interpretations of sound and lyric. The contributors to this volume show how music *mattered* to consumers, participants and protestors.

Of course there is nothing new about the notion that music can be read as a form of political protest and sonic commentary on social and economic conflict. After all, if we didn't have the folk music of the nineteenth and twentieth centuries, it would have been more difficult for us to uncover such cultural-political moments as the Chartist uprisings of the 1830s and 1840s, the miners' disputes in 1898, 1921, 1926, and the industrial conflicts of the interwar period. Music is a form of political memory both as a vehicle for preserving and popularising narratives of protest, and as a soundtrack to particular events, episodes and personal feelings.

This collection takes as its starting point a similar moment from recent history where protest and popular music self-consciously converged with the market forces of the entertainment industry. We use the 1980s as a pivot between the mid-twentieth century and today, a time when academic experts were emerging, ready, willing and able to try out their new ideas of subcultural resistance on each and every expression of youth discontent. The eighties certainly provided enough examples of street-level anger, fuelled by the intermingling of politics and culture, and expressed as spectacles of dissent and division. It was there in the battles between anti-racists and the far-right, and in the riots that broke out in 1981 in major British cities (and four years later in a number of smaller towns). To do this, the book brings together a variety of accounts and methods in order to make sense of popular music related cultures from the 1950s to the present day. It moves through the urban conflicts of 1980–85 to see what they offer as a way of reading the riots of 2011 and recent concerns about 'on road', or gang culture. In the process, we hope to shed new light on the earlier period, and suggest some ways in which we might understand popular culture, rooted in the local, as a central historical driver for conflict, resistance and conformity. At the heart of these essays is the idea that although eruptions of street rioting might be the most spectacular expressions of youth disconnect, they are best understood in the longer context of slow resistance and everyday ways in which making a noise makes a difference to young people's lives.

Some of the historical comparisons have already been made for us. The riots and public disorder of 2011 emerged in the wake of student protests against tuition fees and cuts to the Educational Maintenance Allowance (EMA), a means-tested payment that went directly to students who attended further education colleges. The EMA was designed to encourage working-class students to stay on at school by alleviating the financial burden of delaying full-time work. It also worked as an incentive to punctuality and attendance. The state seemed to be retreating from its responsibility to ensure young people's education, yet becoming more interventionist in disrupting aspects of youth culture and the perceived threat of gang activity. In 2011, Mark Duggan was shot and killed by the police in Tottenham. Accusations of Duggan's gang association were used to justify his death. To some sections of the population deaths at the hands of the police severed what little trust existed between the police and the policed, particularly those subjected to everyday acts of surveillance and harassment – young people, in particular from the Black and minority ethnic communities. The same state that did not care about working-class education could seemingly sanction death at the hands of the police. The spate of rioting that followed was immediately understood through the lens and the memories of the riots under Thatcherism. Spurred by the release of official records from the period, some uncanny resonances (Royal Weddings, the Falklands War, cuts to welfare spending, the miners' strike) and a racialised discussion of security and immigration, these recent riots replayed (and rebooted) those of the 1980s.[1]

Studies of gang culture in the post-war period opened up new modes of understanding the political potential of delinquent behaviour. Historically, gangs solicited fear of young people's collective identification with place and local networks; identification which often trumped deference to authority, the aspirations of the workday week and traditional forms of working-class respectability.[2] Notable examples of such studies included work on the teddy boys of the 1950s, mods of the 1960s, and skinheads in the 1970s. Contemporary 'moral panics' around 'on road' gang culture have also been interpreted through these models of resistance and the criminalisation of young people in public.[3] If we understand what happened in the 1950s and 1980s, and how it was responded to at the time, then perhaps we will be able to unpick the work that the past does for us in the present. Importantly for this collection, it allows us to rework the role of popular culture in everyday resistance and public acts of unrest in the 1980s through to and beyond 2011.

British cities have well established traditions of unrest and rioting. But from the end of the Second World War until 1980 there were few notable uprisings (as distinct from those in the six counties of Northern Ireland). The attacks on minorities in Nottingham and Notting Hill in 1958 led to violence and prosecutions, but large-scale disruptions did not reappear until the economic and social problems of the 1970s. The violence that marred the Notting Hill Carnival in 1976 was seen as an aberration by carnival organisers, the police and the press. Discussions around unrest and challenges to the infrastructure were largely focussed on trade union activities through the 1970s, but delinquent youth, inflected by issues of race, gender and class, increasingly came to feature on the political agenda.

The post-war generation came to be defined by their refusal to reap the rewards of the post-war settlement in simple terms. Instead they took new popular cultural spaces like cinemas, clubs and concert halls, and used them to build new collective identities. For example, young girls' sexuality and romantic desires worked against the faultlines of the prescriptive literature they read. They were being sold the dream of the happy-ever-after ending, but in the process they became aware of themselves as sexual agents. It was apparent that young people did not necessarily want to do as they were told and sought to make a difference by making a noise.

The series of riots in the 1980s can be seen as an extension of these trends, and as a way of mapping longer-term cultural networks of resistance across the latter half of the twentieth century and into the present day. Popular culture – its words, sounds, spaces and identities – offered young people a form of political expression. It was not 'mere entertainment', nor was it consumerist propaganda; it was a means of articulating and resolving the contradictions of advanced capitalism.

Against a background of tightening immigration policy, the visible growth of the far-right and everyday experiences of police harassment, riotous disorder became a racialised and localised practice in Thatcher's Britain. When violent unrest broke out in the St Paul's district in Bristol in April 1980 it was originally understood as an aberration. Historians have tended to endorse this reading of events and have failed to put the riots in their historical context. In fact, academic and critical histories of the 1980s, that question the dominant narrative, are yet to be written. Social scientists have sought to measure the levels of social and economic deprivation that are assumed to justify riots, largely focussing on explaining how riots happen (and by implication how can we stop them happening)).[4] Historians of the late twentieth century have not really engaged with the wider question: What do riots mean within a continuum of resistance and resilience? Rather than seeing riots as the special moment, the explosive 'game changer', this collection situates rioting and public resistance in local cultures and networks.

A year after the Bristol disturbances in 1980, three days of serious disorder broke out in Brixton. The television cameras were there to record it all and relay it into the nation's homes. The July that followed saw violent battles between skinheads and members of the local Asian community break out in Southall. Later the same day, some areas of Liverpool 8 took to the streets; the next day Moss Side in Manchester saw rioting. Press coverage often imposed simplistic models of rioting as racialised, misreading the complexities of local identities in the process. Despite the familiar press images of Black rioters on these streets, rioters arrested in Manchester, for example, were predominantly White. By the next week riots were reported in Handsworth, Birmingham, Sheffield, Nottingham, Hull, Slough, Leeds, Bradford, Leicester, Derby, High Wycombe and Cirencester. The riots that followed certainly involved issues of race, but they were also responses to material conditions, of unemployment in a context of economic downturn and the disproportionate burden this placed on the lives of young Black men and women in particular areas.

On 15 July 1981, Brixton again erupted. 176 police officers raided eleven houses in Railton Road. This location had its own long-established history as a place where a whole variety of activists, community organisers and subcultural tribes had their bases side by side. No evidence of the suspected illegal drinking or petrol bombs was ever found. Eventually, the Metropolitan Police had to pay out £8,500 in compensation for the damage caused during the raids.[5]

In September 1985, riots broke out in the Lozells Road area of Handsworth. Some public unrest broke out in 1982, but on a far reduced scale. A shift in police tactics saw a crackdown in Handsworth in Birmingham; 150 police officers raided the Acapulco Cafe, leading to seven arrests. Other disturbances, explained at the time as 'copycat' riots, took place in Moseley, Wolverhampton, Coventry and St Pauls.[6] At 7 a.m. on 28 September, the police shot Mrs Dorothy 'Cherry' Groce in the spine whilst raiding her home in Brixton looking for her son. By 6 pm that evening violent disorder had broken out in Brixton lasting for 8 hours. 724 crimes were reported, including the fire bombing of a local police station. Two days later, rioting again broke out in Liverpool 8 when four Black men were denied bail in court. A further wave erupted on 6 October, precipitated this time by the death of a mother during a police search for her son. Mrs Cynthia Jarrett, whose son Floyd Jarret, a local community worker, was stopped and arrested under suspicion of driving a stolen car, collapsed during the search. Family and police accounts of the death differed. The inquest found her death to be accidental. News spread fast and riots once more broke out.[7] During riots on the Broadwater Farm Estate, Tottenham, 20 members of the public and 223 police were injured and Police Constable Keith Blakelock was stabbed to death. The news media carried images of the slash marks in his uniform, showing each spot where he had been repeatedly knifed by numerous individuals. Questions were raised over the style of policing as the list of trigger events emerged. Tension grew in Nottingham and Plymouth. This was not just a response to increased police activity but also to the background of slow-burning fuses – unemployment, immigration, press representation and far-right activity. The riots may have been primarily about race in the way they were seen and experienced, but ethnicity intersected with class, ideas of community and understandings of place.

Like the riots of the 1980s, the riots in 2011 can be seen as acts of memorialisation and calls for justice against the police. On 4 March 2011, Mark Duggan, who lived on the Broadwater Farm Estate, was shot and killed by police after they stopped a taxi in which he was the passenger. A police officer was shot but survived. Although the police claimed that Duggan had fired a gun on the police first, there was also evidence that

Duggan was unarmed when he was shot. On the 15 March, Britain's first home-grown breakthrough rapper Smiley Culture, who had produced novelty crossover records like 'Police Officer', stabbed himself to death in extraordinary conditions during a police search of his home. The episode not only raised the spectre of deaths involving the police, but his music provided an ironic soundtrack over the next few months as unrest grew. On 26 March 2011 a march organised by the Trades Union Congress (TUC) against austerity cuts brought together student activism, grass roots resistance and heavy police tactics to ferment a perfect storm. Over 200 people were arrested in the disorder that followed.

On 6 August, a group of family members and friends of Mark Duggan and local community residents marched to Tottenham Police station to bear witness to police brutality and to demand answers to questions about the death. By the end of the day disorder had erupted not only in Tottenham, but also in Wood Green, Enfield, Hackney, Waltham Forest and Brixton. Within a week most of London was affected and riots were being reported in Liverpool, Birmingham, Nottingham, Manchester Bristol, Leeds and Huddersfield. Although events calmed down in London, other areas of the country were still experiencing riots, including Birmingham, Gloucester, Nottingham and Liverpool.[8] It is estimated that between 13 and 15 thousand people engaged in rioting or looting in four days of August 2011. The disorder has been measured as costing £50 million to police; £43.5 million to clean up; £80 million in lost business and £300 million in damage.[9] Almost 2000 individual offenders were officially identified as the cause; 462 were found guilty and 315 were sentenced. The majority of prosecutions were for burglary, violent disorder and theft.[10]

The 2011 riots were met immediately with comparisons to the unrest of the 1980s. Memories of the 1980s helped communities, commentators, politicians and the press to make sense of the events of that August. Partly this is to do with the role of popular culture, as both a form of historical work (recalling/analysing the past) and as a form of political activity in the present, as both a rallying cry and an affective community. The two periods of rioting became a measure of what had changed since the spring and summer of 1981. The stories and memories of both periods wove together in the wake of Margaret Thatcher's death and a new royal wedding. It seemed as though we were re-enacting, or re-imagining the 1980s in the second decade of the millennium. *The Guardian* and the London School of Economics (LSE) collaborated on a research project on the events of 2011, *Reading the Riots*. It noted that 'both [periods of unrest] took place while a Conservative Prime Minister grappled with the effects of global economic down turn and rising unemployment'.[11]

The death of Smiley Culture coincided with the anniversary of the death of Groce 26 years after she sustained her original injuries. From a politician's perspective, the riots of 2011 were measured against the riots in the earlier decade to criticise the present and revise the past. Paul Gilroy pointed out at the time that quantifiable indicators of inequality were worse in 2011 than they had been in the 1980s. In terms of day-to-day experiences of being stopped-and-searched by the police on the street, of disproportionate levels of unemployment, and of school exclusion, figures were all higher in 2011. And yet the comparisons between the two periods often positioned the past as explicable, if not justifiable, but not the present. We ended up in the surprising position of commentators pretty much representing the 1980s as 'good riots' and 2011 as 'bad riots'. As Evan Smith pointed out in his article 'Once as History, Twice as Farce', the comparisons with the riots of 1981 largely focused on the extent to which rioting could be 'justifiable'.[12]

So, for example, Kenneth Clarke MP was interviewed by ITV news to comment on the 2011 riots. Clarke had served as a cabinet minister throughout the 1980s. He told ITV, 'I remember riots 30 years ago, but these were very widespread, very serious and the sheer casual criminality troubles me. You know, it was almost instantly; people were responding on their BlackBerry or mobile and turning out just to loot what they wanted. There was absolutely no undertone of anything except ... criminal people, just away, going out to repeat crimes they had already been convicted of in the past. Quite outside the values of the ordinary, decent people in this country'.[13] The riots in 2011 were set up both as larger in scale and less justifiable, motivated by greed and spread like a virus through social networking technology.[14] In comparison the eighties were regarded as less about shopping and technology, and more about response to social context.

In this volume, we are less concerned with whether the contexts are (or are not) materially equivalent, but, rather, how the experiences, memories and legacies of youth are conveyed, organised and acted upon. This is why we focus first on the way riots are communicated, but also on how music informs identities and how gangs create an institutional form for action. Rather than seeing riots as moments of unrest or the result of a spectacular tipping point, this collection examines the networks, communities, shared interests and mediating role played by music and social media. Riots might be the most exciting press stories of a period, but they were just one part of an ongoing continuum of resistance and resilience that helped communities stick together, and pick up the pieces once the riot vans and news reporters had gone.

A historical view of the 'everyday' and the 'spectacular' underpins this volume. Our aim is not to explain the riots. Instead, we are asking how people are enabled to make a difference and make sense of their lives. For example, how do the emotional lives of young girls feed into the possibility of powerful political action? We want to bypass the fixation on riots as the measurement of young people's discontent, and instead connect the exceptional and the unexceptional back into everyday cultural networks and expressions. The following chapters include contributions that explore how riots occur but, as significant we feel, are the contributions that shed light on the everyday; that is, towards an understanding of young peoples' experiences as a driver and response to social change. Looking at events over a longer period allows us to reveal the processes, experiences and actions that order and shape the creation of spectacular moments from the mundane.

When we brought these different chapters together a series of themes emerged across geographical and temporal case studies. The press and politicians' argument that riots were set off by external triggers or outside agitators did not fit a recognisable narrative. Instead, the research presented here uncovers the importance of specific local networks and experience. The story of how a riot 'kicked off' was rooted in the local experiences of a place, and so were the reactions to them in the aftermath. Whether we look to the post-war youth culture or riots in the 1980s or the more recent events of 2011, the importance of pre-existing conditions and pre-existing resilience helps us to put the riot back in its place as a way of making a difference by making a noise.

Rather than pinpointing the immediate cause of extreme moments of explosion, or discovering outside agitators, or copycat mindless crowds, instead we found grass-root networks: sound systems, school catchment areas, shared club and night-time spaces, stairwells, recreation parks, street corners and bedrooms. The popular culture that emerged – spoken, sung, listened to, broadcast or sent through social media – was central to these networks. The popular culture around riots and resistance is more than an illustration of 'what happened'. The songs, poems and tweets offer more than an insight into what life felt like before, during and after those explosive movements. The popular-cultural voice is a driver in community response to the world we live in. Music builds communities, makes sense of the world and finds ways of describing, articulating, and enacting change. Music is also how these events have been memorialised. Popular culture might give us conflicted and often contradictory messages, but that is exactly why it is central to understanding public unrest.

The moments of resistance described in this collection are themselves cultural acts, they have sounds, styles and audiences, just the like songs, poems and videos made about them. Milburn and Hardie's understanding of the riots as a form of 'noise' that disrupts and changes the context is a useful way to understand disorder as a part of popular culture, and popular culture as a form of disorder. Riots have a 'rhythm of resistance'. 'Those who were part of that rhythm [are] bound by weak ties, with the result that he rhythm was mobile, highly responsive and able to grow very quickly as new people adopted, and adapted the beat'.[15] Riots have a rhythm but they are part of longer, fragmented soundtrack to young people's lives.

Fittingly this collection emerged out of its own network: the Interdisciplinary Network for the Study of Subcultures, Popular Music and Social Change. This network is not just a collection of interdisciplinary researchers, but also of the communities in which we each root ourselves. A series of events was funded by an AHRC Network Grant from 2013 to 2015, the first of which took place in Bristol. This event, which triggered many of the contributions herein, recognised the city's place in the history of rioting and popular music over the twentieth and twenty-first centuries. The symposium attempted to explore the experiences of living in British cities and growing up through an association with music subcultures or scenes. Bristol has a unique position in the history of British popular music, feeding into narratives of reggae, disco, punk, club culture and drum 'n' bass. But to start with Bristol also let us move from the local to the national. The associations between and across anxieties about public disorder, subcultural music and 'on road' associative culture all come together in the events and studies presented here. Popular culture, therefore, is not just a useful way into a political, social and economic context as academic evidence, nor is it simply a way of giving voices to the unheeded. As a structure, the network, institutions, knowledges and language of communities built around shared popular culture have been at the heart of what it feels like to make a difference by making a noise.

NOTES

1. E. Smith, 'Once as history, twice as farce? The Spectre of the summer of '81 in discourses on the August 2011 riots', *Journal for Cultural Research*, 17(2) (2013), 124–43 (Smith 2013).
2. The work of the Birmingham University Centre for Contemporary Cultural Studies was obviously integral to this. For an overview and context, see B. Osgerby, 'Subcultures, popular music and social change: Theories, issues and debates, in Subcultures Network (ed.), *Subcultures, Poplar Music and Social Change* (Cambridge, 2014), pp. 1–45 (Osgerby 2014).
3. S. Hallsworth, 'Gangland Britain? Realities, fantasies and industry', in Barry Goldson (ed), *Youth in Crisis? 'Gangs', Territory and Violence* (London, 2011), pp. 183–97 (Hallsworth 2011).
4. Notable exceptions could include J. Rex, 'The 1981 urban riots in Britain', *International Journal of Urban and Regional Research*, 6 (1982), 99–113 (Rex 1982).
5. *Hansard, House of Lords Debates*, 29 October 1981, vol. 424, cc1127–32 (Hansard 1981).
6. John Benyon and John Solomos, 'The simmering cities: Urban unrest during the Thatcher years', *Parliamentary Affairs*, 41 (3) (1988), 404 (Benyon and Solomos 1988).
7. Benyon and Solomos, 'The simmering cities', 406.
8. E. Smith, 'Once as history, twice as farce', *Guardian Shorts, Reading the Riots: Investigating England's Summer of Disorder*, 124–43 (London, 2011) (Smith 2011); D. Briggs, *The English Riots of 2011: A Summer of Discontent* (Sherfield-Upon-Lodden, 2012) (Briggs 2012).
9. Briggs, *The English Riots of 2011*, p. 10; T. Newburn, 'Reading the riots', *British Society of Criminology Newsletter*, 12 (2001).
10. Briggs, *The English Riots of 2011*, p. 14.
11. Guardian Shorts, *Reading the Riots*. T. Newburn, 'Reading the riots'.
12. Smith, 'Once as history, twice as farce', 124–43.
13. Kenneth Clarke, ITV News 15 September 2011, quoted in Briggs, *The English Riots of 2011*, pp. 11–12 (Clarke 2011).
14. S. Milne, *The Enemy Within: The Secret War Against the Miners* (London, 2004) (Milne 2004).
15. K. Milburn, 'The August riots, shock and the prohibition of thought', *Capital & Class*, 36 (3) (2012), 401–9 (Milburn 2012).

REFERENCES

John Benyon and John Solomos, 'The Simmering Cities: Urban Unrest During the Thatcher Years', *Parliamentary Affairs*, 41, 3 (1988), 404.

D. Briggs, *The English Riots of 2011: A Summer of Discontent* (Sherfield-Upon-Lodden, 2012).

Kenneth Clarke, 'ITV News', quoted in Briggs, *The English Riots of 2011*, 15 September 2011, pp. 11–12.

S. Hallsworth, 'Gangland Britain? Realities, Fantasies and Industry', in Barry Goldson (ed), *Youth in Crisis? 'Gangs', Territory and Violence* (London, 2011), pp. 183–97.

Hansard, House of Lords debates, 29 October 1981, vol. 424, cc1127–32.

K. Milburn, 'The August Riots, Shock and the Prohibition of Thought', *Capital & Class*, 36, 3 (2012), 401–9.

S. Milne, *The Enemy Within: The Secret War Against the Miners* (London, 2004).

T. Newburn, 'Reading the Riots', *British Society of Criminology Newsletter*, 12 (2001).

B. Osgerby, 'Subcultures, Popular Music and Social Change: Theories, Issues and Debates', in Subcultures Network (ed.), *Subcultures, Poplar Music and Social Change* (Cambridge, 2014), pp. 1–45.

J. Rex, 'The 1981 Urban Riots in Britain', *International Journal of Urban and Regional Research*, 6 (1982), 99–113.

Smith, 'Once as History, Twice as Farce', Guardian Shorts, in *Reading the Riots: Investigating England's Summer of Disorder* (London, 2011), pp. 124–43.

E. Smith, 'Once as History, Twice as Farce? The Spectre of the Summer of '81 in Discourses on the August 2011 riots', *Journal for Cultural Research*, 17, 2 (2013), 124–43.

Lucy Robinson is Professor of Collaborative History at the University of Sussex. She writes on popular music, politics and identity, feminism, and punk pedagogy. As well as co-ordinating the Subcultures Network, and the open access digital project Observing the 80s, she has recently advised on an exhibition on Jersey in the 1980s.

Keith Gildart is Professor of Labour History and Social History at the University of Wolverhampton and author of *Images of England through Popular Music: Class, Youth and Rock 'n' Roll, 1955–1976* (Palgrave Macmillan, 2013).

Anna Gough-Yates is Head of the Department of Media, Culture and Language at Roehampton University. Her research has focused mainly on the magazine and television industries, and has examined the ways in which the economic processes and practices of production are also phenomena with cultural meanings and effects. She has published a number of articles in this area, and is also the author of two books, *Understanding Women's Magazines: Publishing Markets and*

Readerships, and Action TV: Tough Guys, Smooth Operators and Foxy Chicks, co-edited with Bill Osgerby.

Sian Lincoln is Senior Lecturer in Media Studies at Liverpool John Moores University. Her research interests are in youth culture, private space and identity, and young people's uses of social media. Her book *Youth Culture and Private Space* was published by Palgrave Macmillian in 2012. Her work has also been published in anthologies and journals such as New Media & Society, Journal of Youth Studies, Social Media + Society, and Qualitative Research. She is co-editor of the Cinema and Youth Cultures series (Routledge) with Yannis Tzioumakis.

Bill Osgerby is Professor in Media, Culture and Communications at London Metropolitan University. His research interests focus on modern American and British media and cultural history, and has published widely in the fields of, with particular regard to, the areas of gender, sexuality, youth culture, consumption, print media, popular television, film and music. His books include *Youth in Britain Since 1945, Playboys in Paradise: Youth, Masculinity and Leisure Style in Modern America, Youth Media,* and a co-edited anthology, *Action TV: Tough-Guys, Smooth Operators and Foxy Chicks.*

John Street is Professor of Politics at the University of East Anglia, England. He is the author of several books, of which the most recent are *Music and Politics* (Polity, 2012) and (with Sanna Inthorn and Martin Scott) *From Entertainment to Citizenship: Politics and Popular Culture* (Manchester University Press, 2013).

Peter Webb is a writer, lecturer and musician who specialises in research into popular and contemporary music, subcultures, globalisation, new media, politics and social theory. He is Senior Lecturer and Programme Leader for Sociology at the University of the West of England, Bristol.

Matthew Worley is Professor of Modern History at the University of Reading. He is a co-founder of the Subcultures Network and author of various articles and chapters on the relationship between youth culture and politics. His latest book, *No Future: Punk, Politics and British Youth Culture, 1976–84,* will be published by Cambridge University Press in 2017.

PART 1

Riots

CHAPTER 2

Subcultures, Schools and Rituals: A Case Study of the 'Bristol Riots' (1980)

Roger Ball

The spring and summer of 1981 saw one of the most widespread and intense periods of violent urban disturbance in England in the twentieth century. Recent research has highlighted over 200 daily disorders of varying magnitude during the month of July 1981 alone.[1] These were spread over more than one hundred locations in England, most notably in the cities of Liverpool, London, Manchester, Nottingham, Leicester, Derby and the West Midlands. Outside of these conurbations, Home County towns such as High Wycombe, Luton and Bedford and many other locales experienced 'rioting' which had rarely been seen in the post-war era.[2] During the week of 6–13 July 1981 patterns of disturbance diffusion emerged suggesting that major 'riots' in inner city areas of mixed ethnicity precipitated numerous further disorders in other more ethnically homogenous districts of the conurbations, sometimes considerably distant from the initial 'flashpoints'.[3] The majority of contemporary commentators left these intriguing patterns of apparent contagion unexplained or blandly wrote them off as merely incidents of 'copycat rioting'.

One year before the tumultuous events of 1981 the St Pauls area of Bristol was rocked by an afternoon and evening of serious collective violence which led to the controversial and (in)famous withdrawal of the

R. Ball (✉)
School of Psychology, University of Keele, Staffordshire, UK
e-mail: dodger@brh.org.uk

© The Author(s) 2017
K. Gildart et al. (eds.), *Youth Culture and Social Change*,
Palgrave Studies in the History of Subcultures and Popular Music,
DOI 10.1057/978-1-137-52911-4_2

17

police force from the neighbourhood. The events of 2 April 1980 have since become iconic both in the media and popular memory and were perceived by many commentators to be the first major outbreak of urban 'rioting' on mainland Britain for several decades that was not directly instigated by formal political protest.[4] Although this view has been contested by some authors, in that it ignored violent disturbances centred around police raids on clubs and cafés frequented by ethnic minorities in the 1970s[5] as well as significant disorder at large public events such as the Notting Hill Carnival in 1975 and 1976, the wider perception was that the St Pauls disturbance was 'something new' to England.[6] The event thus became central to the modern history of Bristol and marked a moment where issues of institutional and popular racism were forced into the media spotlight, obliging national and local government bodies to search for explanations and generate policy responses. Consequently, the 'St Pauls Riot' as it was defined by the local media or 'The Bristol Riot' as the national newspapers labelled it, now occupies a racialised place in the popular memory signifying 'race riot' or 'Black uprising'.

On the eve of the 25th anniversary of the St Pauls 'riot' the *Bristol Evening Post* ran a double-page spread entitled 'The Night a Riot Rocked a Nation'.[7] The article included eyewitness statements and comments by a 'community leader', a councillor, a press photographer, 'a resident' and 'the policeman'. The latter, Superintendent Tim Lee the Deputy District Commander of the Avon and Somerset Constabulary in 2005, was a beat constable during the 1980 St Pauls disorders. In the article Lee provided an interesting insight by recalling some further disturbances that occurred in the succeeding days after the St Pauls event: 'What few people know is that for the following nights we had more problems in Southmead than we did in St Pauls because of copycat attacks.'

The significance of the disturbances in the Southmead estate for the Avon and Somerset Police Constabulary was confirmed by the Chief Constable's report of that year which gave them equal coverage to the St Pauls incident and considered them to be 'serious'.[8] However, the Southmead 'riots' were barely reported in the local press, ignored by the national media and relegated to the status of 'copycat attacks' or 'hooliganism' where they were mentioned.[9] Following disturbances over the start of the Easter weekend in 1980 the Monday edition of the *Western Daily Press* carried an editorial entitled 'Lessons for the Young' which stated that 'HOOLIGANISM in Southmead and Knowle West Follows the Riots in Bristol's St Pauls'.[10] The only reference made in the rest of that edition of the newspaper as to what had actually occurred in Knowle West was a short article referring to some slogans daubed on three shops in the area.[11] However, clearly *something had happened* over the weekend of 4–6 April 1980 to spur the comment in the editorial. Further research in the local media, available police reports and similar primary sources failed to locate any reference to the mysterious event in the South Bristol neighbourhood. Bristol's 'other riots' thus passed largely unnoticed and, more significantly, *unheeded* into obscurity. In contrast the St Pauls disturbance reverberated around the nation's media, dominated debates in the Houses of Commons and Lords over the succeeding days and led to a visit by a parliamentary sub-committee.[12] In addition there were several official and unofficial reports, a public enquiry held by trade unions and eventually a number of books and academic papers, which studied the event.[13]

DEMOGRAPHICS AND POLICING

In 1980 Southmead and Knowle West were almost exclusively White areas, the former 6 kilometres north of the city centre and the latter 3 kilometres south (Fig. 2.1). Both of these peripheral self-contained estates had high concentrations of local authority housing with relatively static populations. In contrast, St Pauls, located in the inner city, had a large proportion of ethnic minorities, mixed forms of housing tenure and a notably transient population. All three areas were of similar sized population, principally composed of lower working-class socio-economic groupings, were experiencing very high levels of youth unemployment, household overcrowding and lacked social facilities.[14]

Oral history testimony and other primary sources demonstrate the perceived negative branding of each area by social class (all three) and ethnicity (St Pauls).[15] However, whereas St Pauls was commonly racialised as a closed Black inner city 'ghetto', in fact it was one of the more cosmopolitan areas of Bristol, with a long history of being a reception area for immigrants (Irish, Polish, African-Caribbean, Asian), those in the 'care' and probation systems and others in search of cheap rented housing or squatting. A lively cultural scene attracted a transient population of young people in the 1970s connected to various (youth) subcultures such as Punk and Rastafarianism.[16]

In contrast, the outlying areas of Southmead and Knowle West were actually far more 'closed' by geography, ethnicity and reputation. Oral

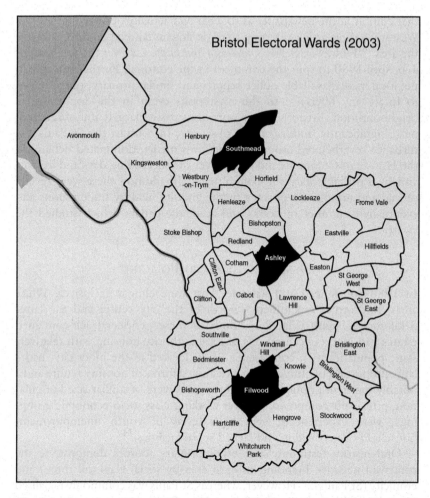

Fig. 2.1   Location within the City of Bristol of the Southmead, Ashley (St. Pauls) and Filwood (Knowle West) electoral wards

histories highlighted violent inter-estate rivalries with neighbouring districts, which inhibited mobility and fraternisation. The negative 'branding' accorded to their neighbourhoods, which inhibited socialising in wealthier nearby areas, compounded these exclusionary aspects of life. Within their estates, struggles for control over social space between local youth and the authorities were common and brought young people into contact with the police on a fairly regular basis.[17]

The most striking similarities in oral history testimonies in the three areas concerned the encounters of young people with the police in the late 1970s and early 1980s. In fact it was possible to interchange these accounts by location, with one exception, that of ethnicity. Almost all the White respondents experienced situations where Black friends and acquaintances had been treated worse than they had in particular situations, and crucially they were fully aware of this fact. In some cases the respondents cited the generalised maltreatment as a basis for solidarity between subcultures and ethnic groups. Neither were these isolated incidents. Several respondents realised in retrospect that, at the time, they had accepted police maltreatment as the norm. This pointed to a history of policing practice that appeared to be area based and in many cases racist and derogatory to certain youth subcultures. Ironically, despite racist myths about St Pauls, several White respondents from Knowle West and Southmead regarded the inner city multiethnic area as a *safer* area for youth than their own neighbourhoods. This inference was based upon on the propensity of 'Black' residents to collectively intervene in police activities on the street, something the Avon & Somerset Constabulary were fully aware of. In St Pauls such confrontations were more commonplace than in the outlying estates of Southmead and Knowle West and may have led to over-policing of specific operations such as raids and other such irregular actions.

Accounts of the 'Bristol' Riots of April 1980

The following three sections summarise the disturbances in St Pauls, Southmead and Knowle West in April 1980.[18]

St Pauls: Wednesday 2 April 1980

On the afternoon of 2 April 1980, the 'frontline'[19] in St Pauls became the flashpoint for a serious disturbance when an operation involving more than 40 police officers was launched to discover evidence of the illegal sale of alcohol in the Black and White Café.[20]Having entered the premises and discovered several hundred crates of beer stored there, the Inspector in charge of the operation made the fateful decision to remove the items, a task which took more than an hour. During this time a large crowd, eventually numbering hundreds, gathered at the site to watch the events unfolding. When a small amount of soft drugs was openly taken through the crowd by plainclothes police officers vacating the café, violence erupted. For approximately an hour, in the immediate vicinity of the 'frontline', police officers were stoned by crowds of Black and White youth, several police vehicles were overturned and one was burned. A number of police officers were trapped in the café and had to be 'rescued' by a military style march of 30 or so officers along Grosvenor Road. Police dog handlers eventually managed to clear the crowds from the immediate vicinity of the café before declaring the area apparently pacified at 5.45 p.m.

The already disastrous 'raid' further degenerated when violence re-ignited an hour later as they attempted to remove a burned-out police car from the scene. This time however, the disorder was not limited to the vicinity of the café, as police officers were driven by stone-throwing crowds out of the 'frontline' onto the main thoroughfares of Ashley Road and City Road. Estimates of the size of the crowds present on the streets at this stage of the disturbance range from hundreds to several thousand. Many were merely observing the action whilst other groups actively fought the police units present.

The first phase of the disturbance had been marked by serious confusion in the chain of command of the Avon & Somerset Constabulary. Despite the arrival of the Chief Constable at the scene, the situation worsened during the second phase of the disturbance, with attacks on the police expanding across the neighbourhood. Three police vehicles that responded to confused calls for assistance drove into a large crowd in the commercial centre of St Pauls and their drivers had to abandon their vehicles and flee the scene. Other groups of police were chased by the stone-throwing crowds, the majority ending up on City Road. At this point the order to deploy 30 riot shields was issued and an attempt to march towards the centre of St Pauls was made. This ended in abject failure as the police line came under severe attack from three sides and was driven back along City Road towards the city centre.

When some of the 'rioters' began to burn the abandoned police vehicles outside the Lloyds bank on Ashley Road there was a final attempt to retake the centre of the neighbourhood using a police Land Rover, a van and a group of officers on foot. This too resulted in fiasco, with the vehicles and the following officers forced to retreat back up Ashley Road under a hail of missiles. As the confidence of the rioting crowds grew, that of the police wavered. Eventually, under attack from all sides, the rabble of police, journalists and TV cameramen was driven down City Road and out of St Pauls. At approximately 7.30 p.m. a 'historic' order was given by the Chief Constable for all police units to withdraw from the area completely. They were not to return for more than four hours.[21]

The departure of the Constabulary was initially met with joyous celebrations amongst large crowds of rioters and onlookers. A huge cheer went up as Lloyds Bank was torched, and this was followed by the selective looting (and burning in some cases) of many businesses including a betting shop, post office and a motorbike dealer.[22] After the opening wave of window-breaking and seizing of high-value goods, older members of the community ventured out to engage in the 'surreal normality' of shopping without having to pay. Crowds of people excitedly chatted around the burning police vehicles exchanging stories and stolen alcohol and cigarettes, as astounded members of the public drove directly through the area now effectively under the control of the 'rioters'.

After several hours of reorganisation within the divisions of the Avon and Somerset Constabulary and requests to neighbouring county police forces for reinforcements, the Chief Constable had managed to assemble over 600 police officers, including a firearms team, in order to retake the St Pauls neighbourhood. The operation began at approximately 11.30 p.m. and met little resistance. By midnight the police had reestablished control over the area.

Southmead: Thursday–Friday 3–4 April 1980

Thursday 3 April 1980, the day after the 'Bristol Riot' in St Pauls, was to the casual observer, a normal day for the residents of the Southmead estate in North Bristol. However the apparent calm belied the fact that, via the numerous media reports, the majority of the area's adult residents were fully aware of the previous day's events in St Pauls. Other groups, especially some younger people, had received or were receiving first-hand accounts of the 'Bristol Riot' via their peers and school friends from St Pauls.

The apparent normality in the Southmead estate was punctured in the evening when small dispersed groups of youths began to stone passing police vehicles as they drove along Greystoke Avenue adjacent to the symbolic gathering point for youth known locally as the 'Green'.[23] This relatively minor incident led to the call for back up police units, which entered the estate and congregated at the nearby Arneside shops close to Southmead Youth Centre. The arrival of the police reinforcements attracted more youths, creating a crowd from which several began to stone the collected police and their vehicles. This crowd was estimated by residents to be a hundred strong, mainly composed of male youths and 'including skinheads and punk rockers'.[24] In response to the attacks the police officers called further reinforcements in vans. These units helped formed a 'wall' of vehicles in front of the shops at the junction of Arneside Road. As the barrage of missiles continued several shop windows were broken, including a butcher and hairdresser, but there were no attempts to loot any premises.

At approximately 10 p.m. the senior police officer made the decision that enough manpower had been assembled for them to take more aggressive action. The police officers formed a line and, along with police dogs, began to advance across the 'Green' towards the crowd, who began to disperse across the estate. As the youths scattered, the police fanned out in groups in an attempt to make arrests. Twelve youths and adults were detained, the majority being seized outside the Standard of England public house opposite the 'Green'.[25] Despite these incidents the police managed to achieve the dispersal of the crowd without having to negatively engage with a wider section of the community. To all intents and purposes the incident was over. However, the following evening was to see a significant escalation of violence.

For the senior police officers of 'C' Division the heightened atmosphere after the nationally perceived 'defeat' of the police in St Pauls and the subsequent disturbance in their own 'manor' on the Thursday night in Southmead put them under some pressure to react. Their normal policy of non-interactive vehicular patrols was altered on the following day. One oral history respondent recalled:

> The following day and the following evening it was noticeable that vans of police was just tucked away, dotted about Southmead... up the little quiet bits of Southmead... sat in vans... hidden away in the shadows just waiting, on watch almost.[26]

The change in policing routine was immediately noticed by many of Southmead's residents, especially younger people who were traversing the estate. The feeling that the neighbourhood had been secretly 'occupied' and that they were under surveillance from the estranged police force heightened the tension. The confidence provided by their experience of the previous night's attack on the police and the perceived ineffectual response, combined with the news of the 'successful uprising' in St Pauls that had both travelled by word of mouth and via the mass media, was a potent brew. Consequently, larger numbers of youths, several hundred strong, were engaged in the disturbance on the Friday night and after nightfall they began to act.[27]

The disturbance commenced at around 9 p.m. with youths breaking the windows of some shops close to the Southmead Youth Centre. According to one account this was a tactic to draw the police units who were dispersed around the estate into a confrontation: 'As it was the police who were the targets, they first needed to be lured from out of the back streets and in to the open, so shop windows on Greystoke Avenue were duly smashed, causing the desired effect.'[28]

The tactic was successful as vanloads of police left their 'hiding places' on the estate and sped to the scene, eventually gathering as a large group close to the Arneside shops. For the next hour or so the situation descended into a stand-off, with the police seemingly corralled and the groups of youths facing them across the 'Green' intermittently stoning them. Between 10 and 10.30 p.m. people began to arrive from nearby houses and the two nearby pubs, The Pegasus and The Standard of England, which stood on opposite sides of Greystoke Avenue. As the crowds of onlookers of all ages gathered to watch, some of the new arrivals to the disturbance began to take an active rather than tacit role in the disturbance:

> It was at that point that a lot of these blokes [from the pubs] began advising the kids about what to do. So some of these blokes were kind of guiding and giving advice. They had a lot of suss actually... they could kind of plan it. They could tell these kids what to do, how to go about it.[29]

One particular moment appeared to unite the 'rioters' and the onlookers as was recalled by one eye-witness:

> Somebody chucked a block ... it went high up into the sky and landed full onto the window of a police van ... It just smashed it and that was quite a sight. All these people, all about just roared. A massive cheer went up. But that was quite illuminating to me because it kind of showed all of these local Southmead

people, of all ages, not condemning this and actually thinking and saying out loud 'yeah, that was a good one'. That was an amazing moment to see this kind of unified applause. It showed again this kind of unity and it showed we've actually got a lot in common all of us lot. It showed that none of us were supporting the police, of all ages. That nobody was disgusted by this. They was applauding it. It defined the position of the police to us as a community. It showed explicitly that the police was not of the community ... that there was a division between us and that nobody gave much backing to the police.[30]

The disturbance eventually petered out as the night wore on with the police making nineteen arrests.

Knowle West: Saturday 5 April 1980

The lack of written primary sources concerning events in Knowle West in the wake of the St Pauls disturbance dictates a turn to oral histories from participants. One particular respondent, a White teenage Punk from Knowle West who had social links to St Pauls and had travelled with his friends to the disturbance on Wednesday 2 April, remembered the beginning of the Easter weekend (4–5 April) in Knowle West:

The word went round Knowle that we were all going to meet up and have a 'riot' ... there must have been three hundred people, three hundred youths in Filwood Broadway, just hanging around, all tooled up, bottles, ready to go.[31]

The chosen meeting point for the 'riot' was again a symbolic location, 'The Green' at the top of Filwood Broadway, the main shopping street in the local area and close to the centre of the Knowle West estate. The respondent recalled the effect that the St Pauls 'riot' had on the youth in the area:

Everybody was like gee'd up about St Pauls and the feeling was that the whole of Britain was gonna go ... it was a few days after the St Pauls riots 'cos that sort of, you know inspired a lot of people.[32]

He also provides an interesting insight into the organisational forms and mechanisms for the transfer of information between the youth of Knowle West prior to the incident:

It was just word of mouth round the streets. Kiddies would just come around on their bikes. 'Cos we used to ... when we were in Knowle West there used to be gangs of kids... So what you used to do was to hang out then and go and hang around by the chip shop. We all knew each other and we were all mates, it weren't gangs that was... you know ... but where different people used to hang out... People would go round on bikes saying 'We're meeting at the thing, we're meeting at the thing.' It all went round and everybody sort of met there. It was a word of mouth thing really.[33]

The respondent explains that the gangs should not be understood as warring factions, but instead that 'We all knew each other and we were all mates.' The gangs were not defined by specific subcultural or similar allegiances but merely spatially located according to where young people lived and had attended junior school in the area.

Organisational forms above the local gang level had been part of the history of Knowle West youth in their inter-estate 'wars' with nearby rivals from Hartcliffe.[34] The respondent went on to explain:

If there was trouble with Hartcliffe, we used to try and get a crew together... so people used to go around 'Right there's trouble, they're coming' ... we'd try and get a crew together and go down and see what was going on. And obviously the more you get together the more intimidating you are.[35]

The same method for spreading news and gathering the youth gangs together was used to organise the 'riot' in Filwood Broadway; this time, however, rather than their nearby rivals, it was the police that were the target. The hundreds of youths that did gather on the 'Green' were, according to the respondent, the biggest 'crew' he had ever seen and it brought out older residents in the neighbourhood:

We all went up there [to Filwood Broadway], there were loads of people out as well, load of the locals were out on the street, and you know, some for, some against... It got round the older people as well, what was gonna go on...[36]

The youths were met by a massive proactive police response, which in itself is a testament to the importance the Avon and Somerset Constabulary gave the potential of such incidents in the wake of the disturbances they had recently experienced. According to the respondent he had never seen so many police in Knowle West:

They [the police] were already there ... there must have been about twenty vans lined up. And each van was packed. So they knew what was going on and they were prepared. A few bottles got thrown and they just marched on us and we all sort of dispersed.[37]

The Knowle West 'riot' was effectively 'snuffed out' before it could begin, as a result of advance intelligence and, on the day, by weight of police numbers. The event effectively remained unreported in the local media, and obscured as hooliganism or vandalism where it was alluded to.

CONTAGION, 'COPYCAT', AND CONSCIOUSNESS IN THE SPREAD OF DISORDER

Pyschological analysis of the spread of collective violence such as urban 'riot' has produced several competing theoretical explanations. Historically these have been related to concepts such as contagion or mimicry which deny to varying degree the individual or collective agency of participants. The concept of 'contagion' is related to early crowd theories which posited the collective unconscious as a behavioural driver such that: 'individuals in a crowd could be "infected", or swept away by the collective body by a kind of unconscious, primitive craze passed from individual to individual'.[38]

In the aftermath of the August 2011 'riots' in the UK the concept of contagion was extended from a single crowd event to an explanation of the spread of disturbances across the country:

Slutkin argued that 'groupness' is akin to a virus that infects the mind and causes 'a collective, communal group-think motivated violence'. Once one mind is infected, he further contended, others will inevitably become infected through 'the "contagious" swap of feelings'. In time this contagion 'ripples throughout a crowd driving them toward (often violent) action'. This frame of reference explains that once the trigger had occurred in Tottenham the 'epidemic' then moved irresistibly 'from person to person' and 'town to town'.[39]

The related concept of 'copycat riots' which rose to prominence as a result of the unrest in the summer of 1981 emphasizes the inability of individual or collective receivers of information about a disturbance to analyse, critique and make conscious objective decisions about its content.[40]

Instead, the recipients are seen as passive consumers of information, where their unconscious desires are the driver for their subsequent actions. Attempts to apply this concept to real situations typically concentrate on visual media such as television as the conduit for information and the young (particularly children) as the receivers, on the basis that they are more vulnerable to this influence and less critical than adults.[41]

In contrast with these theories of mindless, epidemic-like behaviours alternative approaches are concerned with conscious, rational and evaluative decision-making based upon the real experiences and the actual social relations of those both giving and receiving information about disorder. For example:

> diffusion [of 'riot'] is a rational form of inter-actor influence in which potential actors observe and evaluate the outcome of others' behaviours and then make a decision about whether to adopt the behaviour.[42]

Other theories share this conscious evaluative understanding of the spread of 'riot' but stress that assessment of incoming information is on the basis of collective 'social identities'. So if the receivers of the information recognise the source of the information as being 'in-group' and acting normatively, they are more likely to act in a similar manner. Influence is thus not contingent merely upon exposure to information but upon answering questions such as 'is this an appropriate thing for *us* to do?' and thus upon how 'us' is defined. This suggests that there is another element to the transmission process. That is, behaviours do not merely depend on the identity and actions of the original source itself (say rioters in another part of a city), but also on the reactions of immediately present co-actors which determine whether we see that source as legitimate.[43] Social identity theories thus escape the bind of metaphysical speculation as to the content of the unconscious and thus the need to situate the driver for disturbances in the supposedly gullible *very young* or in the assumed irrationality and savagery of subordinate social classes.

SUBCULTURES, SCHOOLS AND RITUALS

So, if the St Pauls 'riot' of 2 April 1980 influenced or even precipitated the latter episodes in Southmead and Knowle West, how did this actually occur in practice? Was the transmission of information merely through homogenous visual media, or were other mechanisms in play? And why would mainly White areas such as Southmead and Knowle West respond in such a way to what was being presented in the mass media at the time as a 'Black riot' in a 'Black ghetto'?[44]

The fact that the disturbances succeeding the St Pauls 'riot' occurred within three days of this event suggests there was a causal relationship between them. However, considering the incidents from a spatial perspective appears to confound this connection. Geographically, the three areas are clearly not adjacent to each other or even located in the same districts of Bristol but are in fact separated by several kilometres (see Fig. 2.1). However, oral history testimony from participants in the 'riots' and subsequent research has suggested that despite the spatial separation there were a variety of significant social links between the outlying areas and St Pauls, particularly amongst the young. These are examined in the following sections.

Displaced schooling

In the late 1970s Avon County Council introduced a controversial and unpopular policy to deal with the fact that St Pauls, despite having primary schools in the locality, had no non-selective secondary schools. Consequently, teenagers from the St Pauls ward were transported to nine different schools spread amongst three of the five designated education areas of the city.[45] Two of the schools chosen for the 'bussing' of inner city youth, were the relatively small Southmead secondary schools Pen Park Girls and Greenway Boys, more than 6 kilometres from the pupils' home neighbourhoods.[46] This was reflected in the high percentage of so-called 'Commonwealth immigrant children' (14.8 per cent) in Pen Park Girls School in 1980, despite the fact that the local catchment area had less than 3 per cent of its population of similar origin. One oral history respondent described a similar ethnic mix in Greenway Boys School in 1980:

> At Greenway . . . even though it [Southmead] is a 99 per cent White area, we had probably about 20 per cent Black Africans and Asians so it was a real mix. Even though it was a White area, Black and Asian kids were bussed in and there were kids from St Pauls and from some other areas as well there, you see. So it was a real hodge podge of cultures really. But where we actually lived in Southmead there weren't that many Black or Asian families.[47]

The outcome of the 'bussing' strategy instigated and enforced by Avon County Council was that many of the teenage youth of St Pauls had no choice but to leave their home neighbourhood and travel to distant locales on a daily basis for schooling, with all the potential trauma that entailed. This created effectively a dual identity, living in one environment and displacement into other, sometimes majority White, communities during term time. The inadvertent consequence of this educational strategy was to create direct social links between many of the youth of St Pauls and outlying estates such as Southmead. Several oral history respondents immediately located these connections as being important in both the physical transmission of information about the St Pauls disturbance to the teenagers of Southmead and subjectively as creating awareness and reciprocity between them.[48]

Subcultures and symbolic locations

Another series of social ties between the study areas that facilitated the dissemination of news of the 'riot' amongst participants, created the conditions for active participation amongst the St Pauls rioting crowds, and encouraged working class youth to 'travel' sometimes considerable distances to take part in disturbances, were derived via youth subcultures. Of particular relevance were the Skinhead, Punk, Rastafarian and Ska (rude boy) subcultures, which were prevalent in the late 1970s and early 1980s in some or all of the study areas. Much has been written about the origins of and links between these cultural movements, in particular the effect of Caribbean music forms on the early Skinhead movement in the UK, the linkages between Punk and Reggae in the late 1970s and the fusion of styles and ethnicities in the Ska movement originating in the West Midlands in 1979.[49] Their importance in this analysis is the part they played in bonding youth of different locales and ethnicities, both socially and ideologically, in and around the urban disturbances in Bristol in 1980.

Youth subcultures had the potential to overcome historic spatial divisions between rival areas through shared cultural values, and they also opened avenues of 'escape' into wider Bristol offering new social environments to explore. Knowle West, for example, had an historic connection with Skinhead culture and it was older 'original skins' that opened up these avenues for one respondent:

By that time I was hanging around with a load of older blokes, who were like ex-Skinheads, not fascist Skinheads but like 'Black music White Skinheads'. They were all from Knowle West... they were original Skinheads, very anti-racist, they couldn't believe what the young Skinheads were into. They were constantly going into town and almost getting into scraps with Skinheads because they'd say 'well you're not fucking Skinheads, Skinheads is about Black music' and stuff like that... They were all very open-minded and not racist at all'.[50]

Through his connections to this peer group of 'original skins' the respondent (a Punk) and his friends from Knowle West were introduced to one of the most important meeting points for Black and White Bristolians in the early 1980s:

[name deleted] knew a lot of Black kids in St Pauls ... and it was because of him and [name deleted] that we started going to the 'Dug Out'. Then I started to see some of the kiddies, a couple of Black kids from school, Black Punks. And it was at that time when ... from the London scene where it was a Punky–Rastafarian cross over and it was OK to be in each other's company. In London there was the Roxy scene where there was no Punk music so everyone used to get into Black music... So the 'Dug Out' was our ideal place. It was our equivalent.[51]

The 'Dug Out' club close to the city-centre and St Pauls became a popular haunt of those who couldn't get into 'straight' clubs because of racism, subcultural fashions (Punk, Skinhead, Ska and Rastafarianism) or because they wanted a place where they could listen to 'their' music. The club acted as a hub for these subcultures allowing new relationships to be formed between youth of different ethnicities and locales. It also had a major part to play in the fusing of different musical influences into new styles, which formed a vibrant multiethnic 'underground' scene in the mid-eighties.[52]

Meetings in the neutral space of the 'Dug Out' not only connected youth from outlying working-class estates with inner city St Pauls but also allowed new contacts to be made with 'sussed' youths from nearby rival areas.

When you were like eleven or twelve in Knowle West the only political group, this shows how bad the Left were, was the NF [National Front], and you kind of thought 'they're quite cool like'. When I changed, which was when I was about thirteen, I went to this demo outside Knowle School when the NF were having a meeting there. And suddenly you saw all these cool kids from Hartcliffe and different areas. They were all there protesting. It was the height of the Anti-Nazi League and stuff. I didn't really see them again for ages ... and then you saw all those sort of characters reappear at the 'Dug Out'. It had been very rare to mix with that lot.[53]

The transient nature of St Pauls population, particularly in terms of the large amount of rented accommodation, allied with its historic squatting scene dating back to the early seventies, allowed relatively easy movement from outlying estates to the inner city for unemployed or low-income youth. The main impediment to this movement which the mainly White 'outsiders' had to overcome, was the infamous status the neighbourhood had amongst many White Bristolians. One respondent from Knowle West recalled:

St. Pauls was kind of like mythical. There was a lot of White racism. The classic line was 'It used to be a really nice area 'til they turned up.' So I never went down there then ... But that sort of feeling didn't last very long as soon as I started going down the 'Dug Out', you suddenly realised it's not that bad.[54]

By 1980 there was a significant Punk scene resident in the area, comprising 'natives' and more recent interlopers. This in turn brought more young visitors to the 'neutral zone' of St Pauls, escaping from the area-based rivalries in the outlying estates and entering a friendlier subcultural milieu and (ironically) the safer streets of that neighbourhood.

Another important reason to make contacts in St Pauls, which was linked to these subcultural movements, was the need to purchase soft drugs, particularly cannabis and marijuana. This drug scene, which was intimately connected to Grosvenor Road, the 'frontline', generated many visitors from outlying mainly White estates. For some, initial subcultural contacts led to them visiting St Pauls to buy drugs, thereby meeting local youth who had been influenced by Rastafarian ideas and socialising in the semi-legal 'Blues' clubs in the area. Another White Punk respondent from Knowle West was asked how he developed his contacts in St Pauls:

Just through the Punk scene really and just knowing where dealers lived because ... there was a lot of Punks living in St Pauls because the housing was really cheap ... it was all quite relaxed and mellow really ... between the guys on the street. It was the Old Bill that used to cause the problems, not just in St Pauls but in Knowle West . . . And also a bit later then getting into sort of Reggae music as well 'cos you was hanging out with them guys and going to dances . . . there was Reggae, always a Blues going on . . . the Punks were kind of accepted because they lived in the area . . . it was kind of cool at the Blues, they knew you, they let you in. Most of the Punks were just going there for a late drink, so it was just like normal. You could have a smoke [marijuana/cannabis] and it was relaxed and they played Reggae music.[55]

The 'real' St Pauls was thus discovered by many outsiders through subcultural contacts and became an attractive place to hang out, as it provided relatively safe spaces to party, drink after-hours and consume soft drugs. These initial fraternisations facilitated by youth subcultures not only encouraged some to permanently move to St Pauls from outlying estates such as Southmead and Knowle West but also crucially provided a conduit for information via a 'youth grapevine' between these distant areas.

Second-Generation African-Caribbean Youth Diaspora

The Bristol Punk scene's symbolic *daytime* gathering point in 1970–80 was outside the Virgin record shop in Broadmead shopping centre, where contingents from many working-class areas congregated. This new environment brought together not only supposed enemies from rival areas of Bristol but also in the mix were Black, mixed race and White Punks from St Pauls. One contingent remembered by many respondents was the self-named 'Half-breeds', a group of mixed-race Punks who traversed the ethnic and fashion boundaries of several youth subcultures. Their social and spatial make-up was unusual and directly related to the experiences of first-generation immigrants to Bristol from the Caribbean in the 1950s and 60s.

St Pauls was the initial arrival point for many of these immigrants and became the geographic base for establishing a community. Through the 1960s, however, a number of African-Caribbean residents of the area had relationships with White Bristolians who they met through work or leisure. Often this entailed leaving St Pauls to live in outlying mainly White working-class estates where their mixed-race children were brought up. These relationships effectively created a mixed-race teenage diaspora in the late 1970s and, though dispersed across the city, these young people retained familial links to their original Black community in St Pauls.

The experience of being Black in the outlying estates, with the prevalent racial prejudice of the 1970s allied to the feeling of being both 'different' and somewhat isolated, generated some interesting responses amongst these teenagers. Confrontations between rival groups from mainly White working-class estates were often turned into points of fraternisation by Black youth, as was recounted by one mixed-race female respondent from Hartcliffe:

> If you were a girl there used to be 'girl's fights'. And the girls you could go down to Bedminster to have a fight and it happened when there would be a Fair... and you would go there to have a fight with all the girls from Knowle West. So the boys' fights would happen regularly of a weekend but the girls fights would be... [more ritualised]... And what would happen when you'd go to those fights was if you were Black or mixed-race you'd meet lots of other mixed-race people from those areas like Knowle West and Withywood that you wouldn't ever see before. So you never generally ended up having a fight. You ended up having a chat about who you knew, who you were related to... Yeah, 'cos it was unusual to meet Black or mixed-race people from out on the outskirts.[56]

The shared feelings and solidarity expressed between Black and mixed-race teenagers from different, often rival estates allowed groupings such as the *'Half-breeds'* to organically form in the late 1970s. The linkages between members of this particular group were a both a development and mirror of the movements that their parental generation had made in the 1960s. The resulting ethno-geographic map of Bristol in the late 1970s is recalled by a female respondent, a second-generation mixed-race teenager in the period:

> the [mixed-race] people that were in Knowle West were connected to people that were more central [St Pauls] and what I imagine is that there were ... people from these estates Southmead, Hartcliffe, Withywood that were mixed race that were connected through that mixture. So you would know Black people because the connection would be that would-be Black fathers from St Pauls... that would know White women in those satellite estates. And that's how the connection would be made... for me 'cos I'm mixed-race obviously it would be made through people who were mixed-race and that's where the sort of 'Half-breed' thing comes in, because they would be ... people who collectively would have the ... shared experience of having Black parents from the inner city [St Pauls] but who had White

parents from the outskirts. So that's why those connections were round the outside... those connections and those mixed-race children are evidence of those connections between St Pauls and those peripheral estates... When you would meet other mixed-race people then you would be interested in them... Whatever was happening in St Pauls would radiate via those relationships.[57]

The respondent's analysis presents a sophisticated description of the social and familial networks that were in play in connecting both mixed-race African-Caribbean youth in outlying estates, with each other as well as with the mother district of inner city St Pauls. Fig. 2.2 gives a schematic representation of this ethnographic map based on the oral history. This map effectively outlines the historical

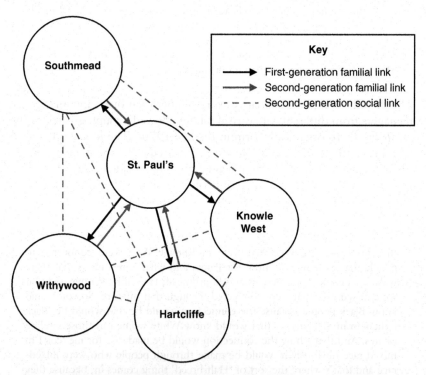

Fig. 2.2   Schematic of ethno-geographic connections between areas of Bristol for first and second generation African-Caribbean residents

framework for the creation of second-generation groupings such as the 'Half-breeds' and explains their pan-Bristol nature. The 'Half-breeds', although connected by the deeper relationships of shared family ties and dual ethnic origin were also functioning in wider youth subcultures such as the Punk scene, which connected them with both White and Black youth. Their 'pan-Bristol' network allowed them to overcome violent inter-area rivalries and importantly opened up opportunities for other members of their shared Punk subculture to meet and eventually move into St Pauls. Groupings such as the 'Half-breeds' not only created bonds between the Black youth of St Pauls and the city-wide Punk sub-culture prior to the 1980 disturbance but also were connected to symbolic locations such as the Black and White Café on the 'frontline' which were central to that disorder.[58]

CONCLUSION

This examination of the social relationships, particularly amongst the young, between St Pauls, Southmead and Knowle West demonstrates that commonly held mythologies of St Pauls as an ethnically closed and ghettoised community in the 1980s were seriously misleading. Instead St Pauls sat at the centre of a web of radial and rhizomic social networks spreading across the city. These were generated between specific outlying working class estates and St Pauls through the effects of displaced schooling, particular youth subcultures and pan-Bristol networks of second-generation mixed race teenagers. These formations overcame spatial separations between areas and usurped the mythical status of St Pauls as a 'no go' area for Whites. Symbolic locations such as clubs like the 'Dug Out', the various 'Blues' drinking-dens in St Pauls and other subcultural gathering points acted as important nodes in this social web.

During and after the St Pauls disorder of 2 April 1980 information radiated out through this web to outlying areas that were 'ripe for riot'. Particular social networks were energised by news of the 'riot', encouraged travelling to St Pauls to take part in the action and were also willing to initiate a local response. Once this information had passed into belligerent local networks amongst youths in Southmead and Knowle West they resorted to their existing organisational forms to plan and launch collective violence against a shared enemy (the police) in their home neighbourhoods. However, these relatively closed, mainly White working-class estates that rose, did so alone, attracted fewer 'travellers' and were apparently hamstrung by inter-estate rivalries.

The complexity of these networks and their contextual importance in overcoming ethnic and spatial divisions suggests shallowness in the concepts of 'contagion' and 'copycat' as explanations for the spread of urban disturbance. The former theory relies heavily on situational relationships, that is, behaviours *within* crowds becoming 'infectious'. It therefore does not adequately explain how temporally and spatially separated events like 'riots' can become 'contagious' or why supposedly 'mindless' behaviours should be restricted to particular social networks or areas. The latter theory relies heavily on the supposed spectacular relationship between the 'unconscious' individual and the mass media. However, what is not explained by the concept of 'copycat' is why there are not more 'riots' due to the inherent lack of human agency and why certain areas fail to 'riot'. In any case the assumption that young people gained information from television reports was challenged by a BBC survey of listening and viewing during the period of the 1981 riots, which suggested that less than 10 per cent of 12–19-year-olds actually watched news bulletins.[59] Instead, police and rioters who were interviewed in the aftermath of the 1981 unrest concurred with the evidence presented here that the 'youth grapevine' provided the conduit for 'detailed information about trouble in their area, where it was taking place and at what time' and this news was garnered in 'the classroom, the street and the pub'.[60]

The multilayered social networks examined in this chapter that were in operation between 'riotous' locales in Bristol in 1980, whether generated by youth subcultures, displaced schooling, a second-generation African-Caribbean youth diaspora or a fusion of all three, demonstrate that the *context* in which information was received was as important as its actual content. This in turn suggests that the extension of social identity theory into the analysis of the spread of urban disorder may provide a better understanding of these processes than outmoded theories based on concepts of unconscious 'contagion' or mimicry.

NOTES

1. R. Ball, 'Violent Urban Disturbance in England 1980–1' (unpublished Ph. D. thesis, University of the West of England, 2012 available at http://eprints.uwe.ac.uk/17958/) (Ball 2012).
2. Denoting collective violence is problematic as the very form of the signifiers represents historically derived bias and what is signified is of course dependent

on the position of the observer. In this chapter the following words have been used to denote collective violence: *riot, disorder, disturbance, unrest, incident* and *event*. In general only the first of these terms has been enclosed by quotation marks (despite similar issues with the second and third terms in the group) as the author felt it was the most contentious (and commonly used) of the collection. However, all of the terms have been used interchangeably in this work and should be considered as such by the reader.

3. Ball, 'Violent Urban Disturbance', pp. 152–201.

4. Violence associated with pickets and demonstrations had been a fairly regular feature of England in the 1970s, with industrial disputes (such as the miners' strikes of 1972–74 and Grunwick in 1977) and political protests against marches organised by fascist parties (notably in London in Red Lion Square 1974, Lewisham 1977 and Southall 1979). The deaths of demonstrators Kevin Gately (1974) and Blair Peach (1979) were a testament to the violence unleashed on these occasions.

5. Notable examples in London include police raids and consequent disturbances at the Mangrove Cafe (1970) and the Metro Youth Club (1971) in Notting Hill, the Swan Disco in Stockwell (1974), the Carib Club in Cricklewood (1974) and the Four Aces Club in Dalston (1975) H. Joshua, T. Wallace, and H. Booth, *To Ride the Storm: The 1980 Bristol 'Riot' and the State* (London, 1983), pp. 59-61.

6. M. Keith, *Race, Riots and Policing: Lore and Disorder in a Multi-Racist Society* (London, 1983), pp. 123–4 (Keith 1983).

7. *Bristol Evening Post*, 1 April 2005. The author is indebted to John Serpico for both highlighting this article and writing the first eyewitness account of the Southmead 'riots' of 3–4 April 1980. See J. Serpico, *The Southmead Riots* (Bristol, 2006): http://www.brh.org.uk/site/articles/the-southmead-riots-2/ (Serpico 2006).

8. Avon & Somerset Constabulary, *Annual Report of the Chief Constable* (Bristol, 1980), p. 40 (Avon & Somerset Constabulary 1980).

9. See, for example, articles in the local papers: *Western Daily Press*, 7 April 1980; *Bristol Evening Post*, 21 May 1980.

10. *Western Daily Press*, 7 April 1980.

11. The slogans were painted on the shops in the early hours of Sunday 6 April and included 'Kill the Bill', 'Kill All Police' and 'Mental Mob'. See *Western Daily Press*, 7 April 1980, p. 2.

12. For the debates in Westminster see *Hansard*, Parliamentary Debates 3 April 1980 982 cc659–68, 1980 and *House of Lords Debates* 3 April 1980 407 cc1469–79, 1980. The visit of the Select Committee on Home Affairs Subcommittee on Race Relations and Immigration is documented in Home Office, *Minutes of Evidence Taken Before the Home-affairs Sub-committee on Race Relations and Immigration* (London, 1980).

13. Reports included Secretary of State for the Home Department, *Serious disturbances in St. Paul's, Bristol on 2 April 1980: A memorandum placed in the library of the House of Commons by the Secretary of State for the Home Department, following the report made to him by the Chief Constable of the Avon and Somerset Constabulary* Bristol Record Office 43129 Box 105: P ST PA B1, P. Stephenson, *Report of Bristol disturbances: April 2nd, 1980* Bristol Record Office 43129 Box 105: P ST PA B1, Equal Opportunities Sub-Committee, Bristol Teachers Association (NUT) commissioned by the Avon Division of the NUT, *After the fire: A report on education in St. Paul's Bristol and multi-ethnic education in Avon* (Bristol, 1980) and D. Bateman and R. Press, *Slumbering Volcano? - Report of an enquiry into the origins of the eruption in St. Paul's Bristol on 2nd April 1980* (Bristol, 1980). The latter contained the findings of the enquiry hosted by the Bristol Trade Union Council. The principal text concerning the disturbances from the period is H. Joshua, T. Wallace, and H. Booth, *To Ride the Storm: The 1980 Bristol 'Riot' and the State* (London, 1983) (Joshua et al. 1983). Several academic papers were produced, most notably the works of the crowd psychologist Stephen Reicher. See S. D. Reicher, 'The St Pauls Riot: An explanation of the limits of crowd action in terms of a social identity model', in J. Murphy (ed.), *Dialogues and Debates in Social Psychology*, Vol. 14 (Hove, 1984), pp. 187–204 (Reicher 1984); S. D. Reicher and J. Potter 'Psychological theory as intergroup perspective: A comparative analysis of "scientific" and "lay" accounts of crowd events', *Human Relations*, 38 (2) (1985), 167–89 (Reicher and Potter 1985).

14. All three areas were referenced in local government reports into poverty in the early 1980s as being areas of significant deprivation and high levels of 'social stress'. See Avon County Council, *Social Stress in Avon, 1981: A Preliminary Analysis* (Bristol, 1983) (Avon County Council 1983); Bristol City Council, *Poverty in Bristol: Final Report* (Bristol, 1985) (Bristol City Council 1985). See Ball, 'Violent Urban Disturbance', pp. 202–74, for a comprehensive demographic analysis.

15. The oral history sources referenced in this chapter are derived primarily from interviews with participants in the three disturbances in Bristol in April 1980 which are quoted in a more comprehensive form in Ball, 'Violent Urban Disturbance'.

16. The classing of Rastafarianism as a youth subculture rather than a religion in this case is not intended to detract from the latter, instead it reflects the important influence it had upon Black youth in the late 1970s. The lack of a central orthodoxy and formal hierarchy in Rastafarianism was important in its adoption and mutation by wider sections of youth and in its subsequent influence on other subcultures such as Punk. See E. E. Cashmore, *Rastaman: The Rastafarian*

Movement in England (London, 1983); idem, *The Rastafarians* (London, 1984) (Cashmore 1983).

17. J. Brent, *Searching for Community: Representation, Power and Action on an Urban Estate* (Bristol, 2009) (Brent 2009).

18. These narratives are based on more comprehensive accounts in Ball, 'Violent Urban Disturbance', pp. 275–346.

19. In the 1970s and 1980s 'frontlines' were associated with inner-city African-Caribbean communities and were often sites of confrontation of between the authorities and the local community, being simultaneously perceived as potential 'no go' areas by the police and as places of sanctuary by many of the local residents. Often within the 'frontline' (usually a street) lay specific clubs, cafés and pubs which became symbolic partly through their reputation for social activities (parties, gigs or 'hang-outs') as well as being locations for obtaining soft drugs, which in the early 1980s were typically cannabis resin or marijuana. They also gained a wider fame from the regular raids that were carried out by the police, sometimes resisted by the customers and nearby local community.

20. The café owner had his licence to sell alcohol removed in 1979 due to police objections. Many residents and customers considered this to be a clear case of racial discrimination.

21. It was subsequently claimed by several commentators that the order was 'historic' because such a withdrawal had never been seen on mainland Britain.

22. A comprehensive analysis of the properties looted and burned in St Pauls on 2 April 1980 is given in Ball, 'Violent Urban Disturbance', pp. 398–409.

23. In 1980 this particular area was at the junction with Arneside Road in front of the Southmead Youth Centre, part of the long flat expanse of green space that lies between the parallel Greystoke Avenues running through the centre of the Southmead estate. It was eventually developed into a car park for a supermarket as noted by Brent: 'One area, 'the green' was used so often as a gathering place and centre of joy-riding and battles with the police, that in 1996 it was built on' (Brent, *Searching for Community*, pp. 20 and 136).

24. *Western Daily Press*, 5 April 1980.

25. *Bristol Evening Post*, 22 May 1980.

26. Ball, 'Violent Urban Disturbance', p. 336.

27. Various estimates of the numbers of youths involved in at least the initial phases of the disturbances on Friday night are given in the sources. One oral history respondent recalled 'On the second night twice as many people and especially kids was up to it' (Ball, 'Violent Urban Disturbance', p. 338, n. 602) and newspapers reported that 'more than 200 youths' were involved (*Western Daily Press*, 5 April 1980), '80 to 120 youths' (*Bristol Evening Post*, 27 April 1980) and '150 youths' (*The Times*, 11 April 1980). The 1980 annual report of

the Avon and Somerset Constabulary stated 'gangs of youths numbering some two hundred' were engaged in the violence (p. 40).

28. Serpico, *The Southmead Riots*: http://www.brh.org.uk/site/articles/the-southmead-riots-2/.

29. Ball, 'Violent Urban Disturbance', p. 341.

30. Ball, 'Violent Urban Disturbance', p. 342. This event is corroborated by a newspaper report of the breaking of a police van window during the disturbances (*Bristol Evening Post*, 21 May 1980).

31. Ball, 'Violent Urban Disturbance', p. 347.

32. Ball, 'Violent Urban Disturbance', p. 347.

33. Ball, 'Violent Urban Disturbance', p. 348.

34. Hartcliffe estate lies on the outskirts of the city of Bristol, approximately 1.5 kilometres south-west of Knowle West.

35. Ball, 'Violent Urban Disturbance', p. 350.

36. Ball, 'Violent Urban Disturbance', p. 351.

37. Ball, 'Violent Urban Disturbance', p. 347 and 352.

38. J. L. Przybysz and D. J. Myers, 'Diffusion of contentious gatherings in England's 1830 Captain Swing uprising', paper presented at the Annual Meeting of the American Sociological Association, Atlanta, GA (2003), p. 4 (Przybysz and Myers 2003).

39. S. Reicher and C. Stott, *Mad Mobs and Englishmen? Myths and Realities of the 2011 Riots* (London, 2011), pp. 349–54 (Reicher and Stott 2011).

40. As the 1981 disturbances were peaking on 11 July, media campaigner Mary Whitehouse sent telegrams to the BBC and ITN broadcasting organisations suggesting that they were responsible for the spread of the 'riots' (*Daily Mail*, 14 July 1981). In November 1981 the Scarman report was published and this made reference to the 'copycat' effect, causing the debate to be reenergised. See Lord Scarman, *The Scarman Report* (Harmondsworth, 1986), pp. 173–175 (Scarman 1986).

41. Good examples from the 1980s are E. Moonman 'Copy-cat hooligans', *Contemporary Affairs Briefing*, 1 (9) (1981) (Moonman 1981) and R. Clutterbuck, 'Terrorism and urban violence', *Proceedings of the Academy of Political Science* (London, 1982) (Clutterbuck 1982), both of which emphasise the involvement of children influenced by television in the disturbances of 1981.

42. D. Myers and J. Przybysz, 'The diffusion of contentious gatherings in the Captain Swing Uprising,' in S. Poole and A. Spicer (eds.), *Captain Swing Reconsidered: Forty Years of Rural History from Below*, Southern History Society, Vol. 32 (Winchester, 2010), p. 3 (Myers and Przybysz 2010).

43. Social identity theories concerning collective violence are explicated in Reicher, 'The St Pauls Riot', pp. 187–204; Reicher and Potter, 'Psychological theory as intergroup perspective', 167–89; Reicher and Stott, *Mad Mobs and Englishmen?*

44. See for example *Daily Telegraph* (3 April 1980), *The Times* (3 April 1980), *Sun* (3 April 19080), *Daily Mail* (3 April 1980), *Daily Star* (3 April 1980), *Western Daily Press* (3 April 1980) and *Sunday Express* (6 April 1980).
45. These were the Northern, Eastern and North Central Areas. See also C. Thomas (dir.), *A Long Way from Home* (Bristol, 1981) (Thomas 1981).
46. Pen Park Girls School had a roll of 657 and Greenway Boys 536 in 1979–80, placing them in the group of the smallest secondary schools in Avon. The majority had over 1,000 pupils. See Avon County Council, *County of Avon Education Department, Multi-cultural Education Centre, Avon Schools at which members of Staff of Multi-cultural Education Centre are Teaching – April 1980* (Bristol Record Office 42974/2 Vol.1 Pt. B).
47. Ball, 'Violent Urban Disturbance', p. 247.
48. These positive outcomes were not always the case. Several oral history respondents and other sources note a stormy period in inter-ethnic relations in Southmead notably as a result of the influence of far-right groups such as the National Front and the British Movement particularly during and after the summer of 1979. See Ball, 'Violent Urban Disturbance', p. 248.
49. See for example E. E. Cashmore, *No Future: Youth and Society* (London, 1984) (Cashmore 1984); D. Hebdige *Subculture: The Meaning of Style* (London, 2008 edition) (Hebdige 2008); S. Jones, *Black Culture, White Youth: The Reggae Tradition from JA to UK* (Oxford, 1988) (Jones 1988).
50. Ball, 'Violent Urban Disturbance', p. 376.
51. Ball, 'Violent Urban Disturbance', p. 376.
52. This led to the 'Bristol sound' and its progenies Massive Attack, Tricky and Reprazent who became world famous in the 1990s. Members of Massive Attack developed out of the Wild Bunch who were regular DJ's at the 'Dug Out' club in the early 1980s. Tricky was well known to oral history respondents from Knowle West his home area. The origins and history of the 1980s Bristol music scene are sketched via the oral histories of the musicians, DJ's and graffiti artists of the period in C. Burton and G. Thompson, *Art & Sound of the Bristol Underground* (Bristol, 2009) (Burton and Thompson 2009).
53. Ball, 'Violent Urban Disturbance', pp. 377–8.
54. Ball, 'Violent Urban Disturbance', pp. 377–8.
55. Ball, 'Violent Urban Disturbance', pp. 380–1.
56. Ball, 'Violent Urban Disturbance', pp. 382–3.
57. Ball, 'Violent Urban Disturbance', pp. 384–5.
58. Social network analysis of 'rioters' present during the 2 April 1980 disturbance in St Pauls demonstrates the role that second-generation African-Caribbean youth, such as the 'Half Breeds', played in traversing ethnic divisions through sub-cultural linkages. See Ball, 'Violent Urban Disturbance', pp. 388–91.
59. H. Tumber *Television and the Riots: A Report for the Broadcasting Research Unit of the British Film Institute* (London, 1982) (Tumber 1982). The findings

in this report were supported by a survey of oral history respondents who participated in the Bristol 'riots' of 1980 in Ball, 'Violent Urban Disturbance', pp. 367–70.
60. Tumber *Television and the Riots*, p. 46.

REFERENCES

Avon County Council, *County of Avon Education Department, Multi-cultural Education Centre, Avon Schools at which members of Staff of Multi-cultural Education Centre are teaching – April 1980* (Bristol Record Office 42974/2 Vol.1 Pt. B., 1980).

Avon County Council, *Social Stress in Avon, 1981: A Preliminary Analysis* (Bristol, 1983).

Avon & Somerset Constabulary, *Annual Report of the Chief Constable* (Bristol, 1980).

R. Ball, 'Violent Urban Disturbance in England 1980–1', unpublished Ph.D. University of the West of England, 2012 available at http://eprints.uwe.ac.uk/17958/.

D. Bateman and R. Press, *Slumbering Volcano? – Report of an Enquiry into the Origins of the Eruption in St. Paul's Bristol on 2nd April 1980* (Bristol, 1980).

J. Brent, *Searching for Community: Representation, Power and Action on an Urban Estate* (Bristol, 2009).

Bristol City Council, *Poverty in Bristol: Final Report* (Bristol, 1985).

C. Burton and G. Thompson, *Art & Sound of the Bristol Underground* (Bristol, 2009).

E. E. Cashmore, *Rastaman: The Rastafarian Movement in England* (London, 1983).

E. E. Cashmore, *No Future: Youth and Society* (London, 1984).

E. E. Cashmore, *The Rastafarians* (London, 1984).

R. Clutterbuck, 'Terrorism and urban violence', *Proceedings of the Academy of Political Science* (London, 1982).

Equal Opportunities Sub-Committee, Bristol Teachers Association (NUT) commissioned by the Avon Division of the NUT, *After the fire: A Report on Education in St. Paul's Bristol and Multi-Ethnic Education in Avon* (Bristol, 1980).

D. Hebdige *Subculture: The Meaning of Style* (London, 2008 edition)

Historic Hansard, Bristol (disturbance), *House of Commons Parliamentary Debates 3 April 1980 982* cc659–68. 1980.

Historic Hansard, *Disturbances at Bristol, House of Lords Debates 3 April 1980 407* cc1469–79. 1980.

Home Office, *Minutes of evidence taken before the Home-affairs Sub-committee on Race Relations and Immigration (22nd May 1980)* Bristol Record Office 42974/1 Vol.1 Pt. A.

S. Jones, *Black Culture, White Youth: The Reggae Tradition from JA to UK* (Oxford, 1988).

H. Joshua, T. Wallace, and H. Booth, *To Ride the Storm: The* 1980 *Bristol 'Riot' and the State* (London, 1983).

M. Keith, *Race, Riots and Policing: Lore and Disorder in a Multi-Racist Society* (London, 1983).

E. Moonman 'Copy-cat hooligans', *Contemporary Affairs Briefing*, 1, 9 (1981).

D. Myers and J. Przybysz, 'The Diffusion of Contentious Gatherings in the Captain Swing Uprising,' in S. Poole and A. Spicer (eds.), *Captain Swing Reconsidered: Forty Years of Rural History from Below* (Winchester, 2010), Southern History Society Vol.32.

J. L. Przybysz and D. J. Myers, 'Diffusion of Contentious Gatherings in England's 1830 Captain Swing Uprising', paper presented at the Annual Meeting of the American Sociological Association, Atlanta, GA (2003).

S. Reicher and C. Stott, *Mad Mobs and Englishmen? Myths and Realities of the* 2011 *Riots* (London, 2011).

S. D. Reicher, 'The St. Paul's Riot: An Explanation of the Limits of Crowd Action in Terms of a Social Identity Model', in J. Murphy (ed.), *Dialogues and Debates in Social Psychology* Vol. 14 (Hove, 1984).

S. D. Reicher and J. Potter 'Psychological Theory as Intergroup Perspective: A Comparative Analysis of 'Scientific' and 'Lay' Accounts of Crowd Events', *Human Relations*, 38, 2 (1985), 167–89.

Lord Scarman, *The Scarman Report* (Harmondsworth, 1986).

Secretary of State for the Home Department. *Serious disturbances in St. Paul's, Bristol on 2 April 1980: A memorandum placed in the library of the House of Commons by the Secretary of State for the Home Department, following the report made to him by the Chief Constable of the Avon and Somerset Constabulary.* Bristol Record Office 43129 Box 105: P ST PA B1. 1980.

J. Serpico, *The Southmead Riots* (Bristol, 2006): http://www.brh.org.uk/site/articles/the-southmead-riots-2/.

P. Stephenson, *Report of Bristol disturbances: April 2nd, 1980.* Bristol Record Office 43129 Box 105: P ST PA B1. 1980.

C. Thomas (dir.), *A Long Way from Home* (Bristol, 1981).

H. Tumber *Television and the Riots: A Report for the Broadcasting Research Unit of the British Film Institute* (London, 1982).

Roger Ball a founding member of the Bristol Radical History Group (BRHG), received his PhD in History from the University of the West of England in 2012 with a thesis entitled *Violent Urban Disturbance in England 1980–81.* Roger is currently employed as a Research Fellow in the School of Psychology at Keele University analysing the anatomy and dynamics of the August 2011 UK Riots as part of the ESRC funded research project *Beyond contagion: Social identity processes in involuntary social influence*. As an active member of BRHG he is involved in several studies focused on Bristol including the Victorian workhouse, the 1831 Reform 'riots' and strikes, mutinies and refusals in the British armed forces during World War One. The author was partially supported during the writing of this chapter by a research grant from the Economic and Social Research Council (ES/N01068X/1).

CHAPTER 3

The Language of the Unheard: Social Media and Riot Subculture/s

Louis Rice

Riots took place in Bristol in 2011. The events began early on 21 April and lasted until the early hours of 22 April; much of an inner-city area in Bristol was blocked by hundreds of protestors, demonstrators and onlookers as well as a large police presence. Whilst the daytime was relatively peaceful, in the evening there were a series of violent exchanges between police and protestors. The violent episodes involved 'riot vans, police in full riot gear with shields' (@pearcafe, 2011a); 'stones and fireworks being thrown at the [police] vans, bins being set on fire' (@efergan, 2011) and 'wheelie bins on fire . . . a police landrover was trashed, with paint tipped all over it and people trying to pull the doors off'.[1] Police and protesters clashed for several hours, which left dozens of people injured as well as damage to buildings and cars in the area.

Many people filmed and photographed events then uploaded this information via social media, along with tweets and other text-based commentaries on the events: 'ripped all the photos over to my laptop, blogged an image'.[2] Commentary, films and photographs uploaded onto social media real-time were watched by (more) people online who subsequently posted their own interpretation of events. Social media was used by individuals to keep informed about the riots as initially there was little

L. Rice (✉)
Architecture and Urbanism, University of the West of England, Bristol, UK
e-mail: Louis.Rice@uwe.ac.uk

© The Author(s) 2017   47
K. Gildart et al. (eds.), *Youth Culture and Social Change*,
Palgrave Studies in the History of Subcultures and Popular Music,
DOI 10.1057/978-1-137-52911-4_3

or no information on mainstream media 'seems the only good source of information for what's going down in Bristol right now is the #stokescroft hashtag' (@robjmills, 2011). So important was the role of social media that one blogger suggested that 'it all started on social media: #bristol's #stokescroft riots'.[3] Even when mainstream media did carry news of the events, mostly the day following the events, many people preferred to source their information from social media.

This research examines the relationships between social media, subculture identity and riots. The first part of the chapter briefly contextualises the key terms within existing literature and then situates the events, in terms of existing social, urban, economic and political context, in the specifics of this inner-city location. The term *'riot subculture'* is adopted here to loosely ascribe those individuals and groups who express support, or sympathy, for these riots and/or riots more generally. The second part of the chapter draws on empirical research concerning the April 2011 riots that broke out in Stokes Croft, an inner-city part of Bristol. The findings show how individuals and groups produce knowledge about the riots that differ, on alternative forms of media. The portrayal of the riot varies significantly between mainstream media and social media. Two representations emerge: the 'official representation' of the police, which is echoed by mainstream media; and 'unofficial representation' which rejects the official view and provides a variety of alternative perspectives of the events. There is an appendix at the end of the chapter detailing the methodological issues raised in this research.

WHAT IS SOCIAL MEDIA?

Social media is a widely used (and abused) term that refers to myriad forms of digital communication. Social media enables users to create and share textual information and visual data such as photographs and video footage.[4] Communications can be shared between friends and groups with common interests but can be disseminated to strangers (and can be anonymously created). All social media operates over the internet or other digital communication networks. Social media is accessed from personal computers and laptops as well as portable devices such as mobile phones and tablets. Social media can be described as the 'many relatively inexpensive and widely accessible electronic tools that enable anyone to publish and access information, collaborate on a common effort, or build relationships'.[5] There are many different providers of social media sites and applications, however those most commonly used in this context are: Twitter, Facebook, Flickr and YouTube. Whilst there are differences between the platforms, all enable users to upload, 'post' or 'tweet' information (textual information and/or visual material) online. Social media as a popular, global phenomenon began in earnest in the mid-to-late 2000s.

SOCIAL MEDIA AND SOCIAL UNREST

Everyone watching these horrific actions will be struck by how they were orga-
nised via social media
British Prime Minister: David Cameron.[6]

Social media has played a significant role in situations of urban and social unrest, protests, riots and revolutions.[7] The 'Arab Spring' is perhaps the best-known example of political unrest related to social media.[8] Starting in 2010, a series of demonstrations, protests and riots erupted across much of the Arab world. The protests involved marches, strikes, rallies, street protests and the occupation of major public spaces.[9] Social media was used to organise, disseminate and raise awareness of these events. The virality of these social media practices concerned the governing regimes. States attempted censorship and blackouts of social media, such was their fear of the role of social media in promulgating these events. The role of social media is particularly pertinent in this context because much of the mainstream media was state-controlled.[10] Social media enabled the production and publishing of content that traditional media channels were prohibited from using. In the same way, social media is linked directly to riots in the UK. The term 'Facebook riot' was used by national newspapers in relation to an incitement to riot.[11] The August 2011 riots in the UK were dubbed the 'Blackberry Riots' due to the the Blackberry[12] messaging service being used as the communication system of organisers of some of the lootings.[13]

THE PRODUCTION OF KNOWLEDGE

Social media permits individuals and groups to publish with (almost) no censorship or controls. Users can create, harvest or produce knowledge and disseminate online via social media. Social media enables the production of knowledge outside of traditional or mainstream media.

It is argued that traditional media mostly involves the 'consumption' of knowledge with television viewers or newspaper readers as passive consumers.[14] The shift from consumption of knowledge to production of knowledge is considered to be a significant change brought about by social media.[15] Perhaps one of the most innovative aspects of 'user-generated content' is the ability to produce content collectively. Users and groups can work together in a 'participatory culture' to produce an account of an event or a shared interest.[16] Eric Schmidt, the CEO of Google, defines the importance of this shift in production as: 'the largest experiment involving anarchy in history'.[17] Anarchy is defined here, not as chaos and disorder, but as a system of self-government in the absence of a controlling authority.[18] The notion of anarchy echoes much of the commentary in relation to the riot subcultures (examined further in the next part of this chapter).

Social media differs from traditional media, such as newspapers and television, in that the content is created outside of large institutions and organisations. According to Schmidt, social media will make it possible for almost everybody to own, develop and disseminate real-time content without having to rely on intermediaries. The absence of intermediaries is also seen as removing powerful corporate or political bias from knowledge production. Newspapers and television broadcasters are sometimes considered to be inherently biased as they invariably need to meet the requirements of advertisers or editorial standards of overtly political organisations and also work within (rather than outside of) established structures of power. Individuals who publish via social media are free from such editorial constraints and pressures. This independence can be seen as enabling social media to allow the 'truth' to be published. However very little of the content of social media content is verified, making it difficult to know which information is speculative or factual. The emerging capacity to create knowledge is liberating in the sense that anyone is free to produce information or disclose previously unreported issues or points of view. Those without the power to speak on mainstream media (or in society more generally) are given freedom to comment. Issues that might be uncomfortable in 'normal' social situations, for example taboo or embarrassing topics, are aired more freely via the anonymity of social media.[19] There are concerns over social media content as radical, revolutionary, seditious and illegal views can be published.[20] Extremist material on social media is very difficult to censor or control.

SUBCULTURES, SOCIAL MEDIA AND IDENTITY PRODUCTION

Social media is a popular forum for many subcultures. A subculture is a group of people with shared beliefs or interests who differentiate or segregate themselves from others within that society.[21] Each subculture shares or adopts artifacts, values, opinions, clothing, mannerisms, language and/or behavioral traits specific to that subculture.[22] Social media can enable subcultures to gather and/or assemble (online) and social media itself may act to propagate a subculture. The *'sub'* in subculture does not denote a lesser nor inferior culture, rather it merely indicates a smaller part or subsection of society in general. A fundamental criterion often associated with subcultures is the adoption of a subversive ideology.[23] The term subversive is broadly defined as those seeking to undermine the power of the established system of authority and control. The ideological position of a subcultural group might be latent or expressed, but is often found underpinning much of the group's shared value system.[24] Ideologies are often based on the rejection of capitalism or the repudiation of the notion of *'work'* – particularly in relation to mass production or regimented lifestyles.[25] The use of social media for following topics such as '#riots' is common to some individuals and subcultures unified by a subversive ideology.

A subculture can develop through social media. It is no longer necessary for a subculture to have a physical space to communicate; this can now occur through social media. In turn, social media can play a role in the development of personal and subculture identity.[26] The process of identity formation in this context is related to the iterative psychic and social performative actions of individuals or groups.[27] Social media's collaborative production can enable 'new' collective identities to be constructed. Furthermore, individuals and subcultures predisposed, or receptive, to a subversive ideology may become radicalised through social media.[28] Social media can play a role in facilitating new identities; however there is scepticism about the impact of social media on individuals or society acting in the 'real world'.[29] There is concern about social media being a platform for illusory agency, with individuals exercising their subversive views exclusively in the virtual domain. The precise influence or power of social media on identity formation and action is contested and unclear. However there are many governments and regimes that are sufficiently convinced about the correlation between social media and riot subcultures that they attempt to block, control and censor social media.

FINDINGS

For the first time in the UK, social media was used on a large scale to report a riot real-time. The research analyses why social media was used and by whom. This analysis provides a clearer understanding of the relationships between social media and riot subcultures. Posts on social media provided differing accounts of the events of the riot. These accounts of the riot are a form of knowledge production and have been categorised into two polarised groups: 'official' knowledge of the riots (which is dominated by the police version of events and subsequently reiterated by mainstream media); or 'unofficial' knowledge (which tends to reject the official account and instead provides a variety of alternative accounts which are mostly hosted on social media platforms). The findings then examine how official and unofficial knowledge is disseminated and *re*presented. Social media becomes the location where riot subculture knowledge is presented and *re*presented. Through this process, social media becomes a representation of the riot subculture itself. The findings are based on analysis of the empirical evidence gathered from the case-study of the 2011 riots in Bristol. The section begins by situating the riots within local conditions, describing the existing sociopolitical and urban context.

THE CULTURAL CONTEXT OF THE RIOT

Stokes Croft is a neighbourhood in Bristol, located in one of the most deprived parts of the UK. It is a 'typical' inner-city area with some derelict buildings and space as a result of post-war planning blight and economic abandonment.[30] Clement contextualises the riots amidst the background issues of 'gentrification, lack of housing and rising levels of inequality; the mixed and multicultural nature of the local population'.[31] The area now houses a diverse demographic: a relatively deprived local population along with a vibrant and active 'artistic' subculture and more recently an influx of wealthier white-collar workers. Whilst similar to many UK inner-city areas, Stokes Croft does have its own unique characteristics and identity. A number of squats were established in the derelict and abandoned buildings. One of these squats, known locally as 'Telepathic Heights' (due to these words written on the building as graffiti) was at the epicentre of the riot. Allied to the squatter population was an influx of artistic/ creative subcultures that set up a number of low-rent galleries and studios as well as independent cafes, bars and nightclubs. There were many protest groups in the area who were trying to address issues such as rejecting expensive residential developments; supporting more affordable housing projects; deterring big property developers from taking control of the area; resisting (perceived) attempts by the local council to enforce a top-down regeneration of the area; and promote 'bottom-up' development. Many of these protest groups could be described as sharing a subversive agenda. The area itself was perhaps most (in)famous for being the 'birthplace' (in the artistic sense) of Banksy, who produced many of his earliest pieces of graffiti here. Whilst graffiti has become much more mainstream, particularly in the case of Banksy whose work is now revered and officially preserved in Bristol, graffiti can still be categorised as an indicator of a specific subculture of protest. Graffiti is *antisocial* media for many councils, local authorities and property owners. This triumvirate of squatters, artists and Banksy lent a distinctive presence to the area.

Much of the violence in these riots was focused on a Tesco supermarket that was located in the heart of the area (opposite the 'Telepathic Heights' squat). As a result of the prominence of the damage to this Tesco supermarket, the riots in Bristol 2011 are sometimes referred to as the 'Tesco Riots'.[32] The supermarket was unpopular with many of the nearby community: it had been granted planning permission in the face of considerable local opposition and protestation. The antipathy towards Tesco relates both to this particular supermarket and more broadly to the practices of large corporations. Tesco is very powerful economically; it is the biggest private employer and retailer in the UK[33] and has attained almost iconic status qua '*capitalism*' as a result of its size and dominance.

THE POLICE ARRIVE...

The immediate precursor event to the riots was the attempted eviction of the 'Telepathic Heights' squat by police. Some commentators point to this as the catalyst for the riots.[34] According to reports on social media the eviction was to be carried out by 'a huge police operation involving 160 armed officers' and 'over a dozen wagons and hundreds of officers'[35] Descriptions of and comments on the eviction were tweeted by locals, who were mostly curious onlookers of the large police presence: 'Squat on #stokescroft is being evicted. 'Copter above us for half an hour. 10+ riot vans. Road closed' (@pearcafe, 2011b). Tweets relating to the eviction were retweeted repeatedly. The eviction operation blocked the main road and caused disruption to the local area. The developing spectacle of a large police presence, a forced eviction, numerous protesting squatters and a gathering crowd of onlookers was being played out directly opposite the recently opened (and much opposed) Tesco supermarket.

SOCIAL MEDIA BROADCASTING

Social media was used to convey the evolving spectacle: 'tens of thousands of people from across the world watched unfolding live in the small hours of the morning as locals tweeted reports and uploaded video footage directly from their phones'.[36] Social media became the frame through which people would follow the events real-time.[37] People in the crowd were using portable devices to record the events: 'lots of pics and videos being taken on camera phones'.[38] Recordings of the events were broadcast through mobile devices on a variety of different social media channels: 'from just before midnight, a local resident going by the Twitter handle @grantikins began to live-stream a video broadcast of the events from his mobile phone'.[39] These broadcasts were followed by people who were also present in the streets and by many others watching remotely: 'seems people rather interested in #stokescroft riot' (@bristol247, 2011); 'soon thousands of people, following the hashtag #stokescroft, were watching and discussing the action online'; 'this #Stokescroft riot is really kicking off. Twitter tells me there may have been one arrest, and possibly no injuries' (@BenPark, 2011).[40] More people followed the events on social media, looking for information and updates on the emerging situation, often following the hashtag #stokescroft (@StokesCroftNews, 2011a). 'Huge spike in traffic overloaded poor server - back up now' (@bristol247, 2011): the number of people following the riot online greatly outnumbered those present on the streets, to the point that internet servers struggled with this demand. Whilst there were several hundreds of people on the street - there were hundreds of thousands watching online.[41]

THE PRODUCTION OF KNOWLEDGE: WHO ARE THE 'RIOTERS'?

Knowledge about the status and meaning of the violent events in the street was produced by a variety of people and groups. Different voices presented and *re*presented the events from alternative perspectives. The outcome of these producers of knowledge is heterogeneous. The depiction of events varies depending on who speaks and for whom they are speaking. These interpretations and narratives involve the production of knowledge. There was a lot of discussion and disagreement on social media about the make-up of the rioting corpus: who are the rioters and/or who are *not* the rioters? Many differing accounts emerged, which can be categorised into two groups: 'official' and 'unofficial'. The 'official' production of knowledge includes the police account of events and those transmitted in mainstream media. The official version consists of a homogeneous, fixed account of the riots from a single-point perspective. The 'unofficial' production of knowledge is polyphonic and includes a myriad of differing accounts of the riot, which mostly differ from the official view. One particular subset of the unofficial view provides an entirely inverse account to the official, characterising the police as the rioters.

OFFICIAL PRODUCTION OF KNOWLEDGE

The most unequivocal presentation of the events was provided by the police force. The police were very clear about the constitution of the rioters. Assistant Chief Constable Rod Hansen describes the event: '300 people congregated and a small minority from that group started small fires and throwing bottles, stones and other items at officers'.[42] The police categorised all 300 people in the street as constituting the 'rioting' crowd. This account of the event partly explains why the police carried out a 'robust operation' on this crowd: 'we used well-rehearsed plans, which involved the use of officers from neighbouring forces to control what had become a volatile situation' – i.e. using batons, shields, police horses, police dogs and riot vans against many of these 300 people.[43] This account was not universally accepted as accurate: 'Police bullshit. Standard' (@AaronBastani, 2011). 'The police then charged through the handful of bottle throwers all the way in to the main section of the "party" which seemed to be a disproportionate and inflammatory response that if anything I was surprised didn't elicit a harsher retaliation from the "party-goers"' (Neurobonkers, 2011).[44] The police report itself referred to a 'small minority' engaged in violent actions, whilst accepting that the majority of the people in the locality were peaceful. According to eye-witnesses, the police did not target just the small minority of violent protestors, but instead carried out their 'robust operations' on some of the innocent bystanders and peaceful protestors. Whilst the vast majority of all comments on social media are critical of the police account of events, some on social media supported the police. 'I am delighted that the crowd seem to be aggressive and the Police not' (The Posie Parker, 2011); 'Lot's of footage saying things like "the police are beating us up and we are not doing anything" but there is no voice from the police saying "people are throwing bricks, stones and glass at us!'" (Ben, 2011).[45] Irrespective of the validity of claim or counterclaims, the official view classified all of the 300 people in the street that evening as part of the riot corpus.

UNOFFICIAL PRODUCTION OF KNOWLEDGE

The majority of the commentators on social media rejected the notion that there was a group of 300 'rioters'. Instead the large number of people on the streets was reported to consist of 'Activists... bystanders and commuters... symbolic anti-capitalist protesters... squatters, local youth, besieged residents, students', as well as a small number of violent individuals.[46] A common re-presentation, as related here by the local MP, rejects the official account and instead offers this account: 'The protestors fell into three categories. There was those lobbing great big lumps of concrete and bottles at the police... Then there were what I'd call "typical Stokes Croft" people, peacefully protesting... And then there was the vast majority of people who were there, like me, to see what was going on. Either on their way home... or locals who had heard the news and were curious.'[47] The largest group were curious onlookers: 'Most, it seemed, weren't there to protest against anything in particular, but rather to see what was a huge police operation involving 160 armed officers'; with 'the majority, just seeing what was going on' (@efergan, 2011).[48] The groups of onlookers comprised local residents, commuters passing through or people who frequented the area for its bars, cafes and pubs. Video footage of the events was used (post hoc) to corroborate claims on social media. The second cohort were 'peaceful protestors': individuals more actively involved in the event as part of protests or demonstrations. The constituency of this group is difficult to pin down precisely as it was so diverse – people with myriad interests and accounts, some of whom described themselves as 'masked up, clued-up activists'.[49] These were people allied to the anti-Tesco protests, anti-police, sympathisers of the Telepathic Height squatters. These more politically motivated people were still overtly 'peaceful' in their intentions. This third cohort also included a corpus of individuals who co-opted the events into a moment for a carnival or festival. 'BEST PRE PARTY EVER!!! #stokescroftriot' (@sam_binga, 2011); 'pretty much felt like St Paul's carnival, but with less dub' (@efergan, 2011); 'The mood began to take on the feel of a small festival, the crowd cheered when somebody started playing some R&B music through a small sound system'. With the roads closed to traffic, some in the crowd chose to be playful: 'We've been chanting 'you're sexy, you're cute, take off your riot suit!'' (@smasherkins, 2011); 'The saxaphone [sic] players on the bus stop are soothing – #stokescroft' (@rossoh, 2011b); with 'revellers' (@Cutl00se, 2011); 'laying their bicycles in the street, playing bongos, a trumpet'.[50] This cohort appropriated the spectacle into an opportunity for revelry and non-productive activities. The unofficial production of knowledge is polyphonic in that many different voices portrayed these events. Whilst resisting an overall single narrative, a loose consensus was assembled through the collective interpretations of the event from bystanders, onlookers (including onlookers accessing the event through social media) and protestors. The third cohort were the 'rioters'; people who engaged in violence towards the police and/or property: 'They're breaking into tesco again. police have driven off. #stokescroft' (@rossoh, 2011a). There was widespread agreement that there was a small minority of people who were actively engaged in violence: 'there were a few who seemed to be just trying to cause some shit... throwing bottles, bricks etc' (@efergan, 2011). The violence was directed sometimes at the police and the local Tesco store but also at other shops nearby, as well as at cars and other objects in the area (bins, doors etc.).

POLICE RIOT

'The police are the rioters' was the message from some of the unofficial producers of knowledge. This discourse asserts that it was the police themselves who rioted. This account of the riot produced knowledge that inverted the official view. According to this view, heavy-handed policing techniques combined with indiscriminate use of force should be reclassified as a 'riot'. There was widespread commentary relating to excessive police force that evening: 'hugely aggressive policing on #stokescroft - protester fleeing with head wounds' (@BristolFloozie, 2011); '#Stokescroft Friend hit across face with riot shield and struck with baton 1 metre from home. Ear stitched. Bad po' (@20thCFlicks, 2011); '#stokescroft police brutality is mental, saw a 16 year old boy beaten by batons whilst unarmed and on the floor' (@CasparBrown, 2011a). 'Police from higher up the road marched down with dogs and cornered the crowd between a row of riot guards and vans' resulting in a 'seriously disproportionate and provocative police action'; 'did police heavy-handedness contribute to the riot?' (@StokesCroftNews, 2011b)[51]. The use of excessive force was also claimed to be poorly directed: 'An officer I spoke to said that they didn't have time to work out who was a threat and who wasn't', which implicated the police in the position of indiscriminate violence against innocent individuals.[52] The police were accused of acting in a manner that met the legal definition of riot'.

The implication of police qua rioters was mostly attributed to incompetent or overzealous police tactics and practices. Some critiques went further and accused the police of being puppets of capitalism. 'If big-business capitalism weren't on its last legs, it wouldn't need to rely on police brutality and political corruption like this'.[53] Part of the reasoning behind this perspective is that the police (qua government) collude with big business (qua capitalism/Tesco) and take action on their behalf, for example 'the country has gone insane when supermarkets are forced onto communities with riot police'.[54] The corollary of this logic is that the violence meted out against the police is justifiable, the violence on the streets is a self-defence mechanism in response to the 'violence' caused by capitalism itself, i.e. 'Tesco . . . brutality' (@SirioCD, 2011); 'Aren't Tesco the bigger hooligans? . . . Or the Tories even bigger hooligans destroying the country?'[55] Justification of this riot was often linked to anti-capitalism: 'an important riot against capitalist oppression' (@CasparBrown, 2011b); 'Capitalist totalitarianism!'[56] 'DESTROY CAPITALISM #stokescroft' (@DSG_DSG, 2011). 'I am clear that the damage caused to Tesco's property last night is relatively insignificant compared to the damage Tesco has been able to inflict on this community'.[57] These point to the 'violence' caused by Tesco/capitalism – the damage caused by multinationals on: the environment, local economies, fragile societies and equality.[58] The riots in Bristol were interpreted not merely as a local protest or grievance, but part of a wider, global, anti-capitalist counter-movement. These critiques all shared an implicit (and sometimes explicit) subversive ideology.

DEFINITION OF A RIOT

A riot is the language of the unheard
Martin Luther King

The use of the term 'riot' and its application in relation to the violent events in Bristol was vehemently contested on social media. Part of the disagreement among commentators stemmed from the diverse meanings of the term 'riot'. This subsection examines these multiple definitions and the purposive application of this language. The production of knowledge, official or unofficial, needs to be understood within the wider context of the term 'riot'. Three areas of controversy surround the use of the term, relating partly to the use of the term colloquially: the legal definition, the purposive use of the word, and concern of the use for political reasons.

The legal definition of a riot is: 'twelve or more persons; used or threatened unlawful violence; for a common purpose'.[59] A minimum of twelve people must be involved, which is rather smaller than a common conception of a riot (a game of rugby might constitute a riot according to these terms of reference!) All of these twelve or more persons must act for a common purpose, which might be political or for a particular cause. The same legislation goes on to state that 'others can commit this offence by aiding, abetting, counselling or procuring the use of violence, e.g. encouraging, planning, directing or coordinating the activities of those involved in violent action'.[60] The effect of this law means that members of the crowd can become designated as rioters even without performing any acts of violence themselves.

Secondly, the police and regulatory authorities purposively replace the term 'riot'. Whilst the terms 'riot police' and 'riot van' are widely used in the UK by the general population, the police themselves refer instead to the 'public order minibus' and 'Police Support Unit'. In the UK, 'read the Riot Act' has become synonymous with a severe or violent reprimand. Similarly, the legislation 'Riot Act' (repealed in 1967) has (effectively) become the much more solemnly titled 'UK Public Order Act'.

Thirdly, many of those commenting on the events were reluctant to accept the term 'riot' as it was a term designated by the police and was both unwarranted in this situation and carried a negative connotation. Instead terms such as 'protest' or 'demonstration' were preferred as these were deemed to reflect more accurately the events as well as implying that these actions carried a political intent. For others, there was a desire to re-appropriate the word 'riot' from the policing/legal interpretation and instead use it in a positive way – taking the term to mean perhaps a carnivalesque event or a festival.[61] 'Riot' can mean having fun or a highly amusing event. The three contested applications of the term partly explain the differing accounts of the events in Stokes Croft.

There were many alternative accounts of what happened during the riots, even those outlined above are a simplification. Whilst there were accounts in mainstream media that depart from the official account, they were rarely afforded the same priority as the official 'news' on the front of a newspaper; instead they came in the form of 'discussion' or 'debate' buried deep in the newspaper. Equally, on social media, there were supporters of the official production of knowledge, but these tended to be posts within an unofficial representation. There were reports of good police, bad police, violent protestors, peaceful protestors, passers-by, families, commuters, squatters, activists, frustrated residents, drunks wandering home, children, party-goers, musicians and local press. The categorisation into official and unofficial is intended to simplify (but not oversimplify) the complex and often conflicting accounts of the riot. This meta-narrative does not attempt to adjudicate on which production of knowledge is correct or not.

REPRESENTATION OF THE RIOTS

Many social media commentators have made explicit claims about the role of social media and mainstream media in relation to the production of knowledge about riots. This section examines the perceived relationships between different forms of media and representations of the Stokes Croft riot. There was a difference between mainstream media's representation and social media's representation of the riots. The representation on mainstream media tended to be closely aligned with the official production of knowledge; whereas social media's representation tended to convey the unofficial production of knowledge. The previous section examined how knowledge is produced and by whom; this section examines the role of how knowledge is disseminated and *re*presented.

Official representation: mainstream media

The morning after the riots, mainstream media published their version of events. Most national newspapers covered the events on their front pages, and a similar level of prominence was given on online news agencies. The representation of the riot in almost all mainstream media accorded with the official representation. These were mainstream media's frontpage headlines:

'Bristol riot over new Tesco store leaves eight police officers injured' [*The Guardian*]
'Bristol mob wrecks Tesco store and attacks police' [*The Times*]

'Eight police hurt during Bristol riot' [*The Telegraph*]
'Police hurt in violent anti-Tesco clashes in Bristol' [*BBC*]

These headlines (and the stories that followed) elicited much reaction from commentators on social media. There were a number of concerns and criticisms of mainstream media. The first criticism concerned the regurgitation of official police reports as their own – with little mediation, corroboration or editing undertaken. 'All I can find on the BBC, practically written by the police' (@paddywagon, 2011); 'BBC, the UK state and police PR agency... #stokescroft' (@b9AcE, 2011); 'It's really eye-opening to see the BBC just copy-paste the police PR. #stokescroft' (@mtdavies23, 2011); 'BBC copy and paste Churnalism from Police PRO's around #Stokescroft' (@soundmigration, 2011). 'Churnalism' is a form of journalism where articles are created from press releases and repeated almost verbatim with little or no checking of veracity. Churnalism.com, a website that checks the degree of churnalism in a newspaper article, by comparing it to e.g. a police report, found that many of the mainstream media articles cut and paste the majority of their public order and crime material directly from police reports. The degree of churnalism was tweeted and retweeted about many times on social media 'BBC coverage of #stokescroft riots is a recycled police press release' (@GuyAitchison, 2011b); 'papers spout the police line unquestioningly'.[62]The process of representation of unedited police reports as news can undermine credibility in the impartiality and independence of mainstream media.[63]

The second criticism of mainstream media representation of the riot was that it was biased and partial. It is self-evident that the mainstream media headlines (above) focused on the injuries suffered by the police. Whilst it was reasonable and justifiable for mainstream media to report on injuries to the police force, social media commentators argued that mainstream media did not sufficiently counterbalance their accounts with, for example, mention of the injuries suffered by the general public, innocent bystanders, or injuries caused to the rioters. Many commentators questioned the BBC and mainstream media's impartiality: 'Wow, amazing that Twitter is actually a better news source than the BBC. It's all so selective and biased! #stokescroft' (@jennieloveday 2011), 'Fuck all about #stokescroft riot in the mainstream media. Thank god for Twitter' (@GuyAitchison, 2011a); 'while there was a proper riot in Bristol, folks from mainstream media were hooked on crack cocaine on the couch. #stokescroft' (@immorali, 2011); and 'so far the mainstream press has reported only the official line on these events'.[64] Despite formal regulations governing impartiality and fairness, many social media commentators do not believe they are followed.[65] Critics of mainstream media pointed out that the definition of 'impartial' means to 'treat all disputants equally'; it was argued, for example, that all people who were injured should be reported and not just a small subgroup (i.e. police officers).[66]

There was a broader criticism: that mainstream media was state controlled.. The concern was that mainstream media clandestinely operated as a state broadcaster – i.e. as a biased propaganda mouthpiece of the ruling elite and their interests. The notion of mainstream media *qua* state controlled media was exacerbated by the absence of coverage of these events. 'Looks to me like the media has been ordered not to run the #StokesCroft riot story' (@SDMumford, 2011); 'how are no news channels picking up this riot #stokescroft' (@CasparBrown, 2011c); 'Thank fuck for twitter #stokescroft' (@spooklouder, 2011); 'searching for info on #StokesCroft uprising in the absence of proper media coverage is like living in fucking China or North Korea' (@meowist_gorilla, 2011). These echo the concern that state-controlled media often blocks or bans reporting of certain events – a proposition that the UK government is considering.[67] All of the criticisms of mainstream media representation: churnalism, lack of impartiality, lack of independence and police collusion formed part of a wider theory that mainstream media was representative of those in power. That is, mainstream media was the mouthpiece of the ruling elite, capitalism and/or the exercisers of hegemony in general.

Unofficial representation: the move away from mainstream media

Fuck you mainstream media, we don't need you anymore
@BrumProtestor (2011)

The frustration with, and suspicions of, mainstream media led many to look towards social media representation for news. 'The lackluster (sic) reporting illustrates why more and more young people are choosing to reject the mainstream media altogether, as they turn to social networks for information perceived as more reliable' (Gallagher, 2011); 'I no longer trust our media reporting of these sorts of incidents' (Laz, 2011); 'Mistrust of the mainstream media has a long history in the protest movement, with good reason' (Martin, 2011).[68] Some set up social media sites themselves in order to provide 'a balanced(ish) view of what happened last night (April 21th) in Bristol (since mainstream media decided it wasn't worth any coverage)' (@marc_in_london, 2011). Social media was used by some individuals as their portal through which to consume knowledge of an event such as this. 'Wow, with everything going on in the world it's awesome that the main story on my feed tonight was #stokescroft thanks to all #solidarity' (@ignite_magazine, 2011). '#StokesCroft tonight. watching it all now (on youtube)' (@HeinzJunkins, 2011). Twitter, rather than mainstream media, was used for accessing information about the events. Social media was often more 'trusted' than traditional media in terms of impartial reporting. 'Those of us using Twitter were on top of the real breaking news'.[69] Twitter feeds became perceived as the trusted news representation, in contrast to the 'state-media' news broadcast on mainstream media.

CONCLUSIONS

The production of unofficial knowledge

Social media documents a number of alternative accounts of history as it unfolds. Myriad witnesses produce a variety of perspectives and interpretations that can be verbal or visual accounts. There were several hundred unofficial 'reporters' at these riots who had first-hand experience of what was happening. Their accounts are an important record, important history, as they provide a direct perspective as it is happening. First-hand accounts, plus additional narratives from social media commentators who access material online, produce unofficial knowledge of an event. Knowledge production is not exclusive to this subculture, but it is a germane and integral aspect of riot subculture ethos. Production of knowledge empowers the author and the shift from consumer to producer challenges existing power relations. Social media permits the production of knowledge that remains outside, or rejects the narrative, of mainstream media. In the posts and comments that followed photographs or videos of the Stokes Croft riot, a variety of differing views were expressed. The views presented and represented on social media were more heterogeneous, polyphonous and conflictual than on mainstream media.

Social media remains a fragile archive for unofficial knowledge. Tweets and other posts were also difficult to retrieve as they are archived relatively rapidly (and require more than basic computer skills to retrieve); even major search engines like Google or Bing struggle or fail to find tweets and posts from this event. Tweets and images have been deleted or removed from social media sites after their original posting. Part of this is due to fear of recrimination (via the UK Public Order Act 1986) or prosecution of the person posting or for fear of incriminating others identifiable in images.

Media subversion

Riot subculture perceives mainstream media representation as biased and partisan. Weakening the power of mainstream media (whilst strengthening social media) is part of a broader subversive ideology. One tactic for achieving this aim is a reduction in the number of 'consumers' of mainstream media. Fewer consumers of mainstream means a diminution in its power as a result of dwindling economic revenue streams from advertisers. The turn to social media 'instead' of mainstream media is part of this subversive tactic. Another tactic for weakening mainstream media is to produce alternative media, in this instance social media (although other forms of media, such as graffiti, may be adopted, and the act of rioting itself is another powerful medium). Taking to Twitter or posting on Youtube, for some, is an attempt to eschew the use of mainstream media. The more use that is made of social media, the greater its power. There is a deliberate employment of social media as a means to produce alternative and unofficial knowledge.

(Social) media is the message

Representation operates in two ways, as in McLuhan's maxim 'the medium is the message' – both the medium and the message are modes of producing knowledge.[70] The portrayal by mainstream media of the riot mostly reproduces the official (*not* the unofficial) version of events. Through this restriction, mainstream medium itself becomes associated with the message, i.e. official knowledge. Social media representation predominantly carries the unofficial (but *not* the official) representation. Through this representation the medium itself becomes the message; social media is unofficial knowledge.

Riot and power

Social media is entangled with the riot subculture; enmeshed in the various shared practices, discourses and traits of the subcultural group. Social media provides an ideologically apposite apparatus for riot subculture expression.

Social media becomes the representation of unofficial language. The adoption, use and promotion of social media increases its power to communicate unofficial knowledge. Simultaneously, the diminution of mainstream media and official knowledge subverts existing power relations. Riot in the streets is the medium through which the unheard is expressed. The violent actions, destruction and aggression are the most obvious significations of this medium. Riots in social media share the same ideology – the subversion of existing power relations.

APPENDIX: METHODOLOGY

The research was based on an empirical study of a single case study based in Bristol, UK. An ethnographic research strategy was used to gather data (predominantly from social media sources). The methodology unearthed some contentious issues and challenges concerning the research process. There are three key methodological concerns around using social media as a data source, particularly in relation to riots: the first is a result of the degree of '*mediation*' inherent in social media.[71] For visual materials, the photographer or film-maker chooses where (and when) to point the camera and hence what the subject and content are (and what is not) and how to frame an event. Many of the online textual accounts are based on footage from secondary sources rather than first-hand experience, which embeds mediation into the data. Secondly, there is a methodological challenge of integrating visual material with textual accounts. Users of social media have few methodological issues blending visual and textual data. However, there is less of a tradition of this in sociological research, as Rose points out 'there remain remarkably few guides to possible methods of interpreting visual materials'.[72] The meaning of textual accounts is relatively straightforward to convey and infer from; there is much less agreement when using visual materials. In this chapter, the interpretation of the meaning/s of visual data is derived from the commentary provided by posts on social media. Thirdly the data gathered are problematic due to the legally contentious nature of riots. In the UK, it is illegal to incite violence or riots using social media (or otherwise), and the boundary of legality is unclear. Posts or comments that incite riots can be censored by regulatory authorities. Some of the original posts, tweets and comments have been removed by their authors, often for fear of incrimination. This generates a void in the online data, as comments in relation to the riot are skewed by legislation. This legal fuzziness also leads to concerns regarding the legality of some content and how data might be interpreted in the future. Only social media data that is public and openly available has been used in this research.

Finally, a note of spelling and grammar. The use of slang and colloquialisms is ubiquitous in social media. All directly referenced social media retains this argot to respect the communicatory intent in bloggers 'own' language. The meaning in these communications remains intelligible, even when the correct usage of the Queen's English has not been applied.

Notes

1. J. McCarthy, 'An Eye-witness Account of the Bristol Stokes Croft/Tesco Riot' [blog], 24 April 2011: http://louderthanwar.com/an-eye-witness-account-of-the-bristol-stokes-crofttescos-riot-from-kerry-mccarthy-mp/. For details of the social media comments not referenced in the text, please contact the author (McCarthy 2011).
2. J. Taphouse, 'BRISTOL RIOT: My Experience', 22 April 2011: https://www.flickr.com/photos/jonathantaphouse/5653010825/ [accessed: 25 August 2011] (Taphouse 2011).
3. Beleaga, 'It all started on social media: #bristol's #stokescroft riots', 30 December, 2011: http://www.interhacktives.com/2011/12/30/it-all-started-on-social-media-bristols-stokescroft-riots/ [accessed: 2 May 2011] (Beleaga 2011).
4. S. Hinton and L. Hjorth, *Understanding Social Media* (London, 2013) (Hinton and Hjorth 2013).
5. D. Murthy, *Twitter: Social Communication in the Twitter Age* (London, 2013) (Murthy 2013).
6. J. Halliday, 'David Cameron considers banning suspected rioters from social media', *The Guardian*, 11 August, 2011 (Halliday 2011).
7. R. Procter, F. Vis and A. Voss, 'Reading the riots on Twitter: Methodological innovation for the analysis of big data', *International Journal of Social Research Methodology*, 16(3) (2013), 197–214 (Procter et al. 2013).
8. P. N. Howard, A. Duffy, D. Freelon, M. W. Hussain, W. Mari and M. Mazaid, 'Opening closed regimes: What was the role of social media during the Arab Spring?' *Social Science Research Network* (2012): http://dx.doi.org/10.2139/ssrn.2595096 [accessed: 12 June 2015] (Howard et al. 2012).
9. L. Rice, 'Occupied space', *Architectural Design*, 83, 6 (2013), 70–75 (Rice 2013).

10. J. O. Hearns-Branaman, 'The Egyptian revolution did not take place: On live television coverage by Al Jazeera *English*', *International Journal of Baudrillard Studies*, 9, 1 (2012), 14 (Hearns-Branaman 2012).

11. O. Bowcott and H. Clifton, 'Facebook riot calls earn men four-year jail terms amid sentencing outcry' (2011): http://www.theguardian.com/uk/ 2011/aug/16/facebook-riot-calls-men-jailed [accessed: 1 September 2014] (Bowcott and Clifton 2011); T. Whitehead and N. Bunyan, 'Facebook riot inciters among those to get toughest jail terms yet' (2011), *Daily Telegraph* online http://www.telegraph.co.uk/technology/face book/8705212/Facebook-riot-inciters-among-those-to-get-toughest-jail-terms-yet.html [accessed: 1 September 2014] (Whitehead and Bunyan 2011).

12. Blackberry is the generic trademark name of a mobile phone manufacturer.

13. P. Lewis, T. Newburn, M. Taylor, C. Mcgillivray, A. Greenhill, H. Frayman and R. Procter, *Reading the Riots: investigating England's Summer of Disorder* (London, 2011): http://eprints.lse.ac.uk/46297/1/Reading% 20the%20riots%28published%29.pdf [accessed: 14 February 2015] (Lewis et al. 2011).

14. G. Debord, *Society of the Spectacle* (Detroit, 1983) (Debord 1983).

15. E. Schmidt and J. Cohen, *The New Digital Age: Reshaping The Future of People, Nations and Business* (Toronto, 2013) (Schmidt and Cohen 2013).

16. H. Jenkins, *Fans, Bloggers and Gamers: Exploring Participatory Culture* (New York, 2006) (Jenkins 2006).

17. Schmidt and Cohen, *The New Digital Age*, p. 4.

18. N. Chomsky, *On Anarchism* (New York, 2013) (Chomsky 2013).

19. T. Jordan, *Cyberpower: The Culture and Politics of Cyberspace and the Internet* (London, 1999) (Jordan 1999).

20. W.C. Hale, 'Extremism on the World Wide Web: A research review', *Criminal Justice Studies*, 25, 4 (2012), 343–56 (Hale 2012).

21. D. Hebdige, *Subculture: The Meaning of Style* (London, 1988) (Hebdige 1988).

22. S. Thornton, 'General Introduction', in K. Gelder and S. Thornton (eds.) *The Subcultures Reader* (London, 1997), pp. 1–10 (Thornton 1997).

23. Hebdige, *Subculture*.

24. R. Barthes, *Mythologies* (London, 2000) (Barthes 2000); S. Hall and T. Jefferson (eds.), *Resistance Through Rituals: Youth Subcultures In Post-War Britain* (London, 1993) (Hall and Jefferson 1993).

25. S. van Gelder, *This Changes Everything: Occupy Wall Street and the 99% Movement* (San Francisco, 2011) (van Gelder 2011).

26. B. Lev Manovich, 'The Practice of Everyday (Media) Life: From Mass Consumption to Mass Cultural Production?' *Critical Inquiry*, 35(2) (2009),

319–31 (Lev Manovich 2009); M. Ito, 'Introduction', in K. Varnelis (ed.), *Networked Publics* (Massachusetts, 2012), pp. 1–14 (Ito 2012).

27. P. Bourdieu and T. Eagleton, 'Doxa and common life', *New Left Review*, 191, (1992), p. 21 (Bourdieu and Eagleton 1992); M. Castells, *The Rise of the Network Society. Volume 1* (Oxford, 1997) (Castells 1997); E. Michelson, 'Carnival, paranoia and experiential learning', *Studies in the Education of Adults*, 31(2) (1999), 140–54 (Michelson 1999); M. Foucault, *The History of Sexuality: The Will to Knowledge, Volume 1* (London, 1998) (Foucault 1998).

28. J. Klausen, 'Tweeting the Jihad: Social media networks of Western foreign fighters', *Syria and Iraq, Studies in Conflict & Terrorism*, 38(1) (2015), 1–22 (Klausen 2015).

29. D. Boyd, *It's Complicated: The Social Lives of Networked Teens* (New Haven, 2014) (Boyd 2014); Jenkins, *Fans, Bloggers and Gamers*; A. Elliott and J. Urry, *Mobile Lives* (London, 2010) (Elliott and Urry 2010); J. van Dijk, *The Network Society* (London, 2012) (van Dijk 2012).

30. A. Tallon, *Urban Regeneration In The UK* (London, 2010) (Tallon 2010); P. J. Larkham and H. Barrett, 'Conservation of the built environment under the Conservatives', in P. Allmendinger and H. Thomas (eds.), *Urban Planning and the British New Right* (London, 1998), pp. 53–86 (Larkham and Barrett 1998).

31. M. Clement, 'Rage against the market: Bristol's Tesco Riot', *Race & Class*, 53(3) (2012), 81–90 (Clement 2012).

32. Clement, 'Rage against the market', 81–90; K. Dutta, 'Police raid over "petrol bomb plot" sparks Tesco riots' (2011): http://www.independent.co.uk/news/uk/crime/police-raid-over-petrol-bomb-plot-sparks-tesco-riots-2273727.html [accessed: 12 October 2013] (Dutta 2011); P. Kemp, 11) 'Tesco riot drives call for supermarket planning review', *BBC Online*, 19 May 2011: http://www.bbc.co.uk/news/business-13431552 [accessed: 21 May 2014] (Kemp 2011).

33. D. Winterman, 'Tesco: How one supermarket came to dominate', *BBC Online*, 13 September 2013: http://www.bbc.co.uk/news/business-13431552 [accessed: 21 Oct 2014] (Winterman 2013).

34. Local Boy, 'Observing the Stokes Croft Riot' (2011): https://www.opendemocracy.net/ourkingdom/local-boy/observing-stokes-croft-riot [accessed: 2 June 2011] (Local Boy 2011).

35. Local Boy, 'Observing the Stokes Croft Riot'; G. Miller, 'The Stokes Croft Riots – Three years later...' [blog] 18 April 2014: https://g1rm.word press.com/2014/04/18/the-stokes-croft-riots-three-years-later/ [accessed: 21 July 2015] (Local Boy 2014).

36. L. Penny, 'On Tesco and the Battle of Stokes Croft', *News Statesman* (2011): http://www.newstatesman.com/blogs/laurie-penny/2011/04/stokes-croft-police-tesco [accessed: 14 May 2011] (Penny 2011).

37. Beleaga, 'It all started on social media ...'

38. McCarthy, 'An Eye-witness account ...'
39. Penny, 'On Tesco and the Battle of Stokes Croft'.
40. Penny, 'On Tesco and the Battle of Stokes Croft'.
41. Taphouse, 'BRISTOL RIOT'.
42. R. Hansen (cited in) BBC, 'Police hurt in violent anti-Tesco clashes in Bristol', 22 April 2011: http://www.bbc.co.uk/news/uk-england-bristol-13167041 [accessed: 7 July 2015] (Hansen 2011).
43. BBC, 'Police hurt in violent anti-Tesco clashes in Bristol'.
44. Neurobonkers, 'The Battle of #StokesCroft' (2011): http://neurobonkers.com/2011/04/22/the-battle-of-stokes-croft/ (Neurobonkers 2011).
45. The Posie Parker, comment posted in Taphouse, 'BRISTOL RIOT': https://www.flickr.com/photos/jonathantaphouse/5653010825/ [accessed: 25 August 2011]; Ben, comment posted in Neurobonkers, 'The Battle of #StokesCroft' http://neurobonkers.com/2011/04/22/the-battle-of-stokes-croft/ [blog] 18 April 2011 [accessed: 21 July 2011].
46. Clement, 'Rage against the market', 81–90.
47. McCarthy, 'An eye-witness account ...'
48. Local Boy, 'Observing the Stokes Croft Riot'.
49. Penny, 'On Tesco and the Battle of Stokes Croft'.
50. McCarthy, 'An eye-witness account ...'
51. Taphouse, 'BRISTOL RIOT'; Clement, 'Rage against the market', 81–90
52. R. Legg, 'The Battle of Stokes Croft: an account of the riot. A first-hand account of last night's dramatic riots and police aggression in Stokes Croft, Bristol' 22 April 2011: http://www.counterfire.org/index.php/articles/163-resisting-austerity/12066-the-battle-of-stokes-croft-an-account-of-the-riot [accessed: 21 April 2011] (Legg 2011).
53. Flora [comment posted in] neurobonkers, 'The Battle of #StokesCroft': http://neurobonkers.com/2011/04/22/the-battle-of-stokes-croft/ [blog] 18 April 2011 [accessed: 21 July 2011] (Flora 2011).
54. Laz [comment posted in] neurobonkers, 'The Battle of #StokesCroft': http://neurobonkers.com/2011/04/22/the-battle-of-stokes-croft/ [blog] 18 April 2011 [accessed: 21 July 2011] (Laz 2011).
55. Scott [comment posted in] McCarthy, 'An eye witness account ...'.
56. Flora [comment posted in] neurobonkers, 'The Battle of #StokesCroft'.
57. S. Allen, 'Bristol City council must support the community and reject Tesco', *The Guardian*. 22 April 2011: http://www.theguardian.com/commentisfree/2011/apr/22/bristol-riot-tesco [accessed: 14 May 2011] (Allen 2011).
58. N. H. Stern, *The Economics of Climate Change: The Stern Review* (Cambridge, 2007) (Stern 2007).
59. UK Public Order Act 1986, (Section 1: Riot) Crown Prosecution Service: http://www.cps.gov.uk/legal/p_to_r/public_order_offences/#General_Principle [accessed: 1 October 2014].

60. UK Public Order Act 1986, (Section 1: Riot) Crown Prosecution Service: http://www.cps.gov.uk/legal/p_to_r/public_order_offences/ #General_Principle [accessed: 1 October 2014].
61. L. Rice, J. Davies and M. Cains, *Bristol Riots* (Bristol, 2011) (Rice et al. 2011).
62. Martin [comment posted in] R. Gallagher, 'Reporting a riot in Britain: How the police spun the Battle of Stokes Croft' (2011): https://www.opendemocracy. net/ourkingdom/ryan-gallagher/reporting-riot-in-britain-how-police-spun-battle-of-stokes-croft [accessed: 12 June 2011] (Martin 2011).
63. N. Davies, *Flat Earth News: An Award-winning Reporter Exposes Falsehood, Distortion and Propaganda in the Global Media* (London, 2011) (Davies 2011).
64. Penny, 'On Tesco and the Battle of Stokes Croft'.
65. Office of Communications (Ofcom) Broadcast Code, 2015; National Union of Journalists ethical code, 2011; BBC Editorial Guidelines, 2015.
66. R. Gallagher, 'Reporting a riot in Britain'.
67. BBC, 'England riots: Government mulls social media controls', BBC 11 August 2011: http://www.bbc.co.uk/news/technology-14493497 [accessed: 29 November 2014] (BBC 2011).
68. Gallagher, 'Reporting a riot in Britain'; Laz [comment posted in] neuro-bonkers, 'The Battle of #StokesCroft'; Martin [comment posted in] 'Reporting a Riot in Britain'.
69. Beleaga, 'It all started on social media'.
70. M. McLuhan, *Understanding Media: The Extensions of Man* (Massachusetts, 1994) (McLuhan 1994).
71. U. Flick, *An Introduction To Qualitative Research* (London, 2009) (Flick 2009).
72. G. Rose, *Visual Methodologies: An Introduction to Interpreting Visual Objects* (London, 2007), p. xiv (Rose 2007).

REFERENCES

S. Allen, 'Bristol City council must support the community and reject Tesco', *The Guardian*, 22 April 2011: http://www.theguardian.com/commentisfree/ 2011/apr/22/bristol-riot-tesco [accessed: 14 May 2011].

R. Barthes, *Mythologies* (London, 2000).

BBC, 'England Riots: Government mulls social media controls', BBC, 11 August 2011: http://www.bbc.co.uk/news/technology-14493497 [accessed: 29 November 2014].

Beleaga, 'It all started on social media: #bristol's #stokescroft riots', 30 December 2011: http://www.interhacktives.com/2011/12/30/it-all-started-on-social-media-bristols-stokescroft-riots/ [accessed: 2 May 2011].

Ben [comment posted in] Neurobonkers (2011) *The Battle of #StokesCroft. 28 April* [Available from]: http://neurobonkers.com/2011/04/22/the-bat tle-of-stokes-croft/ [blog] 18 April [accessed: 21 July 2011].

P. Bourdieu and T. Eagleton, 'Doxa and Common Life', *New Left Review*, 191, (1992), 21.

O. Bowcott and H. Clifton, 'Facebook riot calls earn men four-year jail terms amid sentencing outcry', 2011: http://www.theguardian.com/uk/2011/aug/16/facebook-riot-calls-men-jailed [accessed: 1 September 2014].

Local Boy, 'Observing the Stokes Croft Riot' 2011: https://www.opendemoc racy.net/ourkingdom/local-boy/observing-stokes-croft-riot [accessed: 2 June 2011].

D. Boyd, *It's Complicated: The Social Lives of Networked Teens* (New Haven, 2014).

M. Castells, *The Rise of the Network Society. Volume 1* (Oxford, 1997).

N. Chomsky, *On Anarchism* (New York, 2013).

M. Clement, 'Rage Against the Market: Bristol's Tesco Riot', *Race & Class*, 53, 3 (2012), 81–90.

N. Davies, *Flat Earth News: An Award-winning Reporter Exposes Falsehood, Distortion and Propaganda in the Global Media* (London, 2011).

G. Debord, *Society of the Spectacle* (Detroit, 1983).

K. Dutta, 'Police raid over "petrol bomb plot" sparks Tesco riots' 2011: http://www.independent.co.uk/news/uk/crime/police-raid-over-petrol-bomb-plot-sparks-tesco-riots-2273727.html [accessed: 12 October 2013].

A. Elliott and J. Urry, *Mobile Lives* (London, 2010).

U. Flick, *An Introduction To Qualitative Research* (London, 2009).

Flora [comment posted in] neurobonkers, 'The Battle of #StokesCroft': http://neurobonkers.com/2011/04/22/the-battle-of-stokes-croft/ [blog] 18 April 2011 [accessed: 21 July 2011].

M. Foucault, *The History of Sexuality: The Will to Knowledge, Volume 1* (London, 1998).

R. Gallagher (2011) *Reporting a riot in Britain: how the police spun the battle of Stokes Croft.* [Available from]: https://www.opendemocracy.net/ourking dom/ryan-gallagher/reporting-riot-in-britain-how-police-spun-battle-of-stokes-croft [accessed: 12 June 2011].

W.C. Hale, 'Extremism on the World Wide Web: a research review', *Criminal Justice Studies*, 25, 4 (2012), 343–56.

S. Hall and T. Jefferson (eds.), *Resistance Through Rituals: Youth Subcultures In Post-War Britain* (London, 1993).

J. Halliday, 'David Cameron considers banning suspected rioters from social media', *The Guardian*, 11 August, 2011.

R. Hansen (cited in) BBC, 'Police hurt in violent anti-Tesco clashes in Bristol', 22 April 2011: http://www.bbc.co.uk/news/uk-england-bristol-13167041 [accessed: 7 July 2015].

J. O. Hearns-Branaman, 'The Egyptian Revolution Did Not Take Place: On Live Television Coverage By Al Jazeera *English*', *International Journal of Baudrillard Studies*, 9, 1 (2012), 14.

D. Hebdige, *Subculture: The Meaning of Style* (London, 1988).

S. Hinton and L. Hjorth, *Understanding Social Media* (London, 2013).

P. N. Howard, A. Duffy, D. Freelon, M. W. Hussain, W. Mari and M. Mazaid, 'Opening Closed Regimes: What Was the Role of Social Media during the Arab Spring?', *Social Science Research Network*, 2012: http://dx.doi.org/10.2139/ssrn.2595096 [accessed: 12 June 2015].

M. Ito, 'Introduction', in K. Varnelis (ed.), *Networked Publics* (Massachusetts, 2012), pp. 1–14.

H. Jenkins, *Fans, Bloggers and Gamers: Exploring Participatory Culture* (New York, 2006).

T. Jordan, *Cyberpower: The Culture and Politics of Cyberspace and the Internet* (London, 1999).

P. Kemp, 11 'Tesco riot drives call for supermarket planning review', *BBC Online*, 19 May 2011: http://www.bbc.co.uk/news/business-13431552 [accessed: 21 May 2014].

J. Klausen, 'Tweeting the Jihad: Social Media Networks of Western Foreign Fighters', *Syria and Iraq, Studies in Conflict & Terrorism*, 38, 1 (2015), 1–22.

P. J. Larkham and H. Barrett, 'Conservation of the Built Environment Under the Conservatives', in P. Allmendinger and H. Thomas (eds.), *Urban Planning and the British New Right* (London, 1998), pp. 53–86.

Laz [comment posted in] neurobonkers, 'The Battle of #StokesCroft': http://neurobonkers.com/2011/04/22/the-battle-of-stokes-croft/ [blog] 18 April 2011 [accessed: 21 July 2011].

R. Legg, 'The Battle of Stokes Croft: an account of the riot. A first-hand account of last night's dramatic riots and police aggression in Stokes Croft, Bristol' 22 April 2011: http://www.counterfire.org/index.php/articles/163-resisting-austerity/12066-the-battle-of-stokes-croft-an-account-of-the-riot [accessed: 21 April 2011].

B. Lev Manovich, 'The Practice of Everyday (Media) Life: From Mass Consumption to Mass Cultural Production?', *Critical Inquiry*, 35, 2 (2009), 319–31.

P. Lewis, T. Newburn, M. Taylor, C. Mcgillivray, A. Greenhill, H. Frayman and R. Procter, *Reading the riots: investigating England's summer of disorder* (London, 2011): http://eprints.lse.ac.uk/46297/1/Reading%20the%20riots%28published%29.pdf [accessed: 14 February 2015].

Martin [comment posted in] R. Gallagher, 'Reporting a Riot in Britain: How the Police Spun the Battle of Stokes Croft' (2011): https://www.opendemocracy.net/ourkingdom/ryan-gallagher/reporting-riot-in-britain-how-police-spun-battle-of-stokes-croft [accessed: 12 June 2011].

J. McCarthy, 'An Eye-witness Account of the Bristol Stokes Croft/Tesco Riot' [blog], 24 April 2011: http://louderthanwar.com/an-eye-witness-account-of-the-bristol-stokes-crofttescos-riot-from-kerry-mccarthy-mp/.

M. McLuhan, *Understanding* Media: *The Extensions of Man* (Massachusetts, 1994).

E. Michelson, 'Carnival, Paranoia and Experiential Learning', *Studies in the Education of Adults*, 31, 2 (1999), 140–54.

G. Miller, 'The Stokes Croft Riots-Three Years Later...' [blog] 18 April 2014: https://g1rm.wordpress.com/2014/04/18/the-stokes-croft-riots-three-years-later/ [accessed: 21 July 2015].

D. Murthy, *Twitter: Social Communication in the Twitter Age* (London, 2013).

Neurobonkers, 'The Battle of #StokesCroft' 2011: http://neurobonkers.com/2011/04/22/the-battle-of-stokes-croft/.

The Posie Parker [comment posted in] Taphouse, J. (2011) *BRISTOL RIOT: my experience*. 22 April. [Available from]: https://www.flickr.com/photos/jonathantaphouse/5653010825/ [accessed: 25 August 2011].

L. Penny, 'On Tesco and the Battle of Stokes Croft', *News Statesman* (2011): http://www.newstatesman.com/blogs/laurie-penny/2011/04/stokes-croft-police-tesco [accessed: 14 May 2011].

R. Procter, F. Vis and A. Voss, 'Reading The Riots On Twitter: Methodological Innovation For The Analysis Of Big Data', *International Journal of Social Research Methodology*, 16, 3 (2013), 197–214.

L. Rice, J. Davies and M. Cains, *Bristol Riots* (Bristol, 2011).

L. Rice, 'Occupied Space', *Architectural Design*, 83, 6 (2013), 70–75.

G. Rose, *Visual Methodologies: An Introduction to Interpreting Visual Objects* (London, 2007), xiv.

E. Schmidt and J. Cohen, *The New Digital Age: Reshaping The Future of People, Nations and Business* (Toronto, 2013).

N. H. Stern, *The Economics of Climate* Change: *The Stern Review* (Cambridge, 2007).

A. Tallon, *Urban Regeneration In The UK* (London, 2010).

J. Taphouse, 'BRISTOL RIOT: My Experience', 22 April 2011: https://www.flickr.com/photos/jonathantaphouse/5653010825/ [accessed: 25 August 2011].

S. Thornton, 'General Introduction', in K. Gelder and S. Thornton (eds.) *The Subcultures Reader* (London, 1997), pp. 1–10.

J. van Dijk, *The Network Society* (London, 2012).

S. van Gelder, *This Changes Everything: Occupy Wall Street and the 99% Movement* (San Francisco, 2011).

T. Whitehead and N. Bunyan, 'Facebook riot inciters among those to get toughest jail terms yet', *Daily Telegraph*, 2011: http://www.telegraph.co.uk/technology/facebook/8705212/Facebook-riot-inciters-among-those-to-get-toughest-jail-terms-yet.html [accessed: 1 September 2014].

D. Winterman, 'Tesco: How one supermarket came to dominate', *BBC Online*, September 2013: http://www.bbc.co.uk/news/business-13431552 [accessed: 21 October 2014].

Twitter References

@20thCFlicks (2011) #*Stokescroft Friend hit across face with riot shield and struck with baton 1 metre from home. Ear stitched. Bad po.* [Twitter]. 22 April. https://twitter.com/20thCFlicks/status/61357009844449281 [Accessed: 30 August 2011].

@AaronBastani (2011) #*twitter claims #stokescroft riots, police say "it is unfortunate a minority gathered and attacked officers" Police bullshit. Standard.* [Twitter]. 21 April. Available from: https://twitter.com/AaronBastani/status/61217187163148288 [Accessed: 12 June 2011].

@b9AcE (2011) *BBC, the UK state and police PR agency. http://www.bbc.co.uk/news/uk-england-bristol-13167041 #stokescroft* [Twitter]. 21 April. Available from: https://twitter.com/b9AcE/status/61273390949994496 [Accessed: 12 June 2015].

@benpark (2011) *This #Stokescroft riot is really kicking off. Twitter tells me there may have been one arrest, and possibly no injuries.* [Twitter]. 21 April. https://twitter.com/BenPark/status/61217946629976064?lang=en-gb [Accessed: 30 August 2011].

@Bristol247 (2011) *Huge spike in traffic overloaded poor server - back up now. Seems people rather interested in #stokescroft riothttp://ow.ly/4EW62* [Twitter]. 22 April. [Available from:] https://twitter.com/bristol247/status/61369292842741760 [Accessed: 14 June 2011].

@BristolFloozie (2011) *Hugely aggressive policing on #stokescroft - protester fleeing with head wounds* [Twitter]. 21 April. https://twitter.com/BristolFloozie/status/61216130513125376 [Accessed: 30 August 2011].

@BrumProtestor (2011) *Twitter has been great tonight, thanks to all #stokescroft people tweeting, fuck you mainstream media, we don't need you anymore* [Twitter]. 21 April. https://twitter.com/brumprotestor/status/61229511764750336 [Accessed: 12 June 2011].

@CasparBrown (2011a) #*stokescroft police brutality is mental, saw a 16 year old boy beaten by batons whilst unarmed and on the floor. whats wrong with the world* [Twitter]. 21 April. https://twitter.com/CasparBrown/status/61257545024671744 [Accessed: 30 August 2011].

@CasparBrown (2011b) #*stokescroft @BBCBreaking manage to cover wedding suits but not an important riot against capitalist oppression. ITS A JOKE* [Twitter]. 21 April. https://twitter.com/CasparBrown/status/61263453683331072 [Accessed: 30 August 2011].

@CasparBrown (2011c) *how are no news channels picking up this riot #stokescroft* [Twitter]. 21 April. https://twitter.com/CasparBrown/status/61258181468356608 [Accessed: 30 August 2011].

@Cutl00se (2011) *#stokescroftriot Police car attacked by revellers* http://m.youtube.com/#/watch?v=0cdScUCPIzI ... [Twitter]. 22 April. https://twitter.com/Cutl00se/status/61548187214807040 [Accessed: 30 August 2011].

@DSG_DSG (2011) *ENJOY SAX / DESTROY CAPITALISM #stokescroft.* [Twitter]. 21 April. https://twitter.com/DSG_DSG/status/61223564606578688 [Accessed: 30 August 2011].

@efergan (2011) *stone and fireworks being thrown at the [police] vans, bins being set on fire* [tumbler] 22 April. Available from: http://efergan.tumblr.com/post/4833274687/stokescroftriot [Accessed: 12 June 2011].

@GuyAitchison (2011a) *Fuck all about #stokescroft riot in the mainstream media. Thank god for Twitter.* [Twitter]. 21 April. https://twitter.com/GuyAitchison/status/61210593411072000 [Accessed: 30 August 2011].

@GuyAitchison (2011b) *BBC coverage of #stokescroft riots is a recycled police press releasehttp://bbc.in/fn9t0phttp://bit.ly/hAwLZw via @TenPercent* [Twitter]. 21 April. https://twitter.com/GuyAitchison/status/61237105996730368 [Accessed: 30 August 2011].

@HeinzJunkins (2011) *missed all the madness at #StokesCroft tonight. watching it all now > http://www.youtube.com/watch?v=O46-k00I_nU* [Twitter]. 21 April. https://twitter.com/HeinzJunkins/status/61300893227823104 [Accessed: 30 August 2011].

@ignite_magazine (2011) *Wow, with everything going on in the world it's awesome that the main story on my feed tonight was #stokescroft thanks to all #solidarity* [Twitter]. 21 April. https://twitter.com/ignite_magazine/status/61269925049798656 [Accessed: 30 August 2011].

@immorali (2011) *"While there was a proper riot in Bristol, folks from mainstream media were hooked on crack cocaine on the couch. #stokescroft"* [Twitter]. 21 April. https://twitter.com/immorali/status/61262487647031297 [Accessed: 30 August 2011].

@jennieloveday (2011) *Wow, amazing that Twitter is actually a better news source than the BBC. It's all so selective and biased! #stokescroft* [Twitter]. 2 April. https://twitter.com/jennieloveday/status/61354209634816000?lang=en-gb [Accessed: 30 August 2011].

@marc_in_london (2011) *Stokescroft riots - the timeline.* [Storify]. 22 April. https://storify.com/marc_in_london/stokescroft-riots-the-timeline [Accessed: 30 August 2011].

@meowist_gorilla (2011) *The absence of proper media coverage is like living in fucking China or North Korea.* [Twitter]. 21 April. [Original tweet deleted - copy cited in:] https://www.opendemocracy.net/ourkingdom/ryan-galla

gher/reporting-riot-in-britain-how-police-spun-battle-of-stokes-croft [Accessed: 12 June 2011].

@mtdavies23 (2011) *@Hdfisise It's really eye-opening to see the BBC just copy-paste the police PR. #stokescroft.* [Twitter]. 21 April. Available from: https://twitter.com/mtdavies23/status/61246713704353793 [Accessed: 12 June 2011].

@paddy_wagon (2011) *All I can find on the BBC, practically written by the police. We get news from Misrata but not #stokescroft http://tinyurl.com/3kgdks6* [Twitter]. 22 April. Available from: https://twitter.com/search?q=%20%40paddy_wagon%20%20misrata&src=typd [Accessed: 12 June 2011].

@pearcafe (2011a) *10+ riot vans, police in full riot gear with shields. Mad atmosphere. #stokescroft http://twitpic.com/4nqd7o* [Twitter]. 21 April. Available from: https://twitter.com/pearcafe/status/61177857279401984 [Accessed: 12 June 2011].

@pearcafe (2011b) *Squat on #stokescroft is being evicted. 'Copter above us for half an hour. 10+ riot vans.Road closed http://twitpic.com/4nqawe* [Twitter]. 21 April. Available from: https://twitter.com/pearcafe/status/61175373869752321 [Accessed: 12 June 2011].

@robjmills (2011) *seems the only good source of information for what's going down in Bristol right now is the #stokescroft hashtag.* [Twitter]. 21 April. Available from: https://twitter.com/robjmills/status/61218013722066944 [Accessed: 25 August 2011].

@rossoh (2011a) *They're breaking into tesco again. police have driven off. #stokescroft.* [Twitter]. 21 April. Available from https://twitter.com/rossoh/status/61252377608585216 [Accessed: 30 August 2011].

@rossoh (2011b) *looks like I'm not gonna get to sleep any time soon. Though at least the saxaphone players on the bus stop are soothing - #stokescroft* [Twitter]. 21 April. Available from: https://twitter.com/rossoh/status/61236658103787520 [Accessed: 12 June 2011].

@sam_binga (2011) *BEST PRE PARTY EVER!!! #stokescroftriot* [Twitter]. 21 April. Available from: https://twitter.com/sam_binga/status/61198311847239682 [Accessed: 12 June 2011].

@SDMumford (2011) *Looks to me like the media has been ordered not to run the #StokesCroft riot story. Sounds to me completely botched by the police.* [Twitter]. 21 April. Available from: https://twitter.com/SDMumford/status/61339114112421888 [Accessed: 12 June 2011].

@SirioCD (2011) *all bbc can say is 4 police officers hurt? No mention of Tesco's or police brutality? bbc.in/gLt7V5 #stokescroft.* [Twitter]. 22 April. [Original tweet deleted - copy available at:] https://storify.com/marc_in_london/stokescroft-riots-the-timeline?awesm=sfy.co_5On&utm_campaign=marc_in_london&utm_content=storify-pingback&utm_medium=sfy.co-twitter&utm_source=direct-sfy.co [Accessed: 30 August 2011].

@smasherkins (2011) *We've been chanting 'you're sexy, you're cute, take off your riot suit!' but no avail. The police have no sense of humour. #stokescroft* [Twitter]. 21

April. Available from: https://twitter.com/smasherkins/status/63754077133225984 [Accessed: 12 June 2011].

@soundmigration (2011) *BBC copy and paste Churnalism from Police PRO's around #Stokescroft. Same process as in Ireland http://twitpic.com/4nsu5u* [Twitter]. 21 April. Available from: https://twitter.com/soundmigration/status/61240697390501888 [Accessed: 12 June 2011].

@spooklouder (2011) *Thank fuck for twitter #stokescroft* [Twitter]. 21 April. Available from: https://twitter.com/spooklouder/status/61228544554057728 [Accessed: 12 June 2011].

@StokesCroftNews (2011a) *Also, how nice to see #stokescroft up there on the TT's next to Bieber and Finding Nemo!* [Twitter]. 22 April. [Available from:] https://twitter.com/StokesCroftNews/status/61267319166472192 [Accessed: 14 June 2011].

@StokesCroftNews (2011b) *Is all the focus on Tesco #stokescroft distracting from what the real debate should be - did police heavy-handedness contribute to the riot?* [Twitter]. 27 April. [Available from:] https://twitter.com/StokesCroftNews/status/63203946881236992 [Accessed: 14 June 2011].

Louis Rice is an architect, urban designer, academic and educator. Spending over a decade as a practising architect in France and the UK, he is now a senior lecturer in Healthy Architecture and Urbanism at the University of the West of England, Bristol, where he co-ordinates the undergraduate architecture dissertation, supervises PhD students and leads the Masters in Architecture design studio. His research focuses on the intersection between health, lifestyles, architecture and cities; and completed his PhD in 2015. His latest book is: *Transgression: Towards an Expanded Field of Architecture,* which is an edited collection of research that examines the relationship between transgressive acts and the urban environment.

CHAPTER 4

'My Manor's Ill': How Underground Music Told the Real Story of the UK Riots

Sarah Attfield

The events of August 2011 interested me greatly. From Australia I watched footage of the riots (and associated events) occurring in and near my old neighbourhood in north-east London. I switched between the BBC, *The Guardian* online, Twitter and Al-Jazeera, and checked on Facebook status updates from people close to the action. Afterwards, I read the commentary in the online versions of the major UK newspapers and looked at the print newspaper headlines and front pages. As Pritchard and Pakes illustrate, despite the events being local in origin, the broadcasts and reports were global.[1] This provided an interesting perspective – I could listen and watch reports from Britain, but also follow commentary intended for a global audience. The response to the riots in the mainstream UK media seemed reactionary and simplistic. The people involved in the riots were immediately labelled as criminals – 'criminality, pure and simple' said a Downing Street statement by Prime Minister David Cameron on 9 August 2011.[2] According to the commentators in the mainstream media, the looters should have the full force of the law thrown at them. They were good for nothing, they were 'flaming morons' and 'thugs and thieves'.[3]

S. Attfield (✉)
University of Technology Sydney, Sydney, Australia
e-mail: Sarah.Attfield@uts.edu.au

© The Author(s) 2017
K. Gildart et al. (eds.), *Youth Culture and Social Change*,
Palgrave Studies in the History of Subcultures and Popular Music,
DOI 10.1057/978-1-137-52911-4_4

This chapter offers a comparative analysis of the mainstream media reporting of the riots and the responses from young British musicians. The aim is to demonstrate that musicians' reactions and commentary were much more nuanced and balanced than that of the mainstream media and Conservative Party politicians. I will provide some biographical context for my interest in the riots and then outline the media's representation of the riots and rioters. I will then look at some of the academic analysis of the riots, before surveying the musicians' responses.

COUNCIL ESTATE LIFE

I grew up on a north-east London council estate. We were officially in Chingford (E4), but identified more as Walthamstow (E17). Our estate seemed totally disconnected from the nice respectable working-class terraced houses of Chingford Mount or the forest backdrop of north Chingford. We were geographically isolated, situated at the end of a long road and backing onto the North Circular. There wasn't a bus onto the estate back then so we had to walk up that road every day. The separation of the estate from the rest of the neighbourhood created a bounded psyche and this was reinforced by the attitude of our Chingford neighbours. People from the estate were perceived as different. We were not respectable hard-working people; we were social security dependants, immigrants and criminals. We learnt that giving our address locally produced a judgemental 'look'. At the same time we were a community, a tight knit neighbourhood, despite the size of the estate. There was camaraderie, an understanding of shared experience, that has lasted to this day. Most of my cohort has left the estate. I left at 19, but returned to live there a couple of times before I moved overseas. My mother lived there until October 2011 (when she was given a council transfer out of London). The old estate people keep in touch. We have a Facebook group and people swap stories of life on the estate.

The council estates were probably the safest places to be during the riots, as the majority of violence seemed to occur on the high streets. The small police station on our estate was damaged though, and two police officers ended up in hospital after being hit by a fleeing car at the end of the street.[4] Many of the young people came from the estates and they appeared to be returning, quietly – according to my mother who was watching young people come and go from her kitchen window. She lived across from the only playground/basketball court on the estate – a popular spot for the estate youth to congregate.

This biographical information is relevant because my council estate upbringing and the single parent status of my family made me sympathetic towards the young working-class people involved in the riots (although this sympathy does not indicate support for violent behaviour). The negative rhetoric used by the mainstream media and politicians about the rioters did not match my experience and understanding of council estate life. As the news of the riots rolled in, I became increasingly angry at the language used and started to look for reactions from those directly involved, or people living in the affected areas. I found it very difficult to believe that the mainstream media's demonisation of the rioters was telling the whole story.

MAINSTREAM MEDIA RESPONSES TO THE RIOTS

There has been some analysis of media reporting of the riots and the way in which mainstream media framed the events and created what has been referred to as a particular 'myth system'.[5] This myth system was built on language such as 'rule of the mob' and 'anarchy'.[6] The violence was described as contagious, with participants infecting neighbourhoods with their actions.[7] They were 'feral youths' (as stated by Kit Malthouse, Deputy Mayor of London and Chair of the Metropolitan Police Authority, in an interview with the BBC on 7 August 2011) and the violence was 'opportunistic' and 'mindless'.[8] The rioters were said to have no reasons or justifications for their actions.[9] Winlow and colleagues suggest that the absence of a clear political message was a chief characteristic of the riots, but as Frost, Phillips and Singleton state in their analysis of the media coverage, there is a difference between having *no* reasons for actions and a difficulty in *articulating* the meaning of those actions.[10] Calling the rioters 'mindless thugs' arguably makes it easier to ignore the message they were trying to convey through their actions.

Attempts to offer an opinion on the cause of the riots were shut down by the mainstream media, most overtly seen in the treatment of author and activist Darcus Howe by the BBC's Fiona Armstrong.[11] Howe was interviewed live on 9 August 2011 and was repeatedly interrupted by Armstrong as he tried to offer some analysis of the situation. Howe attempted to tell Armstrong that he was 'not at all' shocked by the riots because young people had been warning of the inevitability of 'something very, very serious' taking place, and that these warnings had been ignored by the authorities. He referred to the death of Mark Duggan and the experiences of young Black men being stopped and searched by police (including his own grandson). Armstrong asked if his lack of shock meant that he 'condoned what happened in your community last night' and accused Howe of having participated in riots in the past. Howe replied 'of course not' to the suggestion that he condoned violence. He also refuted the claim that he had rioted, stating that he had 'been to demonstrations and ended up in a conflict' and asked Armstrong to 'have some respect' (Armstrong did issue an apology to Howe a few days later).[12] Milburn describes this type of shutdown as a 'prohibition on thought, which was then ruthlessly policed'.[13]

Analysis of the Media Coverage and Causes of the Riots

The mainstream media coverage arguably contributed to the shock experienced by many members of the public. Milburn suggests that the constant replaying of violent images, especially the arson attacks, led to an 'affective reaction' which was heightened by the emotional responses from media commentators and politicians, and which helped to foment a 'right wing backlash'.[14] Grant describes the mainstream media's responses to the riots as 'deeply moralistic and unsatisfying', and points to some of the rhetoric of 'immorality and moral decay' as evidence of this overly moral stance.[15] The media whipped up a strong moral panic (centred on the behaviour of young people).[16]

The reaction from the people who lived in the affected areas was more complex. People were angry and frightened, and deeply saddened and sometimes sickened by what they saw. What they were *not*, was surprised. But the mainstream media seemed completely shocked and outraged by what had happened. The online *Daily Mail* described Tottenham on 8 August as a 'war zone' and captioned photographs with words such as 'shocking', 'devastation' and 'aftermath'.[17] The local people, especially the young people, however, talked about how they knew something like this was going to happen – how it was just a matter of time, how they had seen the tension and the unrest building and how they had seen the situation, especially for young working-class people, get worse and worse.[18]

Despite the analysis of the riots conducted by journalists and academics, there has not been an official government inquiry.[19] The government did commission some research centres to study the causes of the riots, such as the National Centre for Social Research's report, *The August Riots in England: Understanding the Involvement of Young People*, which attempted to determine who participated and why (or why not).[20] David Cameron and Nick Clegg set up an independent Riots Communities and Victims Panel to assess these reports, and their findings were presented to the government in March 2012. The panel visited affected areas and spoke with residents and victims and presented a number of suggestions as to the causes of the riots. These were presented as six key areas: children and parents, building personal resilience, hopes and dreams, riots and the brands, the usual suspects and the police and the public.[21] Poor parenting, personal responsibility (or lack thereof), poor education and lack of employment opportunities, pressure from brand marketing, previous criminal convictions, lack of trust in the police and lack of community engagement were cited as causes of the riots. The government's response to this report picked up on some of these issues, but continued to paint participants as 'mindless' and made links between the riots and the use of social media (as a tool for spreading the violence), gang activity, the result of 'greed', poor parenting issues, youth unemployment and prior convictions – the 'usual suspects'.[22]

Research carried out by *The Guardian* and the London School of Economics (the first phase of which was published in 2011 as *Reading the Riots*) presents a very different list of potential causes of the riots. In the first phase of their research, journalists and academics interviewed 270 people who were directly involved in the events. In the foreword of the study, Alan Rusbridger and Judith Rees acknowledge that the media commentary had not included the voices of those involved and the study was an attempt to give voice to the actual participants (some of whom had been charged with offences and others who admitted to being involved but hadn't been charged).[23]

The evidence collected from the interviews reveals that the majority of participants (85 per cent) believed that anger at treatment by the police was a large contributing factor. Young people particularly felt that the police did not treat them with respect and regularly discriminated against them.[24] While the study supported the Riots Communities and Victims Panel's observations that the majority of participants were from economically and socially deprived areas, the other main reasons cited by the participants were quite different from the Panel's suggestions. The subjects of the study denied that gang membership was a causal factor and stated that gang rivalries had been temporarily suspended during the riots. They did not agree that social media had been a contributing factor, pointing out that most communication between participants occurred via the Blackberry Messenger network and not Twitter or Facebook. Fuchs points to the ways in which 'social media panics' are created and how technology is often blamed because it is easier than addressing causes.[25] It seems that Twitter was mainly used by journalists to report what was happening and provide commentary.[26]

The participants blamed a variety of factors including: the scrapping of the Education Maintenance Allowance, the closure of youth services, a general perception of and anger towards social and economic injustices (such as the shooting of Mark Duggan), a sense of hopelessness and lack of inclusion in British society. However, this was not framed in terms of personal responsibility but due to a lack of interest from those in power. The study reported a 'pervasive sense of injustice' and an interpretation of the events from participants as 'protests' rather than riots.[27] The majority did not think that race had been a factor and rejected any labelling of the events as 'race riots', although some acknowledged that race was a factor in treatment by police (Black youths were much more likely to be harassed by the police). The subjects were very keen to have their side of the story heard. Interestingly, 81 per cent of the subjects believed that another riot could happen.[28] It seems that the disturbance that followed the initial peaceful protest in Tottenham was the catalyst for a very public display of anger and frustration from predominantly working-class youth.[29]

There have been further studies into the causes of the riots, and they have reached a variety of conclusions. Fidelma Ashe points to a crisis of masculinity experienced by the mainly male participants and suggests the events were an 'aggressive claiming of commercial spaces by young people'.[30] Ashe outlines the ways in which fatherless families (and by association, single mothers) were blamed by conservative commentators. She challenges these assertions, highlighting instead the ways in which young working-class men perform a hyper- and sometimes aggressive masculinity in an attempt to gain 'respect, independence and power through developing physical toughness rather than through the conventional middle-class routes of education and career building'.[31] Others, such as Baumann, Moxon and Miles, have studied the role of consumerism and have suggested that the looting aspect of the riots was an attempt by the participants to 'join in' with consumer culture in ways that their economic status did not allow.[32] Baumann described the looters as 'a mutiny of defective and disqualified consumers', and Moxon and Miles point to the ways in which the looters were actually conforming to the values of consumerism rather than resisting them.[33] Further analysis comes from the fields of psychotherapy and the sociology of race.[34]

RESPONSE OF MUSICIANS

Whereas the mainstream media labelled rioters as mindless and avoided discussions of *why* the riots may have happened, and politicians promised that all rioters would be dealt with severely, another group reacted in a much more measured way. This group articulated what was happening and how people felt. They offered a nuanced commentary that operated as a counterpoint to the overly judgemental mainstream media.

I would argue that UK grime[35] artists and rappers offered intelligent and articulate opinions on why young people had taken so violently to the streets. The musicians suggested that what happened was an inevitable result of the continuing squeeze on young working-class people who did not have access to decent education or training, who could not get jobs and who felt constantly harassed by the police but ignored by society, while the excess and greed of those at the top was being flaunted. There was a sense that these hip hop artists were saying 'I told you so' and 'we warned you, but you wouldn't listen'. They contradicted the statements made by the media and politicians that the riots were mindless and pointed to the role of systems of power.[36]

Later, some mainstream media and politicians tried to blame this genre of music for the riots. Paul Routledge from the *Daily Mirror* stated that rap music was to blame because it 'glorifies violence and loathing of authority and trashy materialism'.[37] The suggestion was that the lyrics of songs dealing with violence, poverty, racism, gang culture, anti-police sentiment and so on were causing the problems rather than reflecting the reality for many young people. Routledge went so far as to call for 'poisonous rap' to be banned from the airwaves. The sentiments of Routledge are not without precedent – as John Street points out, this fear of the effects of music and desire to blame or censor music is centuries old. He also points to the long history of attempts by authority to close down popular music events due to concerns over potential 'bad behaviour' of fans.[38]

Dan Hancox offers an alternative view.[39] Writing for *The Guardian,* he outlined some of the responses to the riots from UK grime and rap artists and evoked the famous words of Public Enemy's Chuck D, who announced in the 1980s that rap was the 'Black CNN'. Hancox suggested that grime and rap in the UK was the 'BBC News 24 of the British urban working class'. He contended that grime was an important communicative tool for the young urban working class and that grime 'describes the world politicians of all parties have ignored – its misery, volatile energy, gleeful rowdiness, self-knowledge and local pride'. This sentiment echoes that of Hesmondhalgh who states that music has the power to create, consolidate and challenge 'values and attachment', emphasising the role music plays in speaking to fans and shaping their views of the world.[40] Bramwell, in his study of the London grime scene, points to the importance of the music and the scene to young people, stating that participation in the scene helps young people to 'develop a sense of themselves'.[41]

London grime artist Lethal Bizzle responded to the riots by pointing out that he had warned the government about the growing unrest some years before. In a letter to David Cameron that had been published in *The Guardian* in 2006, entitled 'David Cameron is a donut', Bizzle had told Cameron that the government needed to talk to young people or risk anger rising to the surface. Bizzle was challenging remarks made by Cameron about rap music.[42] After being asked how he was going to reduce levels of knife crime, Cameron had directed his comments at Radio 1 disc jockeys and asked: 'do you realise that some of the stuff you play on Saturday nights encourages people to carry guns and knives?'[43] Bizzle felt that Cameron had missed the point and offered him some ways to engage young people.[44]

Grime itself had already been demonised in the UK by other public figures who suggested that the music incited violence,[45] but Lethal Bizzle was keen to counter this negative image and turn the spotlight on the ways in which young people were increasingly marginalised. 'You need to give back to the kids', he said, 'because they're the future of this country. They need to see that their voice counts and that they can get somewhere in life.' In the same article Bizzle claimed that 'a lot of what I do is on a positive tip for the community, but that all gets ignored. I've signed 14 young rappers from east London to my own label; that's taken them off the streets and given them something positive to look forward to.'[46] Bizzle's warnings continued in the words of songs such as his 2007 'Burning the Ghetto'. The song samples 'Babylon's Burning' by reggae punk band The Ruts which was released just prior to the 1981 London riots. Bizzle's song offers the listener 'true stories' and speaks, among other things, of disillusionment with governments. The song and the accompanying video are strikingly prophetic.

Music and politics has a long and well-documented history. Street states that music has been 'a site of political expression' from folk songs to classical music.[47] UK grime can be viewed as another example of politically and socially aware music that can be located within the tradition of protest music.[48] The lyrics are socially and politically conscious, not only reflecting the struggle of the people they represent, but also calling for change. They call for politicians and authority figures to take notice and to listen to young people, they call for wider society to be aware of the ways in which young people, especially young Black working-class men, are becoming increasingly disenfranchised and excluded. They call for the young people themselves to find better ways to express themselves than through gang violence and they attempt to give a sense of empowerment to young people. It is also possible that UK grime operates as a music of resistance because the artists' marginalised positions (as young, mainly Black and working class) mean that any music produced is inherently political, regardless of content.[49] This position is adopted by Walcott, who describes rap as 'cultural criticism', and suggests that for rap artists, the 'very practice of their music is politics'.[50] Huq also points to the potential of rap as 'rebel music', saying that it can be used to resist dominant discourses.[51]

As mentioned before, responses from musicians came through social media and some were republished in a piece by Dan Hancox in *The Guardian* online and the online music magazine *Dummy*.[52] There were responses from high profile artists such as Lethal Bizzle and Professor Green, but also other grime artists such as Skepta, Chipmunk (both from Tottenham), Black the Ripper and Mz Bratt. Many UK MCs commented on the events as they were happening. Some offered solidarity with the rioters – not to condone their actions necessarily, but to express an understanding of their frustration, anger and desperation. Skepta tweeted in reference to the shooting of Mark Duggan: 'I hope the media don't think all these riot videos & pictures are gonna make us lose focus. We're still waiting for answers'.[53] It seems that these MCs wanted to illuminate the causes, not condemn outright the actions. They offered more nuanced reasons for the riots, although, according to *Dummy*, Mz Bratt did, in fact, condemn the violence: 'Burning down other peoples businesses & Homes that's disgraceful'. Hancox reported Professor Green's response, which reflected the complexity of the situation: 'What needs to be understood here is there is a lot of anger in the underclass, and a lot of the youth aren't quite sure where to aim their anger'. Professor Green also pointed to the consequences of growing up with nothing but with 'everything we don't have rubbed in our faces'.[54]

Rap artists seemed to be suggesting that the riots were the young people's way of answering back to this inequality. They talked about the riots as misdirected collective power. They called on the young people to channel their anger into more productive forms of protest and to stop targeting their own neighbourhoods. Some of these artists used music and rap as the medium by which to share their message.[55] On 10 August 2011, London rapper Genesis Elijah uploaded a freestyle a capella rap to YouTube which was directed at young people. In a passionate performance to camera he attempted to make sense of what he had seen on the television – 'they blame the youths dem/but truthfully who wouldn't?/ Stating the obvious but blame ain't solution'.[56] This rap makes it clear that blaming only young people was unfair – 'may the looters, police and government hang their heads in shame'. It also displayed his anger at the behaviour of the young people – 'revolutionaries fight the power, not the powerless'. It seems that many UK grime and rap artists take their responsibility as role models very seriously. They are fully aware of the influence they have on their young listeners and the educational effects of their music. The majority of the artists who responded to the riots come from poor, disadvantaged backgrounds themselves and are likely to know how easy it is to react in destructive ways (and many of them have been down that path themselves).

The musical reactions to the riots appeared almost instantly, which suggests that the artists involved were speaking from a familiar place. The message in most of these responses is clear – they acknowledge the anger and the causes of the riots but they do not condone the actions. They recognise the reasons and target their judgement towards the system that led to the inequalities and caused the problems in the first place. They offer solutions to those in control of the system – stop ignoring the effects of poverty and start to listen to the young urban working class; make young people feel like they should care about themselves and their society.

One artist who released a song immediately after the riots was Young Deacon who recorded and released a track via YouTube on 10 August 2011, while the fires were still burning. In an interview a few days later, the artist stated that his motivation for the song was anger at the injustice suffered by young people and the negative representation of youth in the mainstream media.[57] The track 'Failed by the System' is a spoken word piece, with piano and strings backing, rather than a grime song, although it does demonstrate the kinds of linguistic facility described as a feature of grime by Bramwell.[58] Young Deacon makes it clear who he believes is to blame for the riots. He begins by criticising the violence: 'I can't justify the burning of buildings and businesses/ that sort of attitude there is inexcusable'; but he goes on to offer reasons for the violence. Young Deacon urges society to stop demonising young people and to give them a chance to feel they are worth something: 'we're branded a lot as rioters, looters and murderers ... but like it or not the youth are the future'. He warns that the continued blaming, coupled with squeezing of funds from working-class education and youth-targeted programmes, will lead to more violence: 'everyone wants to pass judgement ... no one wants to take responsibility or nothing'. Lyrics such as 'don't feed on the lies, see the bigger picture/ we all need to unite and build a better future' remind the listener that the young people depicted on the news during the riots are the future of Britain and that those in power must take some of the blame.

There were other musical responses from artists such as 2 K Olderz who sampled Muse in their song 'They Will Not Control Us'; Solocypher's 'Life Worth', which offers a message to the rioters that appeals to their sense of self-worth; West Londoner Nekz's freestyle rap called 'London's Burning'; Naye Forsyth's R&B/rap 'London Riots 2011⊠; and the non-grime/rap song by reggae artist Fresharda called 'Tottenham Riot'. South London collective, The Unit, used a news report format in their music video to tell their story in 'London Riots'. The voices in this track are varied and offer a set of different opinions, while also avoiding the moral panic and judgement of the mainstream media and politicians. The song includes a reporter describing the events and asking various people (played by rappers in the collective) on the streets to speak to him. He speaks to a protester who blames the police, unchecked racism and poverty and suggests that people have reached boiling point; they 'can't hold it in, that's why they call it outrage'. He then talks to a looter who points to a rare sense of solidarity with young people from other areas and a police officer who states that lack of police resources meant the violence was able to get out of control. And finally he speaks to a young man (neither a protestor nor a rioter) who is angry at the violence and the system and ends his verse with, 'but in the end, the poor people will still be poor for sure'.

PLAN B

One of the higher profile responses came from London rapper Plan B, who appears to have embraced a role as a spokesperson for disadvantaged youth. It is possible that Plan B operates as a 'movement artist' – an individual who, according to Eyerman and Jamison, operates as an important agent of cultural change.[59] Eyerman and Jamison point to the ways in which musicians contribute to 'knowledge bearing' and 'identity giving' within social movements.[60] If the actions of young people during the riots – and the responses from artists – can be seen as part of a social movement (one that mobilises young working-class people against austerity measures), then Plan B has the potential to occupy this kind of role. I would suggest that Plan B, and other grime artists, do provide the 'truth-bearing significance' that Eyerman and Jamison attribute to popular music linked with social movements, due to the ways in which grime songs often highlight social injustice and criticise those in authority.[61] The music of artists such as Plan B also points to the potential of songs as 'channels of communication for activists' and vehicles for expressing particular 'feeling of common purpose'.[62]

Plan B wrote an editorial for *The Sun* on 10 August 2011 which, while critical of the looting and destruction of property during the riots, suggested that young people are not being equipped to think through the consequences of their actions: 'the real thing that's going to help these kids is some knowledge and some education about how to live'.[63] In 2010, Plan B had recorded a *TEDxObserver* talk, in which he condemned the continuing demonisation of the poor and described his role as an educator for young rap fans, outlining how socially conscious rap was the only medium that spoke to him as a young disadvantaged and wayward youth. He recalled the ways in which rap guided him and his peers, and how the poetry of rap changed his life and created a desire to change the lives of others.

Plan B has stated in interviews that he understands how young people feel 'that no one cares about them, so they don't care in return' (Plan B in MistaJam, 2012).[64] He is attempting to instil some self worth in young people by making music that acknowledges their experience and empowers young people through a more accurate representation of them. He claims that he has written his rap music for the 'forgotten kids of society – those are the people I'm making it for'.[65] The educational potential of rap has been noted by a number of scholars and the concept of rap pedagogy acknowledged.[66] Plan B points to the power of words and considers his music to be a tool for communication and change, and urges people to make a difference by sharing their knowledge.

Plan B released his track 'Ill Manors' in 2012. This song has been described as 'the greatest British Protest Song in years'.[67] It serves as a response to the riots. According to reviewer Simon Price, Plan B is 'laying bare the causal connections between the macro and the micro, political corruptions and callousness and street level disorder and despair'.[68] The structure of the song is complex and layered, and based on 'Alles Nue' by German musician Peter Fox. It includes samples of Fox's song which itself contains samples of Shostakovich's Symphony Number 7. The musical tone is dark and angry. Plan B shouts: 'Oi, you little rich boy!' and dares the middles classes to venture onto an estate and experience the sort of violence that the young residents are expected to endure. Lyrics – such as 'keep on believing what you read in the papers/council estate kids, scum of the earth/think you know how life on a council estate is/from everything you've ever read about it or heard[69] – challenge the media representation and demonisation of young working-class and underclass people. 'Feed the fear that's what we've learned/fuel the fire/let it burn' also indicates that when people have been constantly depicted as thugs they feel that they might as well act like thugs.

The song is arguably a demand for those in power to listen to what the young urban working class have to say. I would suggest that the message is very clear, and Plan B makes reference to the riots both in the lyric and the video clip. The latter includes footage from new reports of the riots, along with young people filmed on a council estate recreating violent scenes and joining in the song's chorus. In his 2012 interview with MistaJam, Plan B states that the riots were a manifestation of visceral energy needed to shock people into thinking and to open up debate.

CONCLUSION

It is interesting to note how UK grime and rap artists both predicted the unrest of August 2011 and then responded in intelligent and nuanced ways, in stark contrast to the reactionary and moralistic responses presented by the mainstream media. The commentary from musicians continued with a number of artists releasing songs some months on from the riots. This could indicate a recognition that the issues that sparked the riots were not being resolved. Since the riots, further austerity measures, cuts to local services and rhetoric from the Conservative government about problems with 'sink estates' (as breeding grounds for gang activity, crime and causes of the riots), point to a lack of measures to prevent future riots.[70]

If music, as Hesmondhalgh suggests, has the power to challenge the particular 'values' of society, then it is possible that the songs and commentary of grime artists such as Lethal Bizzle and Plan B can contribute to a greater understanding of the complex causes of riots both within the subculture and the wider public.[71] Young people will arguably listen to people like Lethal Bizzle and Plan B (rather than politicians or the mainstream media) and the potentially empowering aspects of the artists' words can also create a positive effect.[72] It has been noted that participation in the grime scene offers young people an opportunity to build self-esteem and develop specific skills (such as those involved in song writing and production) and even some economic reward. Involvement in the scene can also have a politicising effect, as artists and fans engage in their own pubic sphere and share their understanding and criticisms of society, authority and political structures.[73] As a result, the artists who operate as spokespeople for the scene – the 'movement artists' referred to by Eyerman and Jamison – occupy an important and potentially powerful role.[74] It could be suggested that those in power should listen carefully to what musicians and their fans have to say in order to understand better the current situation for working-class youth in the UK and prevent further unrest and violence in the future.

NOTES

1. D. Pritchard and F. Pakes (eds.), *Riot, Unrest and Protest on the Global Stage* (Basingstoke, 2014) (Pritchard and pakes 2014).
2. Cameron's statement can be accessed here: D. Cameron, 'David Cameron on the riots: "This is criminality pure and simple". *The Guardian* (2011): http://www.theguardian.com/politics/video/2011/aug/09/david-cameron-riots-criminality-video [accessed 21 October 2016].
3. *Daily Express*, 9 August 2011.
4. The local incidents were reported here: D. Sutton, 'Waltham Forest: Police injured as unrest spreads to borough'. *East London and West Essex Guardian* (2011): http://www.guardian-series.co.uk/news/9182849.WALTHAM_FOREST__Police_injured_as_unrest_spreads_to_borough/# [accessed 21 October 2016].
5. R. Phillips, D. Frost and A. Singleton, 'Researching the riots', *The Geographical Journal*, 179(1) (2013), 3–10 (Frost et al. 2013).
6. *Daily Telegraph*, 9 August 2011; *Daily Mail*, 9 August 2011.

7. A. Cavanagh and A. Dennis, 'Behind the news: Reframing the riots', *Capital and Class*, 36(3) (2012), 375–81 (Cavanagh and Dennis 2012).

8. *The Sun*, 9 August 2011.

9. Cavanagh and Dennis, 'Behind the news', 378.

10. S. Winlow, S. Hall, D. Briggs and J. Treadwell, *Riots and Political Protest* (London, 2015); Frost et al., 'Researching the riots', 3–10 (Winlow et al. 2015).

11. K. Milburn, 'Behind the news: The August riots, shock and the prohibition of thought', *Capital and Class*, 36(3) (2012), 401–9 (Milburn 2012).

12. PA. 'BBC Apologises over Darcus Howe interview'. *Independent* (2011): http://www.independent.co.uk/news/media/tv-radio/bbc-apologises-over-darcus-howe-interview-2335357.html [accessed 21 October 2016].

13. Milburn, 'Behind the news', 402.

14. Milburn, 'Behind the news', 402.

15. J. Grant, 'Riots in the UK: Morality, social imaginaries, and conditions of possibility', *New Political Science*, 36(3) (2014), 311–29 (Grant 2014).

16. R. Huq, 'Suburbia runs riot: The UK August 2011 riots, neo-moral panic and the end of the English suburban dream?' *Journal for Cultural Research*, 17(2) (2013), 105–23 (Huq 2013).

17. I. Gallagher, 'Did rock-throwing teenage girl's "beating" by police spark London riots? Pictures that show how Tottenham turned into a war zone'. *Daily Mail* (2011):
    http://www.dailymail.co.uk/news/article-2023254/Tottenham-riot-Mark-Duggan-shooting-sparked-police-beating-girl.html [accessed 21 October 2016].

18. *The Guardian* conducted a number of interviews with young people from affected areas, for example, A. Conroy, 'Behind the Clapham riots: 'the police are the enemy'. *The Guardian* (2011): https://www.theguardian.com/society/2011/sep/07/clapham-riots-police-enemy [accessed 21 October 2016].

19. L. Bridges, 'Four days in August: The UK Riots', *Race & Class*, 54(1) (2012), 1–12 (Bridges 2012).

20. G. Morrell, S. Scott, Sarah, D. McNeish and S. Webster, *The August riots in England: Understanding the Involvement of Young People*. National Centre for Social Research. https://www.gov.uk/government/uploads/system/uploads/attachment_data/file/60531/The_20August_20Riots_20in_20England_20_pdf__201mb_.pdf [accessed 21 October 2016].

21. D. Singh, S. Marcus, H. Rabbatts and M. Sherlock, *After the Riots: The Final Report of the Riots Communities and Victims Panel* (London, 2012), p. 6 (Singh et al. 2012).

22. HM Government, *Government Response to the Riots, Communities and Victims Panel's Final Report* (London, 2013) (HM Government 2013).

23. P. Lewis, T. Newburn, M. Taylor, C. Mcgillivray, A. Greenhill, H. Frayman and R. Proctor, *Reading the Riots: Investigating England's Summer of Disorder* (London, 2011) (Lewis et al. 2011).
24. Lewis et al., *Reading the riots*, p. 4.
25. C. Fuchs, 'Behind the news: Social media, riots and revolutions', *Capital and Class*, 36(3) (2012), 383–91 (Fuchs 2012).
26. F. Vis, 'Twitter as a reporting tool for breaking news', *Digital Journalism*, 1(1) (2013), 27–47 (Vis 2013).
27. Lewis et al., *Reading the riots*, p. 24.
28. Lewis et al., *Reading the riots*, pp. 5–10.
29. The original (peaceful) protest staged by Mark Duggan's family and friends, was a demand for more information on his shooting.
30. F. Ashe, '"All about Eve": Mothers, masculinities and the 2011 UK riots', *Political Studies*, 62 (2014), 652–68 (Ashe 2014).
31. Ashe, '"All about Eve"', 657.
32. Z. Bauman, 'Interview: Zygmunt Bauman on the UK riots', *Social Europe* (2011): http://www.socialeurope.eu/2011/08/interview-zygmunt-bau man-on-the-uk-riots/ [accessed 21 October 2016] (Baumann 2011); D. Moxon, 'Consumer culture and the 2011 "riots"', *Sociological Research Online*, 16(4) (2011), 30 November 2011. http://www.socresonline.org. uk/16/4/19.html [accessed 21 October 2016] (Moxon 2011); S. Miles, 'Young people, "flawed protestors" and the commodification of resistance', *Critical Arts*, 28(1) (2014), 76–87 (Miles 2014).
33. Bauman, 'Interview: Zygmunt Bauman on the UK riots'; Miles, 'Young People, "flawed protestors"'.
34. D. Blackwell, 'Reading the riots – London 2011: Local revolt and global protest', *Psychotherapy and Politics International*, 13(2) (2015), 102–14 (Blackwell 2015); J. Solomos, 'Race, rumours and riots: Past, present and future', *Sociological Research Online*, 16(4) (2011): http://www.socreson line.org.uk/16/4/20.html [accessed 21 October 2016] (Solomos 2011).
35. UK grime is a British genre of hip hop (rap music) originating in London, characterised by a fast beat and fast rapping in localised accents.
36. P. Taylor 'Behind the news: The just do it riots, a critical interpretation of the media's violence', *Capital and Class*, 36(3) (2012), 393–9 (Taylor 2012).
37. P. Routledge, 'London riots: Is rap music to blame for encouraging this culture of violence?' *Mirror* (2011): http://www.mirror.co.uk/news/uk-news/london-riots-is-rap-music-to-blame-146671 [accessed 1 March 2017] (Routledge 2011).
38. J. Street, *Music and Politics* (Cambridge, 2012), p. 9 (Street 2012).
39. D. Hancox, 'Rap responds to the riots: "They have to take us seriously"', *The Guardian* (2011): http://www.theguardian.com/music/2011/aug/

12/rap-riots-professor-green-lethal-bizzle-wiley [accessed 1 March 2017] (Hancox 2011).

40. D. Hesmondhalgh, *Why Music Matters* (Chichester, 2013), p. 140 (Hesmondhalgh 2013).

41. R. Bramwell, *UK Hip-Hop, Grime and the City: The Aesthetics and Ethics of London's Rap Scenes* (London, 2015), p. 4 (Bramwell 2015).

42. N. Morris, 'Radio 1 DJs encouraging gun crime, says Cameron', *The Independent* (2006): http://www.independent.co.uk/news/uk/politics/radio-1-djs-encouraging-gun-crime-says-cameron-481491.html [accessed 21 October 2016] (Morris 2006).

43. Cameron made these comments in response to a question at a meeting of the British Society of Magazine Editors in June 2006. He also responded to Lethal Bizzle in a letter to the *Daily Mail* on 11 June 2006, in which he stated that 'young and impressionable people are given the message, in song after song, that guns, knives and other weapons are glamorous' (para 22).

44. S. Attfield, '"There's a world outside of the ghetto": UK grime and the empowering effects of creativity on working-class youth', in *Instruments of Change: Proceedings of the International Association for the Study of Popular Music Australia-New Zealand 2010 Conference*, (Melbourne, 2011), pp. 3–7 (Attfield 2011).

45. Former Home Secretary David Blunkett and former Culture Minister Kim Howells had both attacked rap in separate radio interviews with the BBC in 2003.

46. L. Bizzle, 'David Cameron is a donut', *The Guardian* (2008): http://www.theguardian.com/commentisfree/2006/jun/08/davidcameronisadonut [accessed 21 October 2016] (Bizzle 2008).

47. Street, *Music and Politics*, p. 42.

48. Bizzle, 'David Cameron is a donut'; I. Peddie (ed.), *The Resisting Muse: Popular Music and Social Protest* (Aldershot, 2006).

49. D. Laing, 'Resistance and protest', in J. Shepherd, D. Horn, D. Laing, P. Oliver and P. Wicke (eds.), *Continuum Encyclopaedia of Popular Music of the World* (London, 2003), pp. 345–6 (Laing 2003).

50. R. Walcott, 'Performing the (black) postmodern: Rap as incitement for cultural criticism', in C. McCarthy, G. Hudak, S. Miklaucic and P. Saukko (eds.), *Sound Identities: Popular Music and the Cultural Politics of Education* (New York: 1999), p. 97 (Walcott 1999).

51. R. Huq, *Beyond Subculture: Pop, Youth and Identity in a Postcolonial World* (London, 2006), p. 110 (Huq 2006).

52. Hancox, 'Rap Responds to the riots'. N.A. 'The music world responds to the London riots on Twitter'. *Dummy* (2011): http://www.dummymag.com/news/grime-artists-respond-to-london-riots [accessed 1 March 2017].

53. Skepta (2011). *Twitter*. https://twitter.com/skepta/status/ 100360068662435840 [accessed 21 October 2016] (Skepta 2011).
54. Hancox, 'Rap responds to the riots'.
55. It should be noted that there does not appear to be any musical responses from female artists. Grime and rap is very male dominated (as is rap in general).
56. Genesis Elijah, 'Re: UK Riots'. *YouTube* (2011): https://www.youtube. com/watch?v=f-rQpkvLuv0 [accessed 1 March 2017] (Elijah 2011).
57. R. Gallagher, 'We were raised by a generation of hypocrites', *Open Democracy UK* (2011): https://www.opendemocracy.net/ourkingdom/ ryan-gallagher/raised-by-a-generation-of-hypocrites-youth-riots-london [accessed 1 March 2017] (Gallagher 2011).
58. Bramwell, *UK Hip-Hop, Grime and the City*, p. 4.
59. R. Eyerman and A. Jamison, *Music and Social Movements: Mobilizing Traditions in the Twentieth Century* (Cambridge, 1998), p. 22 (Eyerman and Jamison 1998).
60. Eyerman and Jamison, *Music and Social Movements*, p. 23.
61. Eyerman and Jamison, *Music and Social Movements*, p. 24.
62. Eyerman and Jamison, *Music and Social Movements*, p. 161.
63. Plan B, 'Two views of the riots that shame the UK', *The Sun* (2011): https://www.thesun.co.uk/archives/news/708300/two-views-of-riots-that-shame-uk/ [accessed 21 October 2016] (Plan 2011).
64. MistaJam, 'Plan B interview with MistaJam'. *BBC Radio 1 Xtra* (2012): http://www.bbc.co.uk/programmes/p00plvyr [accessed 21 October 2016] (MistaJam 2012).
65. MistaJam, 'Plan B interview with MistaJam'.
66. A. Ibrahim, 'Taking hip hop to a whole nother level: Metissage, affect and pedagogy in a global hip hop nation', in H. Samy Alim, A. Pennycook and A. Ibrahim (eds.), *Global Linguistic Flows: Hip Hop Cultures, Youth Identities and the Politics of Language* (New York, 2009), pp. 231–48 (Ibrahim 2009; A. A. Akom, 'Critical hip hop pedagogy as a form of liberatory praxis', *Equity & Excellence in Education*, 42(1) (2009), 52–66 (Akom 2009); L. F. Rodriguez, 'Dialoguing, cultural capital and student engagement: Toward a hip hop pedagogy in the high school and university classroom', *Equity & Excellence in Education*, 42(1) (2009), 20–35 (Rodriguez 2009).
67. D. Lynskey, 'Why Plan B's Ill Manors is the greatest British protest song in years', *The Guardian* (2012): http://www.theguardian.com/music/musicblog/ 2012/mar/15/plan-b-ill-manors [accessed 1 March 2017] (Lynskey 2012).
68. S. Price, 'Album: Plan B Ill Manors', *The Independent* (2012): http://www. independent.co.uk/arts-entertainment/music/reviews/album-plan-b-ill-manors-atlantic674-7964105.html [accessed 1 March 2017] (Price 2012).
69. The lyrics quoted from here are available via Plan B's website, http://www. time4planb.co.uk/lyrics/ill-manors [accessed 21 October 2016].

70. David Cameron's plan to demolish so-called 'sink estates' has been widely reported in the media, C. Davies, 'David Cameron vows to "blitz" poverty by demolishing UK's worst sink estates'. *The Guardian* (2016: http://www.theguardian.com/society/2016/jan/09/david-cameron-vows-to-blitz-poverty-by-demolishing-uks-worst-sink-estates [accessed 21 October 2016] (Davies 2016).
71. Hesmondhalgh, *Why Music Matters*, p. 140.
72. Attfield, '"There's a world outside of the ghetto"', pp. 3–7.
73. Bramwell, *UK Hip-Hop, Grime and the City*.
74. Eyerman and Jamison, *Music and Social Movements*, p. 22.

References

A. A. Akom, 'Critical Hip Hop Pedagogy as a Form of Liberatory Praxis', *Equity & Excellence in Education*, 42, 1 (2009), 52–66.

F. Ashe, '"All About Eve": Mothers, Masculinities and the 2011 UK Riots', *Political Studies*, 62 (2014), 652–68.

S. Attfield, '"There's a World Outside of the Ghetto": UK Grime and the Empowering Effects of Creativity on Working Class Youth', *Instruments of Change*, (Melbourne, 2011), pp. 3–7.

Bauman, Zygmunt. 'Interview: Zygmunt Bauman on the UK Riots'. *Social Europe*, 15 August 2011: http://www.socialeurope.eu/2011/08/interview-zygmunt-bauman-on-the-uk-riots/. [accessed: 21 October 2016].

L. Bizzle (2008), 'David Cameron is a Donut', *The Guardian*. http://www.theguardian.com/commentisfree/2006/jun/08/davidcameronisadonut [accessed: 21 October 2016].

D. Blackwell, 'Reading the Riots – London 2011: Local Revolt and Global Protest', *Psychotherapy and Politics International*, 13, 2 (2015), 102–114.

R. Bramwell, *UK Hip-Hop, Grime and the City: The Aesthetics and Ethics of London's Rap Scenes* (London, 2015), p. 4.

L. Bridges, 'Four Days in August: The UK Riots', *Race & Class*, 54, 1 (2012), 1–12.

A. Cavanagh and A. Dennis, 'Behind the News: Reframing the Riots', *Capital and Class*, 36, 3 (2012), 375–81.

Davies, Caroline (2016). 'David Cameron vows to 'blitz' poverty by demolishing UK's worst sink estates'. *The Guardian*: http://www.theguardian.com/society/2016/jan/09/david-cameron-vows-to-blitz-poverty-by-demolishing-uks-worst-sink-estates [accessed: 21 October 2016].

Elijah, Genesis (2011). 'Re: UK Riots'. *YouTube*: https://www.youtube.com/watch?v=f-rQpkvLuv0 [accessed: 21 October 2016]

R. Eyerman and A. Jamison, *Music and Social Movements: Mobilizing Traditions in the Twentieth Century* (Cambridge, 1998), p. 22.

D. Frost *et al*, 'Researching the Riots', *The Geographical Journal*, 179, 1 (2013), 3–10.

C. Fuchs, 'Behind the News: Social Media, Riots and Revolutions', *Capital and Class*, 36, 3 (2012), 383–91.

R. Gallagher, '"We Were Raised by a Generation of Hypocrites"', *Open Democracy UK*, 2011: https://www.opendemocracy.net/ourkingdom/ryan-gallagher/raised-by-a-generation-of-hypocrites-youth-riots-london [accessed: 21 October 2016].

J. Grant, 'Riots in the UK: Morality, Social Imaginaries, and Conditions of Possibility', *New Political Science*, 36, 3 (2014), 311–29.

D. Hancox (2011), 'Rap Responds to the Riots: "They have to take us seriously"', *The Guardian*: http://www.theguardian.com/music/2011/aug/12/rap-riots-professor-green-lethal-bizzle-wiley [accessed: 13 August 2011].

D. Hesmondhalgh, *Why Music Matters* (Chichester, 2013), p. 140.

HM Government, *Government Response to the Riots, Communities and Victims Panel's Final Report* (London, 2013).

R. Huq, *Beyond Subculture: Pop, Youth and Identity in a Postcolonial World* (London, 2006), p. 110.

R. Huq, 'Suburbia Runs Riot: The UK August 2011 Riots, Neo-Moral Panic and the End of the English Suburban Dream?', *Journal for Cultural Research*, 17, 2 (2013), 105–23.

A. Ibrahim, 'Taking Hip Hop to a Whole Nother Level: Metissage, Affect and Pedagogy in a Global Hip Hop Nation', in A.H. Samy *et al* (eds.), *Global Linguistic Flows: Hip Hop Cultures, Youth Identities and the Politics of Language* (New York, 2009), pp. 231–48.

D. Laing, 'Resistance and Protest', in J. Shepherd *et al* (eds.), *Continuum Encyclopaedia of Popular Music of the World* (London, 2003), pp. 345–6.

P. Lewis *et al*, *Reading the Riots: Investigating England's Summer of Disorder* (London, 2011).

D. Lynskey (2012), 'Why Plan B's Ill Manors is the Greatest British Protest Song in Years', *The Guardian*: http://www.theguardian.com/music/musicblog/2012/mar/15/plan-b-ill-manors [accessed: 16 March 2012].

K. Milburn, 'Behind the News: The August Riots, Shock and the Prohibition of Thought', *Capital and Class*, 36, 3 (2012), 401 – 409.

S. Miles, 'Young People, 'flawed protestors' and the Commodification of Resistance', *Critical Arts*, 28, 1 (2014), 76–87.

MistaJam (2012). 'Plan B Interview with MistaJam'. *BBC Radio 1 Xtra*: http://www.bbc.co.uk/programmes/p00plvyr. [accessed: 21 October 2016.

Morris, N. (2006), 'Radio 1 DJs encouraging gun crime, says Cameron', *The Independent*: http://www.independent.co.uk/news/uk/politics/radio-1-djs-encouraging-gun-crime-says-cameron-481491.html [accessed: 21 October 2016].

Moxon, D.'Consumer Culture and the 2011 "Riots"'. *Sociological Research Online*, 16, 4 (2011), 30 November 2011: http://www.socresonline.org. uk/16/4/19.html [accessed: 21 October 2016].

I. Peddie (ed.), *The Resisting* Muse: *Popular Music and Social Protest* (Aldershot, 2006).

Plan B (2011), 'Two Views of the Riots that Shame the UK', *The Sun*: https:// www.thesun.co.uk/archives/news/708300/two-views-of-riots-that-shame-uk/ [accessed: 21 October 2016].

S. Price (2012), 'Album: Plan B Ill Manors', *The Independent*: http://www. independent.co.uk/arts-entertainment/music/reviews/album-plan-b-ill-man ors-atlantic674-7964105.html. [accessed: 22 October 2012].

D. Pritchard and F. Pakes (eds.), *Riot, Unrest and Protest on the Global Stage* (Basingstoke, 2014).

L. F. Rodriguez, 'Dialoguing, Cultural Capital and Student Engagement: Toward a Hip Hop Pedagogy in the High School and University Classroom', *Equity & Excellence in Education*, 42, 1 (2009), 20–35.

P. Routledge (2011), 'London Riots: Is Rap Music to Blame for Encouraging this Culture of Violence?' *Mirror*: http://www.mirror.co.uk/news/uk-news/lon don-riots-is-rap-music-to-blame-146671 [accessed: 10 August 2011].

D. Singh *et al*, *After the Riots: The Final Report of the Riots Communities and Victims Panel* (London, 2012), p. 6.

Skepta (2011). *Twitter*: https://twitter.com/skepta/status/ 100360068662435840. [accessed: 21 October 2016].

Solomos, J. 'Race, Rumours and Riots: Past, Present and Future', *Sociological Research Online*, 16, 4 (2011): http://www.socresonline.org.uk/16/4/20. html. [accessed: 21 October 2016].

J. Street, *Music and Politics* (Cambridge, 2012), p. 9.

P. Taylor (2012) 'Behind the News: The Just Do It Riots, A Critical Interpretation of the Media's Violence', *Capital and Class*, 36, 3 (2012), 393–99.

F. Vis, 'Twitter as a Reporting Tool for Breaking News', *Digital Journalism*, 1, 1 (2013), 27–47.

R. Walcott, 'Performing the (Black) Postmodern: Rap as Incitement for Cultural Criticism', in C. McCarthy *et al* (eds.), *Sound Identities: Popular Music and the Cultural Politics of Education* (New York, 1999).

S. Winlow *et al*, *Riots and Political Protest* (London, 2015).

Sarah Attfield is a Scholarly Teaching Fellow in the School of Communication at the University of Technology Sydney. Her research focuses on how working class experience is represented in popular music, tv, film, literature, art and in the media.

CHAPTER 5

'A Different Vibe and a Different Place': Re-telling the Riots – A Round Table Discussion

Lucy Robinson and Peter Webb

This article is an edited transcript of a discussion that took place as part of a one day event – 'Retelling the Riots' – organised in Bristol by the Subcultures Network. By bringing together participants and commentators we explored the role of the local in youth culture, as well as the role of youth culture in the forms of resistance and rioting seen in cities across the country in the early 1980s and the summer of 2011. Although there was a strong sense of the specificity of local experiences within Bristol, and of the networks that facilitated forms of resilience and resistance in communities, the Bristol experience simultaneously spoke of the national context. What emerged was a complex sense of community building with youth at its heart, and of the role of popular music as both a shared experience and as a way of building a shared historical memory. Participants included

L. Robinson (✉)
University of Sussex, Brighton, UK
e-mail: l.robinson@sussex.ac.uk

P. Webb
University of the West of England, Bristol, UK
e-mail: Peter.Webb@uwe.ac.uk

© The Author(s) 2017
K. Gildart et al. (eds.), *Youth Culture and Social Change*,
Palgrave Studies in the History of Subcultures and Popular Music,
DOI 10.1057/978-1-137-52911-4_5

101

academic Paul Gilroy and musicians Shane Baldwin, Joshua Moses and Mike Darby, who now runs Bristol Archive Records.[1]

INTRODUCTION

In 1980, 1981 and the summer of 2011, urban unrest in Bristol chimed with outbreaks of rioting across the country. The experiences in Bristol were therefore simultaneously specifically local and part of a much wider national context. Community networks in Bristol had helped construct collective identities, particularly over generational or subcultural identity in combination with a strong sense of place. These same networks structured acts of resistance and unrest, and strengthened the resilience of communities to deal with the aftermath of unrest. In the story of the unrest in the 1980s key elements often emerge: the relationships between class and other forms of identity, the relationships between different social and cultural groups, the role of music (and the spaces it is played in) to bring people together and the clashes between the structures of the law and the structures of collective community identities.[2] The riots of August 2011 invited a re-imagining and re-arming of the memory of the 1980s riots in the language of politicians and the press, and in the musical responses of contemporary artists.[3]

Music is central to this story. It was central to the street battleground between communities and the organised far-right, and it was central to the ways in which transgression and dissent were recognised.[4] Music was central to the ways in which young local people, both Black and White, connected with each other; embodied in punk and rasta, music was key to whether or not 'Black and White [could] unite and fight'. At the simplest level the places music was played and listened to were central to the collective identities that developed. But music also marked the lines between and across different identity groups; punks and rastas, as well as established older generations' music cultures and emerging subcultural identities. Music provided a mouthpiece for the concerns of the young Black and White working classes to be heard by each other and to share a narrative together. Music also speaks across time and becomes its own form of popular memory, providing a history of past events, re-imagined in the current context.

The Subcultures Network invited a group of Bristol musicians, community members and commentators who had experienced the events surrounding the riots of the 1980s to come together and share their stories about race, music and riots in Bristol.[5] Bristol, as the venue for this symposium, has a unique position in the history of British popular music and we used that history to explore the relationship between the past and present and between Bristol and the wider national context. The Bristol music scene has produced bands such as Black Roots, Massive Attack, Disorder, Roni Size, Portishead and the Pop Group. Many of these musicians created a narrative in lyrics, aesthetics, imagery and comment on the cultural and political scene within the city and nationally. Bristol's example demonstrates not only the importance of the history of popular music, but also the role of musicians, audiences and music in making history happen. The format of the discussion emphasised the importance of ideas around 'authentic' experience, the importance of the stories that we tell about our communities and the centrality of music in both of these processes. They shone a spotlight on the ways in which the Bristol stories could be simultaneously indicative of the wider national context, and an example of the importance of local specificity. They also showed the central role music played in the communities that were built, and the forms of resilience and resistance that they developed. The role of music as a form of memory, for both punks and rastas, emerged throughout the discussion. This also raises issues around what sort of historical records are left – across the memoirs of public figures, statistics, songs and local heritage projects.

PARTICIPANTS

Shane Baldwin is a member of the Bristol punk band, Vice Squad and played a key part in the development of the punk music scene in Bristol. In the early 1980s, Baldwin and Simon Edwards (also from Vice Squad) set up Riot City Records. Shane says that the only reason they called it Riot City Records was because they were in a city that had some riots in and it wasn't anything deeper than that.

Mike Darby was in the indie-punk Bristol band The Rimshots in the early 1980s and now owns and runs Bristol Archive Records. He has had a central role in reinvigorating the Bristol reggae scene and supporting other independent music produced in Bristol.

Paul Gilroy, Professor of American and English Literature at King's College London is author of numerous work including *There ain't no Black in the Union Jack* (1987), *The Black Atlantic: Modernity and Double Conciousness* (1993) and *Darker than Blue: On the Moral Economies of Black Atlantic Culture* (2010).

Joshua Moses, reggae musician and key member of the community of St Pauls in Bristol. Moses was ever present during the riots of the 1980s and central to the networks of that time.

What follows is an edited transcript of their conversation.

THE ROUNDTABLE

Peter Webb: Just to kind of start off, and to give it a bit of context, this day is partly about the kind of music, subcultures, the kind of stories and narratives about these events and the rise of politics that come from them and I just wanted to ask each person about their identification with their particular cultural, subcultural belonging. Joshua, I'd like to start with you, just to talk a little bit about the kind of development of Rastafarianism in St Pauls; how important the reggae scene was for the development of young people like yourself during the 1970s and 1980s.

Joshua Moses: Yeah, well in them times it was different from now [laughs]. The struggle was more direct and even more confrontational in many ways. Because my generation have to be the first generation of Caribbean who went through the schooling system and the whole system in England. So, therefore, we were like at the frontline of things; we had to be the ones who were breaking down the barriers because our parents never went to school here so they were lacking in certain areas where we as kids who went to school here, we felt we knew as much and we deserve as much as anyone who went to school here. But it was unbalanced and still is, nothing has changed, it is no different.

So that's where the struggle really starts. A sense of injustice. And once that injustice start to spread then you have fractionalised people in the community; you see the sort-of fractionalisation between the community and the government and you see these things just seem to spread and the pressure of life means at that time we were the unconsidered ones; you were the last ones to be considered. And our advice was, at that time, [laughs] we never did want any war; we all lived as Rasta man; ask for peace and love and justice. But that was the kind of community that the system never liked because it was a unity and it was a good, upstanding unity which was attempting to achieve some natural things that we think it was our deserve.

But in this process the policing at that time never favoured us because, you know, there has to be a scapegoat in the system – just as it is today – still nothing's changed. So we were at the frontline and felt most of these pressures, like the SUS law and them kind of thing. And then there was a crucial time, which I don't hear no-one mention, but the policing in this country at that time changed because from my memory they are doing the same thing today; they were actually recruiting Zimbabwean police into the British police force. Now you can see what that lead to straight away, the mentality and the effect that that's going to have in the community.

So once the police was infiltrated with this kind of idealism then we were at the front line and we were feeling the pressure and we were crying out these days and no-one listened, it was as if we were telling lies or making up stories. But those lies and those stories today have to be truth and everyone is now feeling the consequences of not adjusting those lies and those words – it still hasn't been adjusted.

Peter Webb: And where are those stories being told Joshua? Are they being told through music; are they being told through the community?

Joshua Moses: That's what the music is all about. The music I have been involved in throughout all my life ... or most of my life. It's the music of message, which is supposed to bring justice, peace and love to humanity – not a fraction of humanity – but to all humanity. There is only one humanity so I cannot fight against humanity because I will be fighting against myself so the whole point of this is justice, bring peace and love – there is no other way to love unless you start with justice [laughs] – it has to be seen to be just.

Peter Webb: Shane and Mike, the punk rock scene in Bristol was, according to various different accounts, quite a mixed scene. There were lots of White kids, Black kids, someone like Ray Mighty (Musician from the band Smith and Mighty), was a key player in the Bristol music scene and was very much into punk. What are your memories of growing up in Bristol and getting involved in the punk scene? Why was punk so important to you?

Shane Baldwin: Well I came along as the second wave and politics were a lot more straightforward, you know? You hated Thatcher and you hated the police so it was quite straightforward. And it was more political than the first wave of punk do you think Mike?

Mike Darby: Yes, I've known Shane since we were kids and [as] Shane said he was in the second wave of the punk bands but he would have being going to see the original wave of punk bands post-'77. I was late '77 to '78, my wife would have been right at the start and, for me I have to say that punk was like coming out of the suburbs and going into the city and you just found yourself. It was about building your character and building confidence in yourself to look different, be different, be around different ... a different vibe and a different place. I've been a salesman all my life, managing sales people but I believe that my character was built by punk rock and if anybody ever asked me when I was President of the Gloucester

Golf Union, which is ridiculous, I would say I was a punk rocker and I'm proud to say that – and that's what it means to me.

Peter Webb: Paul, you've written a lot about a different set of cultures and subcultures within capitalism, how important do you think these kind of social formations are in terms of developing character and the types of identity that these guys are talking about?

Paul Gilroy: You said, 'are' – I heard them say, 'were'.

Peter Webb: Right.

Paul Gilroy: So I wouldn't want to get into it now, because now it's just the lifestyle – now it's nothing; to have locks is nothing and it's everywhere you look and everywhere you see a head of locks – it's nothing. But before, you could get killed for that choice. I was very heartened that in the discussion that we were having earlier on, people talked about running for their lives; they talked about their lives being at stake. I don't remember who it was but someone talked of being outside and running for your life.

I wouldn't say 'running for your life' can be the defining characteristic of a certain experience during those years. I'm proud to have shared that actually and it is not just a generationally defined experience but one that we hold in common – as the children of migrants and some of us as migrants ourselves – with our parents' generation because they used to run for their lives as well after the pubs were shut. For me, there's a very important distinction we have to draw between what happened in the past and what's happening now. I don't think that there are a lot of continuities there.

From my own perspective, you know, I mean I suppose I was there at the birth of punk because I used to be a musician myself and play music and some of the people I played music with or were in rival bands with me went on to become sort of founding people in that world of punk. When I first went to university, Bill Broad later to become Billy Idol was a friend. I used to borrow his amplifier because it was louder than my own one for gigging. He was a rather serious vegetarian guitarist at that time. So having vegetarianism in common and having an interest in sound in common, this was an important thing. So I would say that living in Brighton and coming up to London during the summer of 1976 I was there when all of that started.

But what's more interesting to me than pontificating about punk in that moment is to think about the impact of Ethiopianism as a contribution to that emergent tradition. Now someone else that I used to be friends with – Dick Hebdige – had this line about punk. He said that, whereas the bass culture of the Caribbean settlers, the bass culture of the Ethiopianist movement raised certain deep questions, ontological questions when the music hit you in the body. Punks turned away from that bass, low frequency sound. This is his argument and not mine and I'm sure that everyone will disagree with it – that's fine. He said that there was what could be called a 'politics of frequency' there. After all, Linton had called it a bass culture; Ralph Ellison had also identified it as a bass culture 20 or 30 years before Linton. The question would be, was punk to treble what Ethiopianism was to all that bass? That's Hebdige's question. I would say that there's something to be explored there in the 'politics of frequency', you know? I mean we all have ears right? But there's an aesthetic aspect that comes to this and, personally, when I go to play I turn the treble right off, you know, because I want the bass notes to come through – that's just my view. I think these become ontological questions really.

The other thing I want to say really strongly is that we have to get the history right. It matters actually what the history says; what the historical record says. This is especially important now. I feel it strongly because the internet's full of rubbish and lies and if you try to even edit something on Wikipedia you'll be attacked by people who tell you that don't have any evidence for it – even if it was your life. So I think there are questions about how life and liberty become information in a digital environment that are very, very important to the kind of work that you will want to do.

1976 – and the period between '72 and '76 for me – was the formative period because that's a period of great conflict with the police at the basic level in community life. The person at the back who was talking about being a skinhead raises an interesting question. I mean the mythology of skinheads now is that they just loved Black people – that's the myth that Robert Elms and company have created in the world. But we know that it's not that simple, right? They loved Enoch too. And anyway, you can love reggae, you can love that sound and still hate the people that made it, right? So there's some real complexity there.

As far as reggae and 1976 is concerned, we need to start that story in '68 with The Cats and all of that stuff. John Kpiaye, later to be the inventor of Lovers' Rock, was the architect of their pop hit 'Swan Lake' – all of that history needs to be made really vivid. The big riot of summer 1976 – the Notting Hill riot – is, for me, the beginning of the arc of this story and that's the one that resonates most strongly with the punk thing. But it's also a broader situation. Everyone today, understandably, has spoken in a very local way. I would say that in 1976 you have to go global to understand what happened then. I can remember standing in the carnival – and I'm sure Lez [Henry] was there as well – you're standing in the carnival – and Chris probably too, sitting at the back, holding his peace for now – from Misty in Roots – you know I can remember standing in the street off Ladbroke Grove and hearing the crowd around me chanting 'Soweto, Soweto, Soweto'. The reason they were doing that was because they had watched what was going on in South Africa and they had seen the strikes of the school students, Hector Pieterson and all of that conflict on the streets of Soweto had been unfolding on the TV. So there is a global element to all of this which I think should be recognised. I understand where the priority must fall today but I also want to emphasise that these things need to be seen in a global frame and there's something about the music and its travels; there's something about the passion for human rights that the music disseminates, which requires us to place it in a global frame.

Peter Webb: Bringing it back to Bristol, Joshua, and thinking about that period in the late '70s, early 1980s leading up to the riot, there's a lot of kind of politics going on in Bristol and across the rest of the country but in Bristol there's definitely a kind of mixing of White and Black but also a kind of separation in places like The British Queen, The Bamboo Club, The Criterion – and you remember these places?

Joshua Moses: It always has been important because we live in England, you know? So having a culture which is like Jamaican – and there were many other cultures in the area – we all had our differences; let's say 'flag' and our music was our flag. And the St Pauls carnival festival I think brings more subcultures out of that where each year, each section of the community would show their trophies like, you know, their music and their dance and thing.

So there was at the same time a gelling of the community. But at the same time there was a separation between I think the community and the government in the cities because the government institute had to be front line; the door we had to go through to get things done. So because of how we are and how we mix with the other communities around us it was a nice time really, it was a sweet, conscious time. As the brethren mention, you know, the formative time, '76, the consciousness of Rasta bring justice and how things should really be amongst humanity was flowing so it was like a movement of spirituality and love – peace and love.

And all these things were simmering in St Pauls and if you ever wanted this, this was the only place to get it so people from all around would come to St Pauls to support that view. And in them days everybody used to be mugging and killing and this and that – no – you were living on a different level. Not that there wasn't fights and violence, there will always be – as long as man is in the equation. So it wasn't as or isn't as drastic as it would appear now.

So, yeah, my community reflected the world as it was all nations and those of us who aspire to the one-world concept, justice, peace and love for humanity we really embraced that and I don't think of going because, guess what, I stayed in Bristol.

Peter Webb: There seemed to be a quite strong dividing line as well as the kind of community that Joshua was talking about. Do you have clear memories of that kind of like class breakdown and that political breakdown during that period of time – the late '70s and early '80s?

Shane Baldwin: Well, politically it was certainly a very dangerous time to be a punk wasn't it? Because in the first band we had, the Tea Breaks, we were attacked by a van-load of men and we were only like 15 at the time and quite badly beaten up and our singer, Ian, was actually brain-damaged and he's not right to this day. So it was a very dangerous time wasn't it?

Mike Darby: Yeah, I can remember looking a bit different in the local youth club and there being a big guy from Patchway thrown in to set me on fire because I had the ... you know, what ... the sort of ... clothing and hair, ... that punk kids used to wear and there was like about 20 kids from school in the toilet at the youth club, hanging ... you know, having a fag or whatever and it was ... I couldn't get out; I thought I was going to die but I managed to get out. But that's just because you looked a bit strange or you looked a little bit wacky or a little bit different and, you know, looking a little bit different as a punk would have been looking no different than having locks, because I can remember as a White guy coming into St Pauls, because I had a Black manager who managed my band – Gene Walsh – and I was on the same record label as Joshua was on in 1980 and Gene used to pick us up from the suburbs and take us into The Blues and I'd shit myself for the whole half an hour that I was in there thinking, 'what the hell am I doing?'.

But it was through ignorance more than anything else that Grosvenor Road and The Black & White and The Frontline were scary – it was through ignorance because now I am, I am proud to say, incredibly friendly with all of the reggae musicians from St Pauls, you know, really,

really, really friendly and if I could have said in 1979 that that would happen – it would be a miracle.

Joshua Moses: But the propaganda against that idea, that is huge. I mean today the same things happen … We have to grow – nothing has really changed. All the problems that my granddad talks about and my dad and I'm talking of, my kids have had – nothing has changed. The school's still need fixing; policing … How long are they going to take to fix schools, policing, nursing, whatever? All of my life? All of my dad's life? So these things are not to be fixed and that's how it appears to me. So really I know if we don't grasp this thing with the message of justice, peace and love the problem will remain and we have to change our ways, on our own, so that we can change the things that need changing. If we continue in the same way, the same thing will happen.

I'm not afraid to say, 'hey, 'I've changed my view'. I'm glad to say I have disarmed myself so, therefore, there can be no war. That's my chance.

Peter Webb: To take Paul's point about getting the history right, [what was] …your understanding of the St Pauls riot night in 1980. Do you want to say a bit about how you saw that unfolding and what you think the causes were and then about the aftermath of the riot?

Joshua Moses: As quickly as I can. The main cause as I said for me was what I seen as injustice mostly brought on by the police. The way they were policing the community was unjust and we knew that and if we left the community we have a problem. So we ain't going to sit down and we're still going to go into the community. So, therefore, our life is now living like a criminal life because you either stay in there and be pressurised or you go out there and be pressurised. No, we're not going to stay in there so we went up there. So wherever we go there seems to be trouble. Why? Because the policing forced us into defending our rights so, therefore, there will always be trouble.

But over the years things build up and St Pauls café, The Black and White, was like the tipping point in the St Pauls riot. On the day they were there all day and, as someone said, yes, when they were taking out the weed someone said, 'no man, enough of this' and someone grabbed it and that's where it started. It was a matter of defending what we believe to be truthful because we smoking weed, we're not causing any problem to our belief in them days; I must say I've grown up a bit so I've got slight reservation about that nowadays but we deemed it to be unjust and that was like the last thing we had because it was like a yearly ritual or a seasonal ritual. At certain time when you know a holiday is coming up, that's when we got most of the stuff so they come in and take it off of us. So those things would cause massive problems – it was the policing that was the problem.

Mike Darby: From my recollections of that era, and correct me if I'm wrong Paul, but St Pauls, whilst the statistics or the percentages of the Black population might be less than in Birmingham or Manchester or London – that was the Black area of Bristol – and, at some point people started to be moved out to the suburbs.

Now one of the scariest stories that I've got on BristolArchiveRecords. com website is from one of my artists, Bunny Marriott, who I think it would be fair to say was a political activist in the late '70s; he was called 'Bunny Red', he had a lot to say in St Pauls and, over a period of time, the council allegedly wanted to get rid of Bunny and Bunny's 74 years of age now and the community's been dispersed; it doesn't exist in St Pauls any more. People are coming back to St Pauls, you know?

Bunny actually lives in Clifton. Now Bunny's originally from Jamaica; he's a 74 year old Rasta. He lives in the poshest parts of town in one of the poshest streets in town in a church flat in the basement. He walks, or catches the bus, every single day from that place in Clifton down to St Pauls to see his friends and then sits, every single day, outside Glen's Jamaican Food takeaway before he walks or catches the bus back to Clifton because that's where the council rehoused him because they wanted to get him out of the community because 'he was trouble'.

Joshua Moses: They're doing it even now because I don't really know [laughs] more than maybe 20 people in St Pauls right now. I feel like a stranger in St Pauls but I guess my attitude's they're different but I do feel as if, yeah, people have been cast out of the area and it's now been built up but not in favour of the inhabitants who ... suffer the consequences.

Mike Darby: It's quite a weird thing but when you run an archive record label and you try to find material, lost gems, some really brilliant, some really average and some not so good at all, you're like a detective. So what you end up doing is you start in a place and then you gradually, over a period of time when you gain trust, work your way out. But what is fascinating from a Bristol perspective is it all starts in St Pauls and then by the time you end-up finding the people [laughs] they're often not in St Pauls because they've been dispersed; they don't live in the area – they've been moved out and their families have moved even wider afield and, you know, it's ...

So I've only learned this through finding music but there's huge political things that I've learned about that have got nothing to do with me wanting to be an academic or reading a book, I just learned it because I had to find somebody and had to find a tune and I just had to go that path.

Peter Webb: Joshua was talking about some of the reasons that he thought the St Pauls riot in 1980 got started; it was a catalyst, it was a tipping point for a whole load of other factors. I mean is that the way you think we should be looking at these kind of events, as a kind of catalyst and tipping points where class, ethnicity and the socioeconomic status of communities are underlying factors that contribute to, and frame these events?

Paul Gilroy: We all agreed about the central significance of policing in this story. And in this time, you know, the people that ran the police force – you called it a police service in those days – I don't know how you feel about calling it one now? The police force looked at what was going on in Ireland and they said they didn't want that to happen anywhere here; if you read the autobiographical archive you'll see that. One of the little rituals that the commissioners of the Metropolitan police did was when they retired they always published their autobiography. There's an amazing archive of autobiographical writing by police commissioners about these times and about their sense of the problems that were most important.

Sir Robert Mark – people don't remember his name much now – he was the one who was in charge of the Metropolitan police at the time of the Spaghetti House siege in London. The Spaghetti House siege was when certain activists from the Black communities in West London decided that they were going to hold up this restaurant and take the money and syphon it into the community. Horace Ove made a good film about it called *A Hole in Babylon*.

If you look in the pages of Sir Robert Mark's book – it's called *In the Office of Constable*, he'll tell you that the things that mattered most to him as a police officer, right, were the question of terrorism and the prospect of the Black communities in Britain – not just in London – following the Irish path and that's, of course, why we have number plate readers and, you know, CCTV and all of these Irish technologies which were bought over to Britain. Innovations in law and control have often been brought in from the colonies, you know, into the life of this island. So I think it's very important to understand that.

Now the other thing that I feel has been left out so far is work. I know people have talked about clubs but they haven't really addressed resistance around work. I want to push towards that in a way, because I want to talk clearly about the past. That means talking about work and it seems to me that the movement that we're all discussing here as a youth culture was, a youth movement about and against certain forms of work. From the point of view of the Black communities in this country, it was a movement which said, 'we are not going to do shit work. Okay? We are not going to do shit work. We have watched our parents play by that rule and we have watched them suffer and we will not do that.'

Now there's been a certain reconciliation with some of that kind of work in the intervening years but at that time, with youth on our side, generationally, in the context of the inflation figures and unemployment figures from those same years; inflation was what; 17/18 per cent for the last four/five years of the '70s. Youth unemployment was extremely high for everyone but sky high in Black communities. Think about the politics of work in an environment like that. That was the context for the criminalisation of our communities. That was the context for it.

And so, you know, I know it probably sounds crude and mechanistic and so-on but the police were on the streets coercing people into a certain relationship with work that couldn't be sustained by the work that was available and I think that's important to remember. And in Black communities – I don't know about here – I mean I assume that in Bristol there's a very particular labour market that's got to do with aerospace and things like that; I don't know who got those skilled jobs? I don't know how they work? I don't know who was filtered out, who was allowed to get in there and things like that?

Mike Darby: Well there are numerous, [laughs] unfortunately, [laughs] there are numerous Black reggae musicians who got jobs at British Aerospace in short periods of time through apprenticeships and then stopped. You know, they stopped.

Paul Gilroy: That would have been ... That would have been ....

Mike Darby: I don't know why they stopped but they went ... Because there was, you know, either south of the river – the cigarette factories or north of the river ... Yeah.

Paul Gilroy: I mean, I just think we should put work into it, because actually if you think about what has changed and what hasn't changed then that's an issue because I know that things are broadly as they were but there are a few things that are different. Because, you know, you've all got a camera in your pocket; that's the difference – that makes a difference to the politics of the way we live.

Joshua Moses: Work is the crucial ingredient.

Paul Gilroy: Yeah.

Joshua Moses: The crucial ingredient because when you feel you have ability and your ability hasn't been allowed to bloom, that's one serious crime because everyone will contribute if you're allowed for your ability to flourish. Everyone would work tirelessly if you're doing what you're truly gonna do. And we all really do want to do something but we're not allowed to be ourselves; to be what we want to be. So we felt as if, yeah, we're not going to allow ourselves to be programmed. There is a different way and that has to be accepted. We are special, you know, so we should choose for ourself and the work in that sense is crucial. Crucial.

Shane Baldwin: When I left school in 1978 the teacher asked, 'put your hand up who's got a job'. And I was the only one who put my hand up in a whole class of 38/40 people – that's what it was like.

Mike Darby: Can I just come in on one thing ... I know I keep preaching on about Bristol Archive Records but, fundamentally, that's probably a unique proposition; ... it possibly is unique in the whole world that Bristol musicians have been trustworthy enough to allow me and my tiny little team to have access to their recordings on a non-exclusive basis on a non-contract basis in virtually every single instance. So the whole of the community, whether that be from St Pauls or the whole of Bristol has come together in one place; Pete's music's involved in that from when Pete was in bands...; the whole point of Bristol Archive Records ... follows on from what Joshua's just said; from my point of view it was to tell the stories of people growing up. It was to allow seeing people, players, not necessarily Shane from Vice Squad who sold hundreds of thousands of records and made tours in America and whatever. Bristol has always been rife with talent and ... Forget that we do every single genre of music, but if you just focus on the reggae for a second; everyone thinks of Bristol who knows anything about reggae as Black Roots and Talisman. Now every single reggae musician who made tunes, whether brilliant or not quite so brilliant, has been recognised so they've got some ... they've finally ...

Joshua Moses: Reward for their work.

Mike Darby: Finally, after all those years have got some tiny little bit of reward and self-respect for that work, yeah?

Joshua Moses: It is true.

Mike Darby: And that's what it's all about – nothing else. It's a historical account of talented people enjoying themselves and making, in some cases, massive cases that nobody's ever heard.

Peter Webb: To finish, I'd like to get each of you kind of reflect on the role of music. How important have the kind of communities around music been in continuing that kind of different, other message about what happened in the riots? What has happened in these communities now? What's happening to them and how important do you think that is now?

Joshua Moses: Well for me music has always been the first mouthpiece for the mass; for the people. Go back as far as you wish, music has always been our weapon; what a beautiful weapon that is to state our case, we stated the music as musicians – well I'm proud to be one of them. Even though I must say I'm a suffering musician [laughter] but you know how it is – I love it, I love it – I wouldn't change nothing.

Shane Baldwin: I talk to ... I'm still sort of involved in music. People that aren't any more that I was in bands with, or just involved in punk, they say that however far away from it they've gone it's always made them question everything; they don't just accept things and they still question things and that is probably the most important thing.

Mike Darby: I get asked to do interviews quite a lot and the thing that really bugs me is that most people want to talk about this Bristol sound that doesn't exist. This word 'Trip Hop' which doesn't exist, it was made up by some London bloke and what is important for me is that people all round the world can find out about talent; find out about characters; find out about a place and come perhaps to visit because of Massive Attack and Portishead but actually learn about equally interesting people who perhaps haven't had the rewards that perhaps they should have done – allegedly and without prejudice.

Paul Gilroy: For me I think it's fantastic what you said about your music and that it made you critical and is keeping you critical and developing a relationship with yourself through that sound that produces that critical perspective on the world and I think that's because there is a glimpse in our relationship with that experience and that phenomenon of a world that's different from this world, you see? So you have something ... you are forced to engage with something that takes you out of this world and gives you a chance to imagine something quite different. And I think that imagination is really the key because imagination is under attack.

Peter Webb: We've unfortunately run out of time because I could continue this discussion for a long, long period. But I'd just like to thank you all very much. [Applause]

NOTES

1. Our thanks go to the St Werburghs Centre, Bristol, for hosting the event, and to Bristol Transcription Services.
2. J. Benyon (ed.), *Scarman and After: Essays Reflecting on Lord Scarman's Report, the Riots and Their Aftermath* (Oxford, 1984) (Benyon 1984).
3. E. Smith, 'Once as history, twice as farce? The spectre of '81 in discourses on the August 2011 riots', *Journal for Cultural Research*, 17(2) (2013), 124–43; Plan B, 'Ill Manors', 679 Atlantic (2012) (Smith 2013).
4. P. Gilroy, 'Two-sides of anti-racism', in S. Duncombe and M. Tremblay (eds.), *White Riot: Punk Rock and the Politics of Race* (London, 2011), pp. 177–87 (Gilroy 2011); D. Hann, *Physical Resistance: A Hundred Years of Anti-Fascism* (London, 2013) (Hann 2013).
5. The roundtable was held at St Werburghs Community Centre, Bristol, on 18 October 2013.

REFERENCES

J. Benyon (ed.), *Scarman and After: Essays Reflecting on Lord Scarman's Report, the Riots and Their Aftermath* (Oxford, 1984).

P. Gilroy, 'Two-sides of Anti-racism', in S. Duncombe and M. Tremblay (eds.), *White Riot: Punk Rock and the Politics of Race* (London, 2011), pp. 177–87.

D. Hann, *Physical Resistance: A Hundred Years of Anyi-Fascism* (London, 2013).

E. Smith, 'Once as History, Twice as Farce? The Spectre of '81 in Discourses on the August 2011 Riots', *Journal for Cultural Research*, 17, 2 (2013), 124–43.

Lucy Robinson is Professor of Collaborative History at the University of Sussex. She writes on popular music, politics and identity, feminism, and punk pedagogy. As well as coordinating the Subcultures Network and the open access digital project Observing the 80s, she has recently advised on an exhibition on Jersey in the 1980s.

Peter Webb is a writer, lecturer and musician who specialises in research into popular and contemporary music, subcultures, globalisation, new media, politics and social theory. He is Senior Lecturer and Programme Leader for Sociology at the University of the West of England, Bristol.

Music

Music

'(Today I Met) The Boy I'm Gonna Marry': Romantic Expectations of Teenage Girls in the 1960s West Midlands

Rosalind Watkiss Singleton

The 1960s heralded a great deal of change in British society.[1] From the late 1950s economic growth, full employment and rising wages resulted in a society where '[t]he people of Britain had more money to spend, and more things to spend it on than ever before'.[2] The general post-war affluence and the specific affluence accredited to the younger generation facilitated a rise in teenage consumption, with Abrams recording in 1958 that their spending power was £900 million per annum.[3] He documented 'distinctive teenage spending for distinctive teenage ends, in a distinctive teenage world'.[4] The purchase of record players, records and magazines accounted for around £50 million per annum[5] and it was the use of these which occupied much of the spare time of teenage girls.[6]

Improved living conditions, in larger homes, allowed bedrooms to become personal living spaces for many adolescents.[7] Closeted within these semi-private rooms they read their magazines, absorbed the advice from the problem pages, decorated their walls with posters of their favourite pop stars, practised their dance moves and transcribed the lyrics of

R.W. Singleton (✉)
University of Wolverhampton, Wolverhampton, UK
e-mail: r.watkiss@wlv.ac.uk

© The Author(s) 2017
K. Gildart et al. (eds.), *Youth Culture and Social Change*,
Palgrave Studies in the History of Subcultures and Popular Music,
DOI 10.1057/978-1-137-52911-4_6

popular records. They were to some extent, as McRobbie has noted, 'organising their cultural life' within the safe parameters of the home and school, thus allaying parental fears of risks pertaining to boys and sex in the world outside.[8] It was here, with the music, magazines and friends, that their initial conceptions of love and romance and their ultimate expectations of marriage were fashioned.

The Swinging Sixties and the permissive society are terms which are sometimes used indiscriminately[9] and, as Masters noted, 'teenage promiscuity is a central part of the legend of the swinging sixties'.[10] However, despite the claims in the memoirs and autobiographies of cosmopolitan and educated journalists and those individuals who became rich and famous via the film and music industries during the 1960s,[11] the evidence from those living in the provinces suggests that many teenage girls (and some boys) took a much more conservative stance with regards to sex and marriage.[12] Despite societal changes, increasing accessibility of birth control, and the President of the Methodist Conference stating in 1963 that: 'this is the first generation of emancipated women',[13] this chapter argues that young women of the 1960s and 1970s adhered to traditional social mores, and their ideas of love and romance were influenced by the expectation that they would find and keep a boyfriend – with marriage as the ultimate aim.

The oral testimony of women born between 1947 and 1958 contradicts Laurie's conclusions of 1965 that the effects of an 'incalculable social revolution' meant that the expectations of British society were changing and women no longer 'had a duty to get married'.[14] The interviews indicate conformity to expected norms rather than rebellion or revolution, and the evidence confirms the findings of numerous social surveys that 'young people in this period were usually quite conservative in their attitude to sex, morality and social values'.[15] This is not to deny that attitudes were slowly changing but suggests that there was a great deal of continuity with pre-war attitudes and expectations. Within society, families and the teenagers themselves, there was an assumption that marriage (despite further or higher education and career) was their destiny and those who failed to find and keep a potential marriage partner were stigmatised – old maid, spinster and 'on the shelf' were still used to describe girls who had been 'left behind'. For many young women who were growing up in the 1950s, 1960s and 1970s the urgencies and pressures from earlier generations remained. As Maureen Wilson recalled, '[T]here was a lot of pressure at that time to get married, especially at a young age, no one wanted to be a spinster or fall pregnant out of wedlock'.[16]

Using autobiographies, memoirs and oral testimony this chapter suggests that the music favoured by teenagers, and the magazines that they read, served to reinforce traditional values of love and marriage and were in not symptomatic of rebellion or revolution. The women who were interviewed were teenagers during the 1960s and the early 1970s, born between 1947 and 1958; they were questioned concerning their tastes in music, magazines and men and were asked to explain the influences upon their expectations of love and romance. They were contacted through over-50 s clubs, adult education classes, keep-fit groups, libraries and via the local history newspaper,[17] although three of them had already briefly discussed love and marriage in previously unrelated interviews.[18] Their subsequent experiences were mixed, with two of the women divorcing in their early thirties and a third divorcing and remarrying in her late forties. One is a widow and the remainder are all still with their original husbands. Wherever possible, efforts were made to locate respondents with different educational experiences in order to ascertain whether living independently for at least three years altered perceptions of marriage as an ultimate goal; some left school at 15 for full-time paid employment and others left school at 18 after completing their A-levels, three attended teacher training college or university. There has been no attempt to categorise the respondents by any system of class or income.[19] The interviews were of a semi-structured nature in order to allow the respondents to provide wide-ranging and unrestricted reminiscences of their teenage years.

MUSIC: 'IT WAS A CRUCIAL PART OF MY LIFE, MEANING EVERYTHING AND GIVING WORDS TO MY FEELINGS'[20]

In 1965, with some justification, Laurie claimed that '[m]usic is the pulse and flow of teenage life'.[21] In Brooke's view, popular music, along with the cinema, has been identified as two of the most important 'vehicles in the circulation of discourses of love and romance in the twentieth century'.[22] His research also highlights the impact of these cultural discourses on ordinary life, but cautions that individual day-to-day existences may well, in fact, resist these discourses.[23] The evidence certainly confirms that the popular music of the period between the 1950s and early 1970s, which was consumed by many teenage girls, provided a backdrop to the emotional turmoil of adolescent dreams and desires. Facilitated by increased earnings, this 'significant new economic group'[24] found that the purchase of music in its various guises provided a means of expressing the excitement, uncertainty and angst of the transition from childhood to adult. Access to music in the new cultural spaces of record shops, coffee bars, clubs and music venues[25] was supplemented in the home by the comparatively cheap Dansette record players[26] and transistor radios which allowed the consumption of music on an unprecedented scale, causing Laurie to claim in 1965 that 'music is central' to teenage culture.[27]

One respondent, born in 1947, confirmed that 'pop music was ours, written specifically for us, expressing our emotions and demonstrating our common experience'.[28] Department stores and independent record shops operated a listen-before-purchase system, with record booths, where friends congregated to listen to new releases; a new cultural and social space, which was attractive to the teenage consumers. Lindy explained that '[g]irls from our area used to go into Wolverhampton where Beattie's had a really big record department and we could listen to records and check out the boys'.[29] 'We used to hang around Stanton's in Dudley, or Walter's in Bilston to listen to the records in those little soundproof booths before we bought the singles. LPs tended to be Christmas or Birthday gifts as they were a bit more expensive'.[30]

For young girls much of the music, was consumed 'within [the safe and protected] the vicinity of the home, or the friends' home'. Thus the culture of the bedroom[31] held particular significance for these adolescents – the place where they listened to music, shared secrets and adorned the walls with pictures of their favourite 'heart-throbs'. They turned, as Donnelly indicated, 'their part of the family home into shrines'.[32] These private spaces facilitated the transition from schoolgirl to womanhood and allowed girls to express their burgeoning femininity, experiment with make-up and practise kissing on their poster, forearms or mirrors, so that they were not unprepared when they attracted the attention of the object of their desire.

Teenage bedrooms echoed to the strains of the latest musical fads and passions, from The Mindbenders (1965) 'Groovy Kind of Love', Tamla Motown hits of the Marvelettes, The Drifters, The Supremes, and The Miracles to the solo artists of the time. The plaintive notes of Billy Fury's 'Once Upon a Dream' (1963) or Adam Faith as he sang of kissing 'Someone Else's Baby' (1960) provided a soundscape as girls prepared for school or, more importantly, for an evening out at the youth club or disco.[33] The needle arm of the Dansette was disengaged so that the record of the moment could play repeatedly as a backdrop to homework and social life. Music was, as one respondent described, 'almost a wallpaper'[34] to adolescent dreams.

Launched in 1954, transistor radios, small enough to be termed pocket radios, provided additional opportunities for teenage consumption. Initially expensive, by the 1960s their prices and sizes were falling and many teenagers received them for Christmas or birthday presents.[35] The transistor radio brought teenagers into contact with a new listening experience; portable so that it could be transported easily, taken into the streets and to schools, but more importantly it could be smuggled under the bedclothes and listened to surreptitiously; a minor act of subversion that was widely practised. From the 1950s Radio Luxembourg on the 208 metre wavelength could be received after dark. It eventually became dedicated to English-language programming after 6 p.m. under the slogan of '208 – Your station'. The eagerly awaited Top Twenty hit records were introduced on Sunday nights at 11 p.m. by Pete Murray – hence the need for 'underneath the bedcovers',[36] as Monday was a school day.

Radio Caroline hit the airwaves in 1964 to circumvent the BBC's radio broadcasting monopoly. Again, listening to a pirate radio station was an entirely innocuous means of expressing teenage rebellion. Radio Caroline became (according to its own publicity) a fundamental part of the music revolution and a prime catalyst of the 1960s 'social revolution', introducing teenagers to new music and radio presenters, also objects of teenage fantasies, now termed 'disc jockeys'. As Linda recalled, 'I really fancied some of the DJs, especially Tony Blackburn; although I'm quite embarrassed now when I think of it (laughter)'.[37]

According to the respondents, regardless of the methods of consumption, the lyrics of the songs which they heard encapsulated adolescent perceptions of love and romance and reinforced traditional expectations that girls would find a suitable, adoring boyfriend, whom they would eventually marry. There was scant evidence of teenage rebellion in either in the interviews themselves or in the songs recalled by the interviewees. As Karen recalled, 'I have no doubt at all that the lyrics of the songs affected my notions of romance or, at least, they reinforced my ideas'.[38] The majority of interviewees recalled specific artists and songs that held a particularly relevance for their teenage years. Adolescent insecurities and inevitable anxieties were revealed when the Shirelles asked 'Will You Love Me Tomorrow?' (1961) and hopes expressed in the Drifters 'Save the Last Dance for Me '(1962). Heartbreak when Billy Fury sang '(I Don't Want

To Say I'm Gonna Miss You but) I Will' (1964); broken hearted, the singer vowed that he would love the girl forever. Trina said 'I thought they were writing the songs for people like me and there was a message you could apply to your life'.[39] Lindy almost believed that 'some songs were directed at me personally, they encapsulated my hopes and fantasies and expressed what I was too shy to admit, and when Donny Osmond sang 'Go Away Little Girl (Before I Beg You To Stay)', a 1971 cover of Bobby Vee's 1962 hit, I felt, somewhat optimistically in retrospect, that the lyrics might explain why he had broken my heart'.[40] Although she eventually married for more prosaic reasons, the sentiments of Suzanne's ideal love song were encapsulated in Ike and Tina Turner's 'River Deep and Mountain High' (1966); she believed that when she met her future husband he would 'sweep me off my feet and that love would be all-encompassing'.[41]

The respondents felt that the lyrics addressed them in personal ways. Lindy thought that, 'When the Troggs sang "(I Want to Spend My life) With a Girl Like You" (1966) I thought that could be me. Someone will want to spend their life with me.'[42] Teresa 'always envied girls with names like Sue, Rosemary or Carol, you know, the sort of name that features in a song. I wanted one for me, a sort of personal acknowledgment of my name. Somehow I thought it would draw attention to me, validate me in some way. The boys at school and the youth club would pay more attention to me. I know it sounds silly now but when you're young ...'[43]

A steady boyfriend was to be achieved as soon as possible and many schoolgirls were unofficially engaged (usually to an older boy who was employed and, preferably, a car owner) – 'All the girls liked someone to have a car'.[44] To have a steady relationship as soon as possible was considered to be ideal, 'it proved that you were attractive to someone and even desirable – to be wanted'.[45] 'You were considered the crème de la crème if you got engaged when you were at school'[46] and the song lyrics beloved of many girls encouraged this. Union Gap's 'Young Girl' (1968) held resonance for Dee[47] as well as several other respondents – the track was playing at a youth club when as a 15-year-old she fell in love with the man she was later to marry. She recalled that it was the very record she'd purchased earlier that day – a sign that he was 'the one'.[48]

The 'ring' was a vital sign of worth and attachment – In 1960 Ricky Valance had a number one hit with 'Tell Laura I Love Her' Tommy (Laura's boyfriend) wanted to 'buy her everything ... most of all a wedding ring' the stock car race he entered to win the prize money led to his death. His dying words – 'tell Laura my love for her will never die' – struck a romantic chord with a number of respondents; Dying in an attempt to provide the requisite tokens of his affection emphasised the importance of a ring and all that it signified.

It was, as one respondent recalled a case of the music 'egging us on in the race to get engaged',[49] of course, an engagement ring was a status symbol – a confirmation that the recipient was loved and public recognition that she was close to womanhood. Linda was clear that, under these circumstances, a compliant boyfriend could be an asset. She recalled with amusement: 'I don't know about love – I could manipulate him (laughter). He was easy. We met when I was 16 and were engaged when I was 18. That was important'.[50] The ring and its significance featured in all the interviews, demonstrable proof that the girl was, in the eyes of her family and the community, successfully fulfilling her anticipated role. It is no coincidence that 'She Wears my Ring' was so popular that it was recorded by Jimmy Sweeny in 1960 and then covered by Elvis Presley, Roy Orbison and Solomon King within the space of seven years. The status of 'having a real boyfriend'[51] and the promise of marriage gave these girls prestige and a sense of worth.

'Break Up songs' were also an important part of the backdrop to teenage lives – Trina spoke of 'The Carnival is Over' (1968), when she was 21, as a song resonant of heartbreak – although she did, eventually marry 'the man'.[52] Freda Payne's 1970 hit 'Band of Gold' was recalled by the majority of respondents – and although Payne was singing of a broken marriage the interviews reveal that divorce was not part of the teenage dream – love and marriage was for life. Marriage was, for many girls, the only real means of transportation from the parental home to the privacy and freedom of conferred by adulthood and home ownership; a true private space. As Freda Payne sang in 1970: 'You took me from the shelter of my mother; I had never known or loved any other.'[53]

Romantic love and the ultimate destination of a wedding intended to last a monogamous lifetime were essential themes of much popular music until at least the mid-1960s.[54] For example, '[t]he lyrics of all of the 49 songs copyrighted by the Beatles during 1963–64 were about boy–girl romance', although their preferred subject matter altered radically in subsequent years.[55] It was the love songs that respondents found most memorable. As Suzanne recalled, 'I loved all kinds of music... but absolutely *loved* pop music. The Beatles happened slightly earlier in Cheshire than elsewhere. My favourite tracks were 'Please, Please Me',

'You Really Got a Hold on Me', 'Till There Was You'. These are all romantic ones, I've just realised that'.[56] The sentiments expressed in the record lyrics were echoed in the magazines that the adolescents consumed.[57]

MAGAZINES: 'I LOVED READING THEM THE STORIES, PROBLEMS, FASHION, THE WHOLE LOT'[58]

The publication of a spate of magazines aimed directly at the female teenage consumer from the late 1950s reinforced the musical messages and provided teenager differentiation from their parents' culture. The angst, the romance and heartbreak of the music was replicated in the magazines, with stories of love containing messages of morality in which 'nice' girls got their man and where appropriate behaviour was rewarded. At the same time, as Tinkler's examination of earlier generations asserts, they still sought to steer young women towards 'heterosexual relationships on the path to marriage'.[59]

The journal titles helped to make their message clear – *Valentine* (1957), *Boyfriend* (1959) – promising, as *Valentine* claimed, to 'Bring you Love in Pictures' and exciting free gifts, from cosmetics to poster of pop idols. Carole Hathorne remembered plastering her lips with 'the free white lipstick' courtesy of Valentine.[60] This plethora of magazines marketed for adolescent girls were eagerly awaited by respondents who read and compared the stories and images with their friends: 'I began with *Valentine* and later moved on to *Jackie* and *Honey*. I think most girls did. You had to keep up with what everyone else was reading'.[61] Liz felt that 'the transition from comics like *Bunty* was an important milestone in the teenage years. Reading *Valentine* and the others was a demonstration that you were no longer a child, at least in your own mind.'[62]

The editorial in Valentine's earliest issue enticed the reader with 'Romance... Youth... Excitement! Romance, which lies deep in the heart of every girl.'[63] *Boyfriend,* priced 4d (less than 2p), provided a celebrity boyfriend feature, linking the pop stars and their lyrics with love and romance. In all these magazines teen culture, romance and marriage were inevitably intertwined, and there was a clear progression from boys to boyfriend and exclusivity culminating in marriage. A number of other magazines followed: *Honey* published in 1960 and *Jackie, Rave* and *Fabulous* in 1964.[64] *Honey's* message was similar to the others, offering advice on how to attract (and more importantly keep) a boyfriend and, as Sandbrook explained, 'how to stop them taking too many liberties, as marriage not sex or love was the prime objective'.[65] *Honey*'s early tagline 'For Teens and Twenties' was replaced in under two years by 'Young, Gay and Get Ahead'. The cover of 1964 edition of *Honey* displayed a youthful image of the actor Michael Caine with a young, attractive woman draped around his shoulders; the headline stated: 'A girl's best accessory is a man'.[66]

Magazines provided guidelines on the transition from adolescent to wife and mother – natural roles, which would lead to ultimate fulfilment. Weddings featured prominently in the stories. In 1961 *Marilyn*'s cover story featured a girl attending the wedding of a former boyfriend who was lamenting that '[i]t could have been me standing there . . . as his bride . . . but I threw away my chances'.[67] The first edition of *Jackie* 'For Go-Ahead Teens' in 1964, featured a youthful Cliff Richard on its cover, a free 'twin heart ring' inside and an article on 'perfume tips for a more kissable you'; the early stories and magazine items reinforced 'traditional social norms'.[68]

The new format of these magazines which linked pop stars and their lyrics to romantic ideals merely found a novel way to deliver a traditional moral discourse[69] – look good, learn to cook, and 'catch a boy' – hold out for marriage.[70] As Gardner claimed of American 'Romance Comics', 'Girls who read them were exposed to different models of female behaviour',[71] and in the magazines consumed by the respondents, during the 1960s, readers were given guidelines for acceptable patterns of behaviour: '[t]he magazines told you what good girls should do, no cheating, two-timing boys. Behave well and you'll get a man.'[72] Storylines often used pop song titles as their inspiration – making a clear connection between the music and relationships, with the singer (or a look-alike) in the role of romantic hero, where 'nice' girls get their man in marriage. In 1963 *Valentine* offered a free gift of 'the most glamorous colour portrait of Elvis' and a cover story entitled 'Happy Ending' which was inspired by one of his 'hit songs'.[73]

> These magazines seemed to give me a blueprint for life. They told me how to do my makeup, how to behave on a first date, right the way through until I would meet my hero, the man of my dreams. We all read them and compared notes. I loved the ones with a pop star as the hero, the idea that I could aspire to someone just like him just like the ordinary girl in the story.[74]

These moral guidelines of the stories and the agony aunts' responses on the problem pages were endorsed by the advertisements in the magazines – for engagement and/or eternity rings and insurance firms suggesting to girls that a policy would enable them to save for a wedding – bridegroom not included. Lines such as 'Oh Please Propose 'were even used on milk marketing adverts – drink milk, become beautiful and he'll propose. The advert describes an 18 year old with the 'tallest, handsomest, richest man she has ever known' and she's waiting for a proposal, which will transpire if she drinks milk.[75]

A happy ending, according to McRobbie, was a couple, but a single girl signified a sad ending, a failed relationship.[76] This world of emotion, music and love in the pages of these publications sanctioned the romantic expectations of adolescent girls and encouraged them to maintain the traditional trajectory – education, employment and marriage. The moral code of the immediate post-war period that was endorsed both in the problem pages and the storylines of these teenage publications was continued in the pages of the women's magazines, which the girls would consume as wives and mothers; it was based up the 'assumption that it [the message] provides the best way to get, or keep, your man'.[77]

LOVE: 'WE ALL WANTED TO BE IN LOVE'[78]

Langhamer recently claimed that '[b]y the 1960s the primacy of love was striking: for many the decade could more accurately be described as a golden age of romance, than an age of permissiveness.'[79] All respondents confirmed that they were seeking love and a lifelong partner. Sex was inextricably linked to love inside marriage, and despite Manfred Mann's (1966) warnings to the girl about to marry 'Semi-Detached Suburban Mr James', the interviews indicate that Mr James was the pinnacle of most girls' adolescent aspirations. The singer congratulates her for 'naming the day' and 'getting her man' and, whilst there was an undeniable excitement for adolescents dreaming of a 'bad boy', most were more pragmatic, looking for love and security within marriage. Many using words like 'he was steady and/or reliable'. As Linda confirmed, 'I knew he was trustworthy and wouldn't let me down.'[80] The minority who, like Trina, temporarily indulged their rebellious streak soon conformed to acceptable social norms. Recalling the song 'He's a Rebel' (1963) she spoke of a painter and decorator boyfriend from the 'wrong side of the tracks': 'I didn't particularly like him as he was quite dull really but to others he seemed dangerous. When I was sixteen and he was nineteen he wanted to marry me.' The consensus within the family was that 'Hitler was a painter'![81]

But love at first sight was still a possibility. During the mid-1960s numerous songs were based around the concept of instant attraction, including: Manfred Mann (1964) 'Doo Wah Diddy Diddy'; Herman's Hermits (1964); 'I'm into Something Good', The Beatles (1965) 'I've Just Seen a Face'; The Monkees (1966) 'I Saw Her Face (Now I'm a Believer)'; and the Beach Boys 'Good Vibrations' (1966). Dee knew when she saw her husband that 'he was the one I was going to marry, I knew, he was good looking, immaculate and his sense of humour – I went home and told my mom that I'd met the one – I knew I'd always be with him'.

A number of respondents recollected comparable scenarios – 14-year-old Betty saw 18 year old Howard at the youth club and for them both 'we knew straight away that we'd never want anyone else'. Fifty-three years later they still express the same emotions – although the continuing strength of their emotions may be atypical in comparison with the other interviewees. Similarly, when 16-year-old Linda saw her future husband in the street he was wearing a suit, shirt and a thin tie and 'I thought then I was going to marry him'.[82] Although Carol described herself as a 'career girl' she recollected that 'when George walked into the room I knew from the moment I set eyes on him that I was going to marry him. And he must have thought something similar as his opening words were "how would you like to be the mother of my children?"'[83] As Lindy recalled, 'I was always looking – wherever I went and saw someone I fancied I thought is he the one? Will he marry me? It's quite sad really that I was constantly thinking that.'[84]

MARRIAGE AND SEX: 'WELL, IN YOUR HEAD THEY REALLY WENT TOGETHER'

Writing in the 1960s, Laurie described the years between fifteen and the early twenties as the 'husband-catching ages'.[85,86] The respondents' views and experiences confirmed Langhamer's conclusions that marriage remained 'incredibly popular' into the 1970s as 'it had penetrated teenage culture and was a key aspect of youthful identity'.[87] Although, Jackie Hyams has claimed that 'I was a rebel ... and didn't accept the general status quo: that a young girl best sit tight and wait for Mr Right'.[88] For many teenage girls the Swinging Sixties and the 'permissive society' was little more than a newspaper headline; carefree sex and the era of free love was not an option for the majority of those interviewed. As Lindy said 'nothing swung where we lived – we weren't allowed'.[89] These words were echoed by Sue who claimed 'unfortunately, nothing much seemed to "swing" in our town – dear old Walsall. I feel that either all the "swinging" must have happened elsewhere or to someone else!'[90] Carol was of the opinion that 'any swinging was in the music and the wafting of joss sticks'.[91]

Despite the availability of the birth control pill from 1961, the 1967 Abortion Act, and post-war social change, there appears to have been little impact upon attitudes to pre-marital sex and the continuing desirability of marriage, and the interviewees generally expressed their aversion to the possible consequences of pre-marital sex resulting in the horrors of single motherhood and illegitimate children. Parents generally, but mothers, in particular, constantly reinforced the messages of 'taking risks' with a boy and reminded girls that they would be the one to bear the consequences of the risks.[92] As Glynis explained, '[d]on't get into trouble was drummed into us. Dad was a Victorian father and he made it clear that we should marry as soon as possible'.[93]

The potential shame of an unplanned pregnancy combined with the 'feeling that you would let your parents down, prevented many of us having sex before the wedding'.[94] Over 40 years later, respondents remembered the names and circumstances of girls who found themselves pregnant outside wedlock, particularly if they were still at school, recounting tales of horror and shame.[95] The stigma of pregnancy outside of marriage remained an important consideration for teenage girls, and their families, in this period[96]: 'My cousin was pregnant as eighteen and the entire extended family felt the shame. So dad wanted me to be prim and proper'.[97] The evidence suggests that into the 1970s it was considered crucial to safeguard the reputation of the adolescent (and that of her family) by avoiding the possibility of an unplanned pregnancy and a 'shotgun wedding'.[98] Those respondents who had sex outside marriage, bar one, were all in committed relationships with engagement rings and the promise of marriage in the near future: 'The pill was just coming in but was seen as a bit scandalous and although we were getting married my parents were shocked that we even considered it'.[99] For all but two respondents there was an inextricable link between the concept sexual partners and future husbands, in the sense that they only consented to sex when marriage had been discussed.

Initially, the bohemian ideas percolating from the London area had scant impact upon the ideas and beliefs of suburban teenagers in the West Midlands: 'It was drummed into us that "nice girls don't"; girls behaved as they would have 30 years before, they said "that's far enough".' Jacquie said 'The free love concept passed me by, I felt strongly that sex before marriage was wrong; pregnancy without a ring was shocking.'[100] Dee expressed somewhat similar views but articulated them even more strongly: 'some of our workmates were getting married because they were pregnant. *I was disgusted*. I'm tactile and flirty but have very strong morals. We went so far and he would probably have gone further but he knew that I wouldn't. Our friends thought we weren't all the ticket because we didn't have sex.' She continued: 'I know I'm old fashioned but I thought sex outside marriage was wrong – I still do. We did nothing till we were married.' Interestingly, although she fell in love with her future husband at first sight at the age of 16 (as mentioned above), Dee was the only respondent to have a long engagement. The couple got engaged when she was 19 but she was 25 before they married. Despite the lack of sex before marriage she claimed that 'I didn't want to get married, I wasn't ready and we had a great courtship. We went out to different places and had fun. It [marriage] wasn't important'. When they eventually 'tied the knot' it was because of pressure from the couple's mothers. However, an additional factor, which was revealed later in the interview, was that her father had 'gone into debt' to pay for her sisters' weddings and 'I didn't want dad to pay for a third big white wedding. We couldn't have married in the register (sic) office it would have broken dad's heart.'[101] Respondents all acknowledged that they felt pressure from boyfriends to indulge in pre-marital sex but tended to resist until they believed the relationship was permanent, often 'holding out' until the marriage was imminent.[102]

The minority who had sex before marriage usually waited until the wedding date was set or they, at least, had an engagement ring. Few respondents had premarital sex – Lesley and Gwen had sex with their fiancés and Trina went on holiday to Ireland with her much older boyfriend (29 years), but nevertheless wore a ring to convince his friends they were married. She was the only respondent who spent a complete night with a boyfriend before marriage.[103] Again, this message was confirmed within the magazines' pages, and the increasing availability of effective contraception was not mentioned until much later. In fact an anonymous contributor to Pressley's research, most likely the first editor of *Honey*, Jean McKinley, recalled that 'Girls' magazines didn't write about contraception in those days. In March 1967, *Honey* ran their first feature on "Birth Control and the Single Girl". I cut it out.'[104] It seems clear that the cultural norms and societal expectations were endorsed within the pages of the teen magazines.

MOTIVES FOR MARRIAGE: 'IT MEANT ADULTHOOD AND AUTONOMY'[105]

The risks of sex outside marriage were made perfectly clear but there were other reasons for 'settling down'.[106] Although the message in the magazines was focussed upon finding 'the one boy' who would provide everlasting love inside a committed relationship, there were other considerations for choosing a husband. If marriage was inevitable, 'it was on the cards, it was something that would happen – I'm not a women's libber or anything like that',[107] the right choice of husband was crucial. Despite feelings of initial attraction, the choice of marriage partner was, in the oral testimony, rarely based upon romantic concepts of love. Although the concept of love promulgated in the music was of great importance to these young women they were also quite pragmatic and their motives for marrying were complex. Jeanette 'always thought I'd get married – wanted to get married to get my own space. You didn't leave home until you married.' The reasons for marriage were often based on practical issues, as much as love or passion. For girls who were still living in the family home,[108] marriage was often impelled by the need for privacy, an acknowledgment that they were adults, for autonomy and freedom from the restrictions placed upon them by parents, the community and society. As Linda explained, 'boys were never allowed into your bedroom, not even a fiancé'.[109] For a courting couple, even engaged couples, privacy was hard to obtain, moments alone were often interrupted by family members: 'Mum used to send my little brother in to the front room to 'see if we were alright'.[110] Again ways of ensuring chastity were endless: 'My Mum used to come into the room with a tray of tea every hour or she would remember things that she had left in the room and suddenly needed to retrieve them, books, knitting, in fact anything that gave her an excuse to burst in.'[111]

Lindy recently found postcards from her younger brother who was on holiday in 1972 with their parents less than two months before her wedding. She was surprised to see that they were addressed care of her grandmother's house – 'I suddenly remembered that mum wouldn't let me stay in the family house alone in case we "got up to something". It was ridiculous now I come to think about it as we had already bought our own place which, by then was virtually ready to move into.'[112] Lesley spoke of 'leaving mom and dad to get married' and, despite the fact that her fiancé was eight years her senior, she 'booked the church to move things forward. We wanted to be independent and have less supervision and that meant a wedding. If I sat on Ken's lap when we were engaged dad got me off. Mom said "your dad doesn't like it".'[113]

The freedom of making autonomous choices and the lack of parental control were vital considerations. For Lindy, 'on one level I was sad to be leaving home and my family but marriage meant no more home by 10.30 and no more mom peering through the bedroom window to see if his car was steamed up. Even at the age of twenty when we were engaged I had to be in on time. My brother, who was only seventeen frequently came in after me – but he was a boy – so in mum's eyes that was all right.'[114] Betty's recollections were similar, 'If we didn't say goodnight quickly mom would come to the gate and say your father wants you in now – he didn't really, it was her! She was worried that we'd get carried away.'

Linda explained the inextricable link between a boyfriend and marriage, making clear the necessity for attaining both as soon as possible: 'That's what happened if you weren't married by 22 – you were bypassed – an old maid – Everybody got married – I probably led him to get engaged – Marriage meant freedom – it meant playing house – I married for freedom and sex – see we were working class and...'.[115] Most of the respondents lived at home until marriage, but even those who had attended university or college returned to the family when they graduated, so for many young girls there was an additional excitement: 'the novelty of the marital home was a great attraction and I couldn't wait to use all the things from my bottom drawer, things I'd chosen because I liked them'.[116]

Despite the encouragement within the magazines, the undoubted romance of the lyrics, and the respondents who spoke of instant attraction or, even, love at first sight, the reasons for marrying were, indeed, leaning towards the pragmatic and prosaic. Four times during the two-hour interview Suzanne reiterated the words 'I thought we could make a go of it.' Although she confessed to being 'a romantic', Suzanne explained that her choice of husband was based upon the feeling that 'I realised that we could make a go of it and he was somebody who would stay the course. Underneath... I realised that he was going to be a good husband and a father too. I knew that he would be deep down – it doesn't sound very romantic.'[117] Later in the interview she returned to the topic. 'I just realised that he was going to be – it's odd because I was so romantic – but underlying it all when it came to marriage I wanted somebody who would be there. 'Even later in the interview she concluded 'I love him – but that side [safety and stability] always wins.'[118] Others spoke of 'settling' for their partner, in the sense that 'he would do, and marriage could be ticked off the list'.[119]

As Wendy explained about her courtship, 'It felt comfortable and there was a feeling that this is right'. She confessed that there was never any feeling of 'being swept away' but concluded that, despite earlier romances, she 'wanted someone to stay the distance' as divorce was never an option. There had been no instances of divorce in her family and she was determined 'never to sully that record'.[120] The determination to stay together regardless of problems was endorsed by all but two respondents, precisely because 'no-one in our family divorces, the stigma you see?'[121] Dee's views were the same: 'If you get married it had to be forever and I wanted it to be like that. Divorce would never have been an option.'[122] Most mothers said 'you've made your bed and now you have to lie on it', meaning that whatever happened you were together for life. It was repeated almost as a family motto, and respondents felt that if a marriage broke down there would be a sense of shame and the stigma would affect the entire family, but especially the parents.[123]

It appears that the choice of a suitable husband, one who was likely to win parental approval and remain loyal (therefore less likely to 'stray')[124] was often a deciding factor if the disgrace of divorce was to be avoided. The phrases which were most frequently uttered in the testimony of 95% of respondents were 'reliable', 'steady', 'good provider', 'stable'; a husband who could be described as unlikely to 'cause trouble' was felt to be an additional bonus. This clearly suggests that romantic love was an aspirational ideal amongst young girls but that practical concerns frequently overrode their choices.

In addition to that, parental expectations were that girls would marry young. The shame and stigma of illegitimate children and shotgun weddings were a consideration into the 1970s. Despite the advent of the birth control pill and the Abortion Act, the reasoning was clear – 'It was drummed into us: Nice girls don't' and 'pregnancy was such a terrible, terrible thing to happen if you weren't married'.[125] Carol Hathorne's grandmother acquiesced with Carol dating boys, 'just so long as yer keep yer "and on yer 'alfpenny"' (sic).[126]

As former Home Secretary, Alan Johnson wrote '[t]he "sexual revolution" was by no means as sweeping as is sometimes supposed: the concept might have been *de rigueur* among pop stars and metropolitan radicals but it certainly didn't filter through to ordinary families, where babies outside marriage was still frowned upon'.[127]

If a daughter married young then that solved the problem, as she would be 'settled'[128] and any children would be legitimate. On the day she left school, at eighteen, Lindy's mother told her that her cousin, also a school-leaver, had got engaged that day and then she looked meaningfully at her. She recalled 'I was very aware that mum expected me to marry and she often made dire threats of what my life would be like if I ended up a spinster like Auntie June. She did this from when I was quite young. Auntie June was dad's sister and they didn't like each other much. Worse still for mum, I think, was if I ended up pregnant and "had to get married". They were her twin fears from when I was very young and they became mine too.'[129] Parental concerns combined with peer pressure were undoubtedly important factors in the face to marry – panic set in as Suzanne explained: 'with each couple that got engaged I wondered was I going to be the last one in our group? Was I going to be left on the shelf? Eleanor Rigby came out on the *HELP!* LP in 1966, the year I began to wonder [whether I would marry] from about then.'[130] She continued, 'sometimes the songs were very influential to my thinking'.[131]

Fear of being left behind and the need to conform to expected behaviour patterns were also important. Decisions made in this way were not necessarily rational or sensible. Explaining her registry office wedding in the early 1970s, Jean explained that '[e]veryone else was [getting married], our group and other couples at our teacher training college.' Subsequently, she expanded on her thoughts of her marriage. 'I may well not have done [married], only our friends did. I wasn't expecting it to last but I'm not sure why. In general I didn't expect it to be forever. Most of our friends stayed together and still are.'[132]

SOCIETAL EXPECTATIONS: 'YOU KNEW THAT EVERYONE EXPECTED YOU TO SETTLE DOWN'

There is no doubt in the minds of all respondents that the impetus to marry was influenced by the expectations of family and society at large, as much as by their own desires.[133] Suzanne spoke for the majority of respondents when she explained: 'I did expect to marry; mum did when she was twenty, it was fairly normal. It sounds silly now but even in your early teens people were talking about saving for a bottom drawer.' She expanded on this: 'my eldest sister didn't get married until she was 24 and all the wider family thought she was on the shelf'.[134] Glynis 'was interested in a career but family expectations were that you married and married young, the teens if possible but if not, the early twenties. My sister married her first boyfriend when she was eighteen and dad wanted me to do the same.'[135] As Liz confirmed 'well, people expected you to get married and so you expected it too. The alternative didn't really bear thinking about. That's what you did. You left school, hopefully already with a boyfriend, got a job and then married. What else was there? You didn't want time to slip away and find yourself without a husband.'[136] There was also a certain amount of, real or imagined, peer pressure to marry and for some girls their self-worth and conception of their attractiveness was inextricably linked to the affirmation of a boyfriend/ fiancé/ husband: 'now it all seems ridiculous but then it made perfect sense. A boyfriend was a demonstration that you were nice-looking and could get someone. This was important you know, to be able to tell friends and family that you had a boy.'[137] She went on to say that 'everywhere you went, school, family do's, church, everyone asked, everyone wanted to know and there was a feeling of failure if the answer was no. I had at least one date with most people who asked, just to see where it would lead.'[138]

Carol's grandparents were particularly assiduous in quest of appropriate suitors; her grandmother suggesting boyfriends who might turn out to be 'Mr Right'.[139] Whilst her grandparents both recognised the urgency felt by many young women who were awaiting a proposal of marriage, expressing the opinion that girls were 'just waiting for some young man to say "snip" [propose] and they would say "snap" [yes]'.[140] This phrase was mentioned by several other respondents and was used on numerous occasions by the author's grandmother, mother and aunts.[141]

These expectations were endorsed within the educational system. Wendy, a grammar school pupil, recalled the unmarried, female deputy head of her school, informing sixth-form girls that they should find a 'suitable career to fit in with the prospect of marriage': teaching, nursing or the civil service.[142] Domestic Science at GCE O-level focussed on how to iron your husband's shirts, and the A-level Household Science practical exam paper required students to cook a three-course meal 'to be ready when your husband arrives home from work'.[143] The local newspaper carried an article, penned by the head mistress of the girl's high school, observing that higher education was often discounted as many parents wanted girls to focus on finding employment as an interim to marriage. She felt that girls were becoming confused by mixed messages.[144]

Anna Mangan's mother was proud of her daughter's law degree, but felt that studying might be detrimental to the ultimate goal of marriage. She hid her daughter's textbooks claiming 'that one will ruin her eyes with all that studying and never get a man'.[145] Failure in the search for a marriage partner was, for these women and their families, untenable: 'everyone expected you to find a husband and settle down to married life. Careers were a way of earning some money to save for your bottom drawer and to fill in time until the big day.'[146] Employers reinforced the messages within their advertisements for new staff. School-leavers were invited to submit applications for work at banks and building societies. The boys exhorted to apply for 'a career in banking', as management trainees and girls to apply for 'a job', subtly underlining the temporary nature of female employment.[147] Schools, parents, the family and wider society, perhaps unwittingly, echoed the significance of marriage as an institution, encouraging teenage girls to focus upon connubial bliss, preferably as soon as was practicable.

CONCLUSION: 'THIRD FINGER, LEFT HAND'

Popular music was indeed a backdrop to teenage lives and had a major influence on adolescent thoughts of romantic devotion and hopes for future happiness.[148] The music reflected the uncertainty of teenage love and aspirations for their adult lives, in the sense of happy endings, marriage, and 'Everlasting Love'.[149] The music and magazines both impacted upon the romantic expectations of the respondents in the sense that they confirmed the beliefs of peers, parents and society, that marriage was the primary goal. The magazines that these teenagers consumed contained narratives based upon the lyrics of popular songs, with the 'pop idol who is the embodiment of the romantic hero',[150] and messages designed to reinforce traditional values of love and marriage. Magazines for a specifically teenage market endorsed the fears and hopes of girls, alongside advice on how to get (and keep) your man, tips on kissing (don't eat onions or wear sharp jewellery),[151] and warnings not to 'give way' to passion outside marriage.[152] The stories generally encouraged girls to settle for the 'prosaic and dependable',[153] exemplified in the 'Semi-Detached Suburban Mr James' who had been excoriated by Manfred Mann in 1965.[154] The 'predominant moral tone' within the magazines generally reflected the views of the respondents and their reluctance to indulge in pre-marital sex.[155]

Together with the music, magazines certainly resonated with the romantic expectations of teenage girls during the 1960s and 1970s; but the interviews thus far reveal very little evidence to endorse accounts of a social revolution or sexual freedom before the late 1970s. The contraceptive pill was available but not always readily accessible: 'It was really difficult to get the pill even in 1967, the height of the free love era. I was at Manchester University and there wasn't a doctor within miles who would prescribe the Pill to students'.[156] Family doctors interrogated young women to ascertain when they would get married before the prescription was written and there was always a worry that he might inform the family.[157]

Permissiveness and 'free love' were generally eschewed in favour of traditional beliefs in marriage and fidelity. This was reinforced in many ways by the education system and even the girls who passed the 11-plus examination and attended a grammar school were told by parents and teachers that, whilst careers were temporary, marriage was the ultimate goal.[158] When Lindy decided to reject a place at a Liverpool Teacher Training College, in 1970, her mother said 'well you'll be married in no time so there's not much use studying really'.[159] Further and higher education was rejected by some parents who felt that education would be 'wasted' on girls who would 'only go and get married'.[160] Early engagements and marriages were the expectations of society, parents and the girls themselves, all of who 'looked forward to marriage as it was our ultimate goal in life'.[161] In 1963 Pierce remarked in the *Sociological Review* that 'marriage has never been a more popular institution'[162]; as Trina confirmed, 'a lifetime commitment – that was it'.[163]

Parents, grandparents, the wider family and, the community encouraged these girls in their romantic expectations, making it clear that 'good' girls would soon 'settle down' with a 'nice boy'.[164] Their behaviour was monitored and regulated by those around them; as Jean recalled, 'I was left somewhat to my own devices as mum was out working but there was always the possibility that someone in the neighbourhood would tell her if I stepped out of line.'[165] Lesley and Jeanette confirmed that 'in Coseley they all knew you and if you were somewhere you shouldn't be, or with a chap who was a bit wild, then someone would report back to your parents and there'd be trouble'.[166]

Overall, the oral testimony from the respondents living in the West Midlands refutes Laurie's claims that in 1965 that there was 'a general feeling that young girls are less eager to sell themselves to a man and embark upon marriage'.[167] The respondents, whilst acknowledging that society was changing, generally desired to find suitable husbands; they wanted to conform to customary expectations. Moral attitudes, at least among the respondents in the West Midlands, remained consistent through the 1960s and into the early 1970s. The much-vaunted sexual revolution had little impact on their conservative attitudes to sex. Further and higher education were more accessible at this time, but even those girls with aspirations to education and career fully expected 'marriage to be on the cards';[168] 'It [marriage] was something that would happen, it was inevitable and sooner rather than later'.[169]

For these adolescent girls growing up during the 1960s, consumption of both music and magazines was integral to their lives, the messages within them contributing to the 'romantic expectations' of teenage girls and preparing them for marriage as a much anticipated and inevitable destination. This objective was underpinned by familial pressure and reinforced by traditional social mores.

NOTES

1. The title of this article comes from Darlene Love, '(*Today I Met) The Boy I'm Gonna Marry*' (1963). In 1963 Love reached number 39 in the American Hot 100 with this track.
2. J. Obelkevich, 'Consumption', in J. Obelkevich and P. Catterall, (eds.) *Understanding Post-war British Society* (London, 1994), p. 143 (Obelkevich 1994); D. Sandbrook, *White Heat: A History of Britain in the Swinging Sixties* (London, 2006), p. 56 (Sandbrook 2006); J. Clarke and T. Jefferson, 'working class youth cultures' in A. Gray, J. Campbell, M. Erikson, S. Hanson and H. Wood, (eds.) *CCCS Selected Working Papers Volume 2* (London, 2007), p. 201 (Clarke and Jefferson 2007); C. Langhamer, *The English in Love: The Intimate Story of an Emotional Revolution* (Oxford, 2013), p. 56 (Langhamer 2013): D. Kynaston, *Modernity Britain: A Shake of the Dice, 1959–62* (London, 2014) (Kynaston 2014); M. P. Donnelly, *Sixties Britain: Culture, Society and Politics* (Harlow, 2005), p. 3 (Donnelly 2005).
3. M. Abrams, *The Teenage Consumer* (London, 1959), p. 7 (Abrams 1959).
4. Abrams, *Teenage Consumer*, p. 5.
5. Abrams, *Teenage Consumer*, p. 10.
6. The concept was first introduced in 1975 by A. McRobbie and J. Garber, 'Girls and subcultures', in S. Hall and T. Jefferson (eds.) *Resistance Through Rituals: Youth Subcultures in Post-War Britain* (London, 1975) (McRobbie and Garber 1975); A. McRobbie, *Feminism and Youth Culture* (Basingstoke, 2000) pp. 4–16 (McRobbie 2000); A. McRobbie and

J. Garber, 'Girls and subcultures' in A. Gray, J. Campbell, M. Erikson, S. Hanson and H. Wood (eds.) *CCCS Selected Working Papers Volume 2* (London, 2007), p. 222 (McRobbie and Garber 2007). For a more recent discussion, S. Lincoln, *Youth Culture and Private Space* (Basingstoke, 2012) (Lincoln 2012).

7. Obelkevich, 'Consumption', p. 146
8. McRobbie, *Feminism and Youth Culture*, p. 9. pp. 22–3; S. Frith, *The Sociology of Rock* (London, 1978), p. 64 (Frith 1978).
9. M. Akhtar and S. Humphries, *The Fifties and Sixties: A Lifestyle Revolution* (London, 2001), p. 80 (Akhtar and Humphries 2001); C. Davies, *Permissive Britain: Social Change in the Sixties and Seventies* (London, 1975), p. 69 (Davies 1975).
10. B. Masters, The *Swinging Sixties* (London, 1985), p. 34 (Masters 1985).
11. J. Hyams, *White Boots and Mini Skirts* (London, 2013) (Hyams 2013); J. Street-Porter, *Baggage: My Childhood* (London, 2004) (Street-Porter 2004).
12. Oral interviews and autobiographies.
13. P. Laurie, *The Teenage Revolution* (London, 1965), p. 23 (Laurie 1965).
14. Laurie, *Teenage Revolution*, p. 152.
15. Donelly, *Sixties Britain*, p. 36.
16. MW in T. Johnson, *The Mill Girls* (London, 2014), p. 311 (Johnson 2014).
17. *The Black Country Bugle*.
18. R. Watkiss, 'Old Habits Persist, Change and Continuity in Black Country Communities: Pensnett, Sedgley and Tipton, 1945–c. 1970' (unpublished PhD thesis, University of Wolverhampton, 2014) (Watkiss 2014).
19. Although for a larger study this would be a necessity.
20. SN.
21. Laurie, *Teenage Revolution*, p. 88.
22. S. Brooke, 'A certain amount of mush: love, romance, celluloid and wax in the mid twentieth century', in A. Harris and T.W. Jones (eds.) *Love and Romance in Britain, 1918–1970* (Basingstoke, 2015), p. 83 (Brooke 2015).
23. Brooke 'A certain amount of mush', p. 82.
24. Abrams, *Teenage Consumer*, p. 1.
25. P. Granger, *Up West; Voices from the Streets of Post-War London* (London, 2009) (Granger 2009).
26. Donnelly, *Sixties Britain, p.* 35.
27. Laurie, *Teenage Revolution*, p. 77.
28. KB.
29. LS.
30. LL, JB.
31. McRobbie, *Feminism and Youth Culture*, p. 4; Lincoln, *Youth Culture and Private Space*.

32. Donnelly, *Sixties Britain*, p. 35; Lincoln, *Youth Culture and Private Space*. In her introduction Lincoln confesses that her bedroom was 'almost becoming a kind of shrine' to the band Bros., p. 4.

33. All artistes and tracks mentioned in this chapter were those recalled by respondents. KB, LS, LH, WS.

34. KB.

35. LS, LL, SN, DF, JB.

36. TM, LS, LL, WS, LH, JB.

37. LJ.

38. KD.

39. TB.

40. LS.

41. SN. See remarks before reference 110.

42. LS.

43. TO.

44. SN.

45. DA.

46. TB.

47. DF.

48. DF.

49. KB.

50. LH.

51. C.A. Stafford and A. Crowe, *Us Kids: Growing Up in Ladywood, 1945–1960* (Birmingham, 1998), p. 156 (Stafford and Crowe 1998).

52. TB.

53. Freda Payne, *Band of Gold* (1970).

54. Brooke, 'A certain amount of mush', p. 86.

55. C. Brown, *The Death of Christian England: Understanding Secularisation 1800–2000* (Abingdon, 2001), p. 178 (Brown 2001).

56. SN.

57. This is true at least until the late 1960s, for some magazines it was much longer.

58. LJ.

59. P. Tinkler, *Constructing Girlhood: Popular Magazines for Girls Growing Up in England, 1920–1950* (London, 1995), p. 3 (Tinkler 1995).

60. C. Hathorne, *Five Minutes' Love* (Dudley, 2006), p. 149 (Hathorne 2006).

61. SN, LS, JB.

62. LJ.

63. *Valentine* (1957).

64. A. McRobbie, 'Jackie: An ideology of adolescent feminity' (Occasional Paper, Women Series: SP No. 53, Centre for Contemporary Cultural Studies, University of Birmingham, 1978) (McRobbie 1978).

65. Sandbrook, *White Heat*, p. 227.
66. *Honey* (1966).
67. *Marilyn*, 3 June 1961, p. 1. Thanks to Dr Mike Cunningham (University of Wolverhampton) for remarking that the storyline had 'echoes of the song *"It Should Have Been Me"'* (1963), written by Whitfield and Stevenson for Kim Weston, covered by Gladys Knight and the Pips (1968) and subsequently by other artistes.
68. *Jackie*, 11 January 1964.
69. Brown, *The Death of Christian England*.
70. L. Stras, 'Introduction: She's so fine, or why girl singers still matter' in L. Stras (ed.) *She's so Fine: Reflections on Whiteness, Adolescence and Class in 1960s Music* (Farnham, 2011), p. 18 (Stras 2011).
71. J. E. Gardner 'She Got Her Man, But Could She Keep Him? Love and marriage in American romance comics, 1947–1954', *The Journal of American Culture*, 36 (1) (2013), 24 (Gardner 2013).
72. LJ.
73. *Valentine*, 21 September 1963, p. 1.
74. KD. This was endorsed by LS, LL and others.
75. Langhamer, *The English in Love*, p. 173.
76. McRobbie, *Feminism and Youth Culture*, p. 86.
77. 'Modes and morals' *The Economist*, 28 November 1953, p. 644. It is, however, important to note that by the mid-1970s the content and the message of the magazines was, almost imperceptibly, changing,
78. WS.
79. Langhamer, *The English in Love*, p. 86.
80. LH.
81. TB.
82. LH.
83. CH.
84. LS.
85. GP.
86. Laurie, *Teenage Revolution*, p. 70.
87. Langhamer, *The English in Love*, p. 210.
88. Hyams, *White Boots*, pp. xiv–xv.
89. LS.
90. SV 'Memories of Walsall in the Swinging 60s' *The Black Country Bugle*, 13 June 2013, p. 11.
91. CH Telephone interview 15 October 2015.
92. TB, LS, LL, JB, LH.
93. GP.
94. DF, LH, SN.
95. LH, JB.

96. LS, SN, LL.
97. GP.
98. DF, LS, SN.
99. CH.
100. JC.
101. DF. When they married, in 1976, she was still considering the financial implications for her father. 'There were only twelve guests at the wedding. I had to have a white dress because mum made me but I had my way over the rest of the wedding. As I was twenty-five it was easier to stand up for myself.'
102. LS, WT, JB.
103. LL, GB, TB.
104. A. Pressley, *The 50s and 60s: The Best of Times* (London, 2003), p. 197 (Pressley 2003).
105. WS.
106. LS, LL, SN.
107. KB.
108. It is interesting to note that even girls who left home to study at university and teacher training college returned home at the end of their training – all except JG who got married and 'gained her freedom'.
109. LH, LL.
110. LS.
111. BT.
112. LS.
113. LL.
114. LS.
115. LH.
116. BT, LS, LL, JB, LH.
117. SN.
118. SN.
119. LS.
120. WT.
121. LS.
122. DF.
123. LS, LL, DF, SN.
124. DF.
125. Pressley, *The 50s and 60s*, pp. 192–7. Anonymous respondents.
126. C. Hathorne, *All Shook Up* (Dudley, 2007), p. 26 (Hathorne 2007).
127. A. Johnson, *This Boy: A Memoir of a Childhood* (London, 2013), p. 274 (Johnson 2013).
128. LS.
129. LS.
130. SN.

131. SN.
132. JG She was the only respondent who admitted 'putting it about a bit' with previous boyfriends. Jean's marriage ended in divorce in 1985.
133. WS.
134. SN.
135. GP.
136. LJ.
137. LS.
138. LJ.
139. C. Hathorne, *Those Were the Days* (Dudley, 2013), p. 80 (Hathorne 2013).
140. CH Telephone interview 15 October 2015; Hathorne, *Those Were the Days*, p. 122.
141. LL, LS, JB, BT, JG.
142. WS.
143. LS, 1970; AEB A-level exam paper.
144. *Dudley Herald*, 2 July 1955.
145. A.M. Mangan, *Me and Mine* (London, 2012), p. 175 (Mangan 2012).
146. LL, TB, WS.
147. *Dudley Herald*, 6 March 1965.
148. Martha Reeves and the Vandellas (1967) '*Third Finger Left Hand*' Gordy Records. '*Third Finger Left Hand*' was on the B side of '*Jimmy Mack*' and was covered in 1970 by British duo The Pearls
149. Love Affair, (1968) '*Everlasting Love*' CBS Records. The single, first released by Robert Knight in 1967, reached 40 in the UK charts in January 1968, but was number one in the singles chart for Love Affair in February 1968.
150. McRobbie, *Feminism and Youth Culture*, p. 101.
151. *Jackie*, 11 January 1964.
152. *Marilyn*, June 1961.
153. Laurie, *Teenage Rebellion*, p. 65.
154. Manfred Mann (1965) '*Semi-Detached Suburban Mr James*', Fontana Record Label.
155. Laurie, *Teenage Rebellion*, p, 65.
156. Pressley, *The 50s and 60s*, p. 196. Anonymous respondent.
157. LS; LL.
158. BT, SN, LS, JG.
159. LS.
160. BT.
161. DF.
162. R. Pierce 'Marriage in the 50s' *The Sociological Review*, 11 (2) (July 1963) pp. 215–40 (Pierce 1963).
163. TB.

164. LL was quoting her grandmother here.
165. JG.
166. LL, JB interviewed together.
167. Laurie, *Teenage Revolution*, p. 153.
168. WS.
169. CH.

REFERENCES

M. Abrams, *The Teenage Consumer* (London, 1959), p. 7.

M. Akhtar and S. Humphries, *The Fifties and Sixties: A Lifestyle Revolution* (London, 2001), p. 80.

S. Brooke, 'A Certain Amount of Mush: Love, Romance, Celluloid and Wax in the Mid Twentieth Century' in A. Harris and T.W. Jones (eds.) *Love and Romance in Britain, 1918–1970* (Basingstoke, 2015), p. 83.

C. Brown, *The Death of Christian England: Understanding Secularisation 1800–2000* (Abingdon, 2001), p. 178.

J. Clarke and T. Jefferson, 'Working Class Youth Cultures' in A. Gray, J. Campbell, M. Erikson, S. Hanson and H. Wood, (eds.) *CCCS Selected Working Papers Volume 2* (London, 2007), p. 201.

C. Davies, *Permissive Britain: Social Change in the Sixties and Seventies* (London, 1975), p. 69.

M. P. Donnelly, *Sixties Britain: Culture, Society and Politics* (Harlow, 2005), p. 3.

S. Frith, *The Sociology of Rock* (London, 1978), p. 64.

J. E. Gardner 'She Got Her Man, But Could She Keep Him? Love and Marriage in American Romance Comics, 1947–1954', *The Journal of American Culture*, 36, 1 (2013), p. 24.

P. Granger, *Up West; Voices from the Streets of Post-War London* (London, 2009).

C. Hathorne, *Five Minutes Love* (Dudley, 2006), p. 149.

C. Hathorne, *All Shook Up* (Dudley, 2007), p. 26.

C. Hathorne, *Those Were the Days* (Dudley, 2013), p. 80.

J. Hyams, *White Boots and Mini Skirts* (London, 2013).

A. Johnson, *This Boy: A Memoir of a Childhood* (London, 2013), p. 274.

T. Johnson, *The Mill Girls* (London, 2014), p. 311.

D. Kynaston, *Modernity Britain: A Shake of the Dice, 1959–62* (London, 2014).

C. Langhamer, *The English in Love: The Intimate Story of an Emotional Revolution* (Oxford, 2013), p. 56.

P. Laurie, *The Teenage Revolution* (London, 1965), p. 23.

S. Lincoln, *Youth Culture and Private Space* (Basingstoke, 2012).

A.M. Mangan, *Me and Mine* (London, 2012), p. 175.

B. Masters, The *Swinging Sixties* (London, 1985), p. 34.

A. McRobbie, 'Jackie: An Ideology of Adolescent Feminity' (Occasional Paper, Women Series: SP No. 53, Centre for Contemporary Cultural Studies, University of Birmingham, 1978).

A. McRobbie, *Feminism and Youth Culture* (Basingstoke, 2000), pp. 4–16.

A. McRobbie and J. Garber, 'Girls and Subcultures' in S. Hall and T. Jefferson (eds.) *Resistance Through Rituals: Youth Subcultures in Post-War Britain* (London, 1975).

A. McRobbie and J. Garber, 'Girls and Subcultures' in A. Gray, J. Campbell, M. Erikson, S. Hanson and H. Wood (eds.) *CCCS Selected Working Papers Volume 2* (London, 2007), p. 222.

J. Obelkevich, 'Consumption' in J. Obelkevich and P. Catterall, (eds.) *Understanding Post-war British Society* (London, 1994), p. 143.

R. Pierce 'Marriage in the 50s' *The Sociological Review* 11, 2 (July 1963), pp. 215–40.

A. Pressley, *The 50s and 60s: The Best of Times* (London, 2003), p. 197.

D. Sandbrook, *White Heat: A History of Britain in the Swinging Sixties* (London, 2006), p. 56.

C.A. Stafford and A. Crowe, *Us Kids: Growing Up in Ladywood, 1945–1960* (Birmingham, 1998), p. 156.

L. Stras, 'Introduction: She's so fine, or why girl singers still matter' in L. Stras (ed.) *She's so Fine: Reflections on Whiteness, Adolescence and Class in 1960s Music* (Farnham, 2011), p. 18.

J. Street-Porter, *Baggage: My Childhood* (London, 2004).

P. Tinkler, *Constructing Girlhood: Popular Magazines for Girls Growing Up in England, 1920–1950* (London, 1995), p. 3.

R. Watkiss, 'Old Habits Persist, Change and Continuity in Black Country Communities: Pensnett, Sedgley and Tipton, 1945–c. 1970'', (Unpublished PhD thesis, University of Wolverhampton, 2014).

Rosalind Watkiss Singleton holds a PhD from the University of Wolverhampton, which utilised oral testimony to examine change and continuity in post-war working-class societies. She works as an independent researcher and is also employed as a sessional lecturer in the History and Politics Department at the University of Wolverhampton and at Ruskin College, Oxford. She has been involved several community projects training volunteers in oral history techniques, including *Women of Wolverhampton* (2013) and the *Block Capital Project* (2014–15). Published work includes 'Crime? No, It Wasn't Really Crime' in *Law, Crime and History*, 1 (2014) and translated for in *Revisita Historia y Justicia*, 6 (2016); '"Doing Your Bit": Women and the National Savings Movement in the Second World War' in Maggie Andrews and Janis Lomas (eds.), *The Home Front in Britain: Images, Myths and Forgotten Experiences* (2014).

CHAPTER 7

Agents of Change: Cultural Materialism, Post-Punk and the Politics of Popular Music

David Wilkinson

In this chapter I offer a summary of the ways in which cultural materialism can help illuminate the politics of British post-punk, a theme I have pursued in greater detail elsewhere.[1] The term 'cultural materialism' has its origins in Raymond Williams' humanist rapprochement with Marxist thought, at just the moment in the 1970s when British Cultural Studies was beginning to drift from both Marxism and humanism.

By drawing on this body of work, I show how Williams' theorisation of the materiality of culture might enrich our understanding of popular music as an integral component of social change; in other words how making a noise really can make a difference. The cultural materialist understanding of hegemony, meanwhile, as a process that is constantly contested and in flux, allows us to reflect upon the complex historical and political legacy of post-punk. Furthermore, a humanist attention to lived experience means that the theory is well equipped to consider how and why music as felt matters. I explore this issue in relation to post-punk with reference to another key thinker of the New Left, Herbert Marcuse. These are theoretical arguments that will, I hope, resonate beyond punk and post-punk studies. Beforehand, however, it's worth explaining the

D. Wilkinson (✉)
Manchester Metropolitan University, Manchester, UK
e-mail: D.Wilkinson@mmu.ac.uk

K. Gildart et al. (eds.), *Youth Culture and Social Change*,
Palgrave Studies in the History of Subcultures and Popular Music,
DOI 10.1057/978-1-137-52911-4_7

motivations behind such a move. What brought me to cultural materialism in the first place as a way of thinking about post-punk?

'POLITICS IS LIFE'

Given Williams' abiding concern with the importance of experience,[2,3] and the focus of this collection on why and how memories of social unrest matter, it's appropriate to start with a personal response. Rather than offering this anecdote as autobiography, though, it has been included as a means of clarifying a broader generational 'structure of feeling', a term used by Williams to capture the complex nuances of a particular period of lived experience whilst acknowledging that our feelings as well as our thoughts are socially and historically determined.[4]

On February 15 2003, my sixth-form friends and myself boarded a coach put on from Stockport to London by largely female baby boomers. I remember them swirling in the sartorial remnants of a hippie past. We joined the biggest protest in British history – around two million – against the imminent war on Iraq. The commonly remembered slogans of the time are usually phrased in the negative, capturing the defensive position of the left after decades of defeat: 'No blood for oil' and 'Not in my name'. However, I remember another one that was floating around at the time, which summed up the fact that many didn't stop at saying 'no': 'Another world is possible.'

As I have hinted, the anti-war protests owed a debt to the legacy of successive post-war countercultures. At the same time as all this was going on, I was discovering post-punk in conjunction with a media-driven revival of interest in it; possibly part of the last generation whose teenage tastes were shaped significantly by print music journalism. I couldn't get enough of reading about post-punk's world of alternative institutions; its aesthetic and political radicalism. At some level, I associated this new cultural consciousness with my developing political consciousness. Others must have done similar; post-punk influences can often be detected amongst today's global network of small-scale DIY bands and their audiences, many of whom seem to share a broadly progressive political outlook.[5]

I left college and started university later in 2003, benefiting, like many young people, from the cumulative post-war expansion of higher education. The pick 'n' mix of cultural theory that my degree introduced me to was fascinating, especially the way it interwove with my political outlook. As my studies continued, however, I started to feel that, with a few welcome exceptions, this pick 'n' mix was what Williams might call a selective tradition. Its cultural politics often tended – and still tend – to flip between an ultimately pessimistic 'resistance' and the compensatory, excessively optimistic stance of celebrating popular culture as inherently democratic and subversive.

Apportioning blame for this situation would be unhelpful. The problems of contemporary cultural theory are, after all, just one more example of the left's rearguard action since the neoliberal revolution. But my experience of the anti-war movement, among other things, gave me an intuitive sense that this frustrating, see-sawing 'structure of feeling' was specific, not total. Eventually this led me to cultural materialism. Williams' work acknowledges how deeply rooted and difficult to change dominant power relations can be. Yet its stress on agency and creativity, and its understanding of society and culture as contradictory human-made processes rather than all-pervasive structures, allows for reasonable hope.

Such a view informs my historical analysis of post-punk's politics. For Simon Reynolds, post-punk's most influential and engaging chronicler, post-punk 'tried to make politics and pop work together but failed'.[6] Without overstating post-punk's impact, I think it's worth telling a slightly different story.

A Resource of Hope

These, then, are some directly experiential reasons for thinking about post-punk in the way that I do. It is also important, however, to justify a renewed cultural materialism by situating such an approach within an academic context. Although Williams' work was hugely influential in the opening up of the humanities to the study of popular culture, and despite his argument that 'culture is ordinary',[7] he rarely engaged with popular music and alternative youth culture. Perhaps this is because of his own generational 'structure of feeling', one that Alan Sinfield has characterised as 'left culturism' – a dissident framing of culture as standing in opposition to commerce, which advocated a state-funded extension of supposedly 'good culture' (literature, drama, fine art, classical music and so on) to all, through institutions such as schools, the Arts Council and public service broadcasting. Those who held this attitude were usually suspicious of 'commercial' forms such as popular music, leading to what Sinfield calls a 'historic missed opportunity' of 'working with – politicising – actual popular cultures, commercial though they are'.[8]

The study of subcultures and popular music – in particular the intuition that they may offer instances of opposition – is dominantly traced back to the Birmingham Centre for Contemporary Cultural Studies. Given the way that this work was breaking theoretically from Williams' influence in the 1970s towards the structuralist Marxism of Louis Althusser (and later a fully fledged post-structuralist jettisoning of Marxist insights),[9] it is perhaps unsurprising that Williams has not been the most obvious 'go-to' thinker for the field.

Williams, did, however, make a hopeful passing comment during the post-punk era. He noted that some forms of popular music were not solely motivated by market imperatives, even if those market imperatives eventually claimed them, and positively contrasted popular music's 'vitality' and social engagement with more nostalgic and navel-gazing examples of contemporary cultural production.[10] And there has been a current within analyses of popular music and subcultures that bears the influence of cultural materialism.[11] What this current offers is a way of thinking about post-punk, and popular music more broadly, as both historically significant and directly imbricated with social change.

HEGEMONY

Antonio Gramsci's theory of hegemony is a familiar enough concept across the humanities and social sciences. Yet Williams' sophisticated reworking of it is one that is too often neglected. For Williams, hegemony is the 'saturation' of 'relations of domination' into 'the whole process of living' so that 'the pressures and limits of a specific economic, cultural and political system' like capitalism often seem like 'common sense'.[12] Although hegemony goes deep, significant and potentially transformative dissidence is still possible. This is because hegemony is by nature partial and selective. It does not and cannot account for all 'human practice [and]... intention'.[13] Thus hegemony 'has continually to be renewed', being 'continually... challenged by pressures not all its own'. One hegemonic response to such cultural and political challenges is the attempt to *incorporate* them.[14]

In Britain in the 1970s and 1980s, this was the response of the Thatcherite New Right to the qualitative disaffection with consumerism expressed by the post-war counterculture, its punk and post-punk descendants and various strands of leftist opposition. This was one of the main reasons why post-punk mattered despite its subcultural marginality: its internal tensions over the meaning of freedom and pleasure, which eventually produced a 'new pop' faction that had some affinity with emergent neoliberalism, were situated directly in the crossfire of a key ideological struggle of the era. Indeed such cultural production had an active and shaping part to play in this struggle, as once-underground bands like Spandau Ballet came to represent 'kids who were into acquisition'[15] whilst others, notably bands like Blue Orchids and The Raincoats, continued to pursue the potential of unknown pleasures.

Following Williams on hegemony allows us to see that left post-punk's 'increasingly out of synch relationship'[16] with the shift to neoliberalism in Britain did not mean that its transformative efforts simply 'failed'.[17] Instead of just being crushed, absorbed and rendered irrelevant by broader structural transformation, post-punk dissidence may still offer a residual resource of hope. The word 'residual' is key here, pointing towards Williams' historically layered sense of hegemony. For Williams, the dominant culture coexists with 'residual' and 'emergent' elements, each of which may feature alternative or actively oppositional counter-hegemonic traits.[18] 'Hope', too, is important – Alan Sinfield notes that Williams' model of hegemony offers an alternative to understandings of dominance as 'unbreakable continuum' derived from Althusser and post-structuralists such as Michel Foucault.[19]

Thinking about post-punk as material production, too, rather than simply a series of historical texts to be ideologically decoded, brings us to another way in which cultural materialism can shed light on its politics and, more broadly, the role of popular music in social change. As Andrew Milner has noted, the cultural materialist attention to specific contexts of production and their determining effects is one of the theory's key strengths.[20] It offers a historically rooted means of assessing the politics of popular music that avoids the wishful, freewheeling subjectivism of recent work such as Jack Halberstam's *Gaga Feminism*. Todd Gitlin has referred to this tendency as 'anti-political populism' – the exaggeration of the radical potential of popular culture as an over-compensatory move in response to the declining fortunes of the left (Gitlin 1997).[21]

INSTITUTIONS

Societies need to produce ... to continue – they need food, shelter, warmth ... a transport and information structure ... and so on. Also, they have to produce culturally. They need knowledges to keep ... production going ... and they need understanding, intuitive and explicit, of a system of social relationships

within which the whole process can take place. Cultural production produces... apparently 'natural' understandings to explain who we are... [and] how the world works. Social conflict manifests itself as competition between stories.
Alan Sinfield[22]

To understand how popular music such as post-punk is part of this social conflict, we need to consider the particular institutions through which it has been produced.[23] Elsewhere, I have focused on the post-punk music industry alongside the significance of institutions such as the British music press and higher education to the politics of post-punk.[24] But it's necessary to step back a little from the instance of post-punk here in order to gain perspective, especially in the case of the music industry. A longer historical view of the productive processes at play in post-war popular music gives us an essential sense of the ground on which the political conflicts of post-punk took place.

Within the music industry, popular musicians operate within the dominance of a 'corporate professional' system, with residual elements of 'post-artisanal' and 'market professional' production.[25] *Post-artisanal* describes a situation where cultural producers enjoy a degree of autonomy at the same time as being partly reliant on others to help them make their work. They then sell their work to further intermediaries, who sell it on for profit. We can identify this in the popular music industry in the instances of distribution companies, studio production and manufacture of music in various listening formats. *Market professionalism* involves the move to copyright and royalties, with the producer developing an investment in the market as a whole in the form of sales figures, rather than simply receiving a lump sum for their work. The *corporate professional* system involves direct and sustained employment by large companies and commissioning from above 'of planned saleable products' for 'a highly capitalised market'.[26] Whilst this is more formally organised in industries like publishing, it is a central feature of the music industry, embodied for example in contracts and marketing.

Jason Toynbee calls the relative freedom of the post-artisanal elements of popular musical production 'institutional autonomy'. He argues that historically, companies have often ceded control of cultural production to musicians. This production has often been 'spatially dispersed in small units', and there is 'a strong continuity between consumption and production (often within an over-arching subculture)'.[27] Because of this distance from straightforward capitalist functionality, Toynbee notes that although 'musicians aspire to enter market relations ... at the same time the market is held to corrupt the non-commercial values to which successive corps of music makers ... have subscribed'.[28] Geoff Travis, founder of post-punk independent label Rough Trade, thus recalls the 'disappointing' moment when The Clash and the Sex Pistols signed to major labels.[29]

CULTURALISM

We could also frame this by arguing that much popular music has tended to inherit the *culturalist* distinction of the arts from commerce and civilisation. This distinction is critically analysed in its English, largely literary, form in Williams' classic first book *Culture and Society 1780–1950*. It is part of a broader European tradition of aesthetics,[30] which, as Francis Mulhern summarises, 'took shape in the later eighteenth century as a critical, usually negative, discourse on the emerging symbolic universe of capitalism, democracy and enlightenment ... a process of social life for which a ... French coinage furnished the essential term: *civilisation*'.[31]

Culturalism has taken many forms and adopted various political hues. In Britain, it has been present in romanticism, modernism and the post-war nexus of the counterculture and the New Left, amongst other formations. It is historically rooted in what Sinfield has called 'middle class dissidence'; disdain for the 'philistine' branches of the middle class – 'businessmen, industrialists and empire-builders' – to which it opposes a celebration of 'good' culture.[32] This is not to say that culturalism cannot be adapted and taken up by other classes. Working-class bands like The Fall and the Blue Orchids did precisely this, in their different ways. The Fall's Mark E. Smith asserted 'there's entertainment and there's culture, and we're on the cultural side of the line',[33] whilst Una Baines of the Blue Orchids claimed of the band: 'we're not for people to escape to.'[34] More recently, she has fulminated against the contemporary music industry, with a strong awareness that the market creates and meets pleasures moulded by dominant values rather than simply catering to free individuals: 'Now look at it, Simon Cowell and all that nonsense, where they just take the soul out of everything and regurgitate this shit at people, and people want it. Their lives are being narrowed down.'[35]

The reasons for culturalism's emergence and the shapes it has taken are complex. It was in large part, though, a reaction to the growing historical subordination of cultural production to the vagaries of the market rather than the previous positions of cultural producers within state and religious hierarchies or as the beneficiaries of patronage.[36] Stripped of higher purpose in a marketplace that reduced the qualitative specifics of use value to the quantitative commensurability of exchange value, cultural producers required a new justification for their work. Amid the anxieties produced by the expanding and rapidly changing world of industrial capitalism, culture began to be explained both as a product of 'the "inner life"... in effect a metaphysics of... the imaginative process' and organic 'ways of life', distinct from the march of abstract, rational 'civilisation'.[37]

It might seem like a stretch to detect the workings of culturalism at play within post-war British popular music, given culturalism's tendency to make authority claims about cultural value and its suspicions of 'the commercial' discussed earlier. Yet by the 1960s, these assumptions were challenged by the class mobility, the new forms of popular culture and the expanded consumerism and educational opportunities of the post-war political settlement. Sinfield notes that 'young people had acquired the confidence not to compromise... the kind of attention usually given to "good" culture was lavished on popular and commercial forms'.[38]

Simon Frith and Howard Horne relate this in institutional terms to the art schools that produced many of the key figures of British popular music in the 1960s, including Pete Townshend and Ray Davies. They argue that 'the idea that artists are natural rebels gained wide cultural exposure during the student occupation of Hornsey College of Art in 1968', which incidentally included the key New Left thinker Tom Nairn. With their bohemian beliefs of living spontaneously and creative autonomy, the students resented new pressures to direct their skills toward feeding the culture industry, in a classic example of the culturalist distinction of culture from commerce. The Hornsey occupation, Frith and Horne claim, 'reflected specific institutional contradictions, but fed into a much wider counter-culture... By 1968... the loose "hippie" movement had created its own version of aesthetic revolt'.[39] Paul Willis's ethnographic research on 1970s hippie subculture in the West Midlands observes an antipathy towards a 'ratio-technical order', held responsible 'for the complete impoverishment of human sensibilities'.[40] Crucially, the means of expression for such revolt now took popular cultural forms, including rock, fashion and journalism.

Simon Reynolds has argued convincingly that 'post-punk ... reconnects ... to all those sixties ideas about rock-as-art',[41] and institutional factors played no small part in this: bands like Gang of Four, Scritti Politti and the Raincoats, along with scores of others, were the products of those art schools like Hornsey where many 1960s rebels ended up teaching. Nor was this a coincidence – Green Gartside of Scritti Politti explained his decision to study at Leeds Polytechnic thusly: '[It] was toted [sic] as a very trendy place to go, as you had lecturers there that made names for themselves in the sixties.' [42] Those who were not art school or university graduates, such as The Fall, inherited their culturalism from a long-established tradition of working-class autodidactism that, in the post-war era, had begun to relate to the emerging counterculture as a 'discourse of escape and a call to action'.[43]

The aesthetic revolt of culturalism is not without its issues and contradictions. The distinction of culture from commerce, for instance, is an untenable one if we are discussing cultural production embedded in capitalist market relations. Theodor Adorno's critique of popular music acutely observes that the very elements of culture which are said to be opposed to commerce are sold back to us (Adorno 1991),[44] or, as Gang of Four succinctly put it, 'ideal love a new purchase/a market of the senses'. Also, culturalism's distinction of culture from civilisation can tend to discourage straightforward analysis of the politics of culture. Often, culture actually comes to stand in for politics in culturalist discourse.[45] Furthermore, notions of artistic genius, individualism and outsider status associated with culturalist movements like romanticism may chafe against leftist hopes for democracy, egalitarianism, solidarity and co-operation. Despite all this, there is something highly valuable from a left perspective in the prevailing belief that popular music should be about more than capitalist imperatives[46] – specifically, about aspects of human life neglected or suppressed by such imperatives. It is surely what Ari Up of The Slits was getting at when she claimed: 'When you're into a thing for money then your heart drops out and the heart is made out of rhythm and if you ain't got the heart, then the rhythm ain't there.' [47] Culturalist attitudes are also at the heart of popular music's concern with freedom and pleasure, as we will see below.

POPULISM

Culturalism, already a fraught political battlefield, does not exhaust the institutional determination of the politics of popular music. Arguing that popular music rests on the ideal that 'popular musicians come from the common people', Toynbee claims that the political agency of popular musicians requires an engagement with *populism*.[48] As early as 1960, Ray Gosling, writing in *New Left Review*, characterised young British rock 'n' roll figures like Marty Wilde, Cliff Richard and Billy Fury as representative of the preoccupations of a new era: 'He is your son, the nation's hope, the child of the emancipated common man, the idol of a moneyed age, the hope in a world full of fear. His face comes out in the third dimension from the screen to appeal to the mother, the daughter, the youngest son; to epitomise this new glossy world of boom.' [49]

There are various sources of this ideal of the popular musician as everywoman and man. First and foremost, there has been no official and potentially elitist route through qualifications to become a popular musician.[50] Secondly, there has been a historical trend of collective self-management that includes 'the notion of a direct relationship between audience and musicians'. Toynbee dates this as far back as swing bands and contrasts it with the individualist role of 'pop star'.[51] Thirdly, we should add, popular music is a mass-market cultural form that potentially reaches many people. The royalties system means that there is a financial incentive to reach more people too.

These factors haven given popular musicians the opportunity of a public platform for political debate, the ability to act as a representative force for progressive political movements and marginalised groups and the potential to act as a reminder that 'ordinary people are creative too', often in a 'structurally democratic' manner at odds with the hierarchies and individualist ideologies of capitalist production.[52] Toynbee notes, though, that popular music often underlines inequality by failing to represent marginalised groups. Furthermore, because of the commodification of the creative self that the pop process entails, vainglory and elitist individualism threaten democratic ideals. We should observe, too, that popular musicians have used their public platform to intervene in politically reactionary ways – as in the case of Eric Clapton's racist comments in 1976 that helped provoke the Rock Against Racism movement, which would go on to shape the political context of post-punk.

Post-punk's sometime support for causes such as feminism and anti-consumerism meant that at times it represented the concerns of the libertarian left. It gave broad exposure to such ideas not only in songs, but also in the published discourse of the music weeklies upon which it was reliant. Style journalist Peter York observes: 'It reached the kids ... who never saw ... [libertarian left magazine] *The Leveller* ... quite ordinary working or lower middle class kids who nonetheless wanted to be in touch with *something else*.'[53]

Post-punk's continuation of punk's hostility to stars, and of punk's egalitarian injunction to 'do it yourself', were a particularly pronounced form of populism. There was sometimes a desire for populist reach at the level of consumption as well as production, expressed in Mark E. Smith's claim that 'The Fall had to appeal to someone who was into cheap soul as much as someone who liked [the] avant-garde. I even wanted the Gary Glitter fans.'[54] Post-punk, though, was challenged on this score by its 'new pop' outgrowth, which ironically revived stardom at the same time as it staked a claim to populism. This was a tension in which the broader political stakes were high, as I have already indicated. 'Don't they want to make the money?/Don't they want to be The Beatles?',[55] mused Green Gartside of his peers as he prepared for stardom. Journalist Paul Morley, an ideologue of the new pop, asserted that: 'no longer is there an acceptance of the cobwebbed corner ... [new pop groups] want a big display in the supermarkets, not to be stuck on a high shelf in the corner shop.'[56] The language of commerce indicates the increasingly instrumental direction taken by new pop in terms of populism.

ANTI-CULTURALISM

Culturalism and populism help frame much of the politics of post-punk. However, there is a third institutional factor to the political possibilities of popular music. Its history has been further characterised by what I call *anti-culturalist* tendencies - an umbrella term for any position that consciously recognises the weakness of the culturalist distinction of culture from commerce and civilisation. The most obvious determining element of anti-culturalism is the dominance of corporate professionalism within the music industry; popular musicians are usually the contracted employee of a business, with all the insecurity and exploitation this has historically involved. They experience first-hand the power of the music industry to define what counts publicly as musical creativity in its construction of specific markets, its policing of genres and its influence over what does and does not get released.[57] We should note, in other words, that the 'creative freedom' of institutional autonomy is only a relative condition. In the face of this, it is not difficult to see how doubt might creep in about one's role as an artist whose concerns transcend the grubbiness of the commercial world.

There have also, however, been institutional influences on anti-culturalism from outside the music industry itself. Pop Art in Britain combined the formal techniques of modernism with the 'danger of US popular culture' and an acknowledgement of commerce and consumerism. In so doing, it focused the challenge of the 1960s generation to the 'nannying' institutions of 'good culture', influencing bands like the Who and the Beatles.[58] Pop Art presumptions would consolidate themselves in the educational institutions and milieus that went on to influence later waves of British popular music. Here, the work of Simon Frith is again instructive; with Howard Horne, he has highlighted the centrality of such ideas to the formation of punk and post-punk.[59]

Frith and Horne, though, tend to over-emphasise the potentially conservative consequence of anti-culturalism: once culturalism is sacrificed, popular music can tend to get equated with capitalist imperatives. This is an issue, and it's a theme that often haunted post-punk's new pop turn. But anti-culturalism has also been marked by more incisively critical strands: Sinfield notes that Pop Art 'facilitated a ... breakthrough into political work' through 'its disrespect for the dignity of art'.[60] And more straightforwardly politicised approaches to culture, including Marxism and feminism, also circulated within the same milieus, as the counterculture divided between devoted radicals and more non-committal hedonists (Savage 2005).[61] At times, this strand of anti-culturalism has produced acute awareness and criticism of the unjust economic processes of popular musical production (thus dissolving the culturalist distinction of culture from commerce) and of the social and political significance of creative practice and form (thus dissolving the culturalist distinction of culture from civilisation).

In an early interview, Gang of Four guitarist Andy Gill argued 'I believe that all art is political. Whether it's a painting, a movie or a song, you're making some kind of statement.' [62] This was only one example of the prevalence of 'demystification' in post-punk discourse.[63] Theodore Gracyk has characterised post-punk as an 'anti-romantic strain of artistic modernism' (Gracyk 2011).[64] And it is true that through immersion in the world of art schools and the counterculture, the bohemian legacy of successive avant-gardes filtered through. Importantly, the attraction was often to movements like Dada, and figures such as Bertolt Brecht, where there had been a reaction against the rarefied status of culture even as this status was residually preserved. However, the source of this anti-culturalism was not always or solely modernism. Nor was attendance at art school or university the sole institutional origin. Sometimes anti-culturalism arose more from the diffusion of libertarian left concerns through the counterculture, as with the links of The Raincoats, The Fall and the Blue Orchids to the women's movement, or Scritti Politti's Eurocommunist connections.

FORMATIONS

Though attention to the institutions that shaped post-war popular music in Britain gives a broad idea of its political scope and its role in social change, Williams notes that an understanding of cultural processes 'is also a question of *formations*; those effective movements and tendencies, in intellectual and artistic life, which have significant ... influence on the active development of a culture, and which have a variable ... relation to formal institutions'.[65] By considering how formations like post-punk relate to their historical circumstances and how they contain internal differences and tensions, this kind of analysis acts as a bridge between generalised accounts of cultural production and studies of individual contributions.[66]

It's important to characterise post-punk as a specific formation, and as a broader subculture. This is crucial to an understanding of its politics. Two features marked post-punk out from first wave punk, both of which are central to an understanding of its politics. Each recalls the organising principles that Williams suggests bring cultural formations together. Firstly, post-punk broke away formally, a feature succinctly characterised by Reynolds: 'Groups that had been catalysed by punk but didn't sound 'punk rock' in the classic ... sense ... they interpreted punk as an imperative to keep changing.' [67] In other words, there was 'the common pursuit of some specific artistic aim'.[68] Often, this innovation was consciously or unconsciously politicised. Jon Savage defended the electronic experimentation of Cabaret Voltaire against the 'new conservatives'.[69] Young Communists Scritti Politti advocated 'scratchy-collapsy ... enthusiastic' attempts at innovation, linking them to 'new ideas' and 'commitment',[70] whilst This Heat tied their 'all channels open' musical approach to a 'liberating' anti-hierarchical stance'[71] and a desire to 'fight back against these bastards who were ruining the world'.[72]

Post-punk's second break was its close association with the independent label boom in the wake of punk,[73] distinguishing it from the abandonment of the DIY ideals often present in the first wave of punk as 'the top bands without exception followed the traditional rock route and looked for the best major label deal they could get'.[74] Few post-punk bands signed to established majors, and those that did so were often interrogated as to their reasons. This aspect of post-punk recalls Williams' definition of alternative and oppositional formations, which develop 'alternative facilities' for cultural production.[75]

STRUCTURES OF FEELING

A stress on formations, bound by shared aims and practices, also helps to convey a sense of more immediate and personal investment in popular musical production than institutional analysis; a feel for the values and the moods that brought post-punks together as a retrospectively recognisable tendency. Here, Williams' concept of 'structure of feeling' is also useful. The term avoids the notion of a 'formalised belief system' implied by 'ideology'. It captures the more complex and often contradictory 'felt' nature of social experience.[76]

The concept of 'structure of feeling' also frames my emphasis on freedom and pleasure as key issues that mediated the political concerns of post-punk and its broader historical conjuncture. Freedom and pleasure are surely among the most deeply, personally 'felt' experiences within an encompassing hegemonic process. They are irreducible to purely abstract and conceptual understandings if their varied expressions – dominant or oppositional – are to have any genuine hold.

FREEDOM AND PLEASURE

We have already touched on why freedom has been a common theme in popular music in the discussion of the creative freedom allowed by institutional autonomy. The concern with pleasure in popular music comes largely from the same source. Culturalism tends to view the arts as the terrain of individual experience, the imagination and the bodily senses.[77] Such a focus is highly conducive to questions of pleasure and personal fulfilment. Historically, rock in particular captured the frustration and longing of young people to whom post-war welfare capitalism had extended schooling, even as it maintained class stratification.[78] Education was only part of the story – welfare capitalism generated aspirations on a far greater scale than its capability to fulfil them, producing widespread disaffection.[79] Ray Gosling quoted a young soldier who claimed

that 'life is a permanent wank inside you'.[80] Thus popular music became a
way to imagine alternative fulfilment, however hazily defined.[81] Martin
Bramah of the Fall and the Blue Orchids recalls that 'we were really just
factory fodder. It was our way out from what the world was offering us (Ford
2003).'[82]

Freedom and pleasure's shared origin in the institutional autonomy of
popular musical production, and their twin historical articulation in the
disaffection of post-war youth, mean that they are often inextricable
themes within popular music, as in the case of post-punk. The emphasis
on musical experiment that marked post-punk was often inseparable from
a sense that this creative freedom was not simply formal self-indulgence.
Rather, it was tied to an interrogation of the freedoms and pleasures
associated with certain creative practices and an attempt to suggest new
ones, sometimes with utopian intent.

The pleasure of popular music, though, cannot be abstracted from
hegemony (Middleton 1990).[83] It's wise, if depressing, not to be too
optimistic about pleasure's radical potential. Just as culturalist creative
freedom may work against leftist collectivism, despite disdaining 'com-
mercialism', so the pleasures and fulfilments promoted by popular
music are often marked by dominant articulations of these themes,
even as they express disaffection. 'Rock music', Sinfield argues, is in
many instances 'consumer capitalism writ too large ... developing its
recommended values (conspicuous consumption, material aspirations,
masculine aggression) with an unacceptable excess'. This excess is one
that does not seriously disturb the dominant culture.[84] Indeed, it may
even rejuvenate it; Jim McGuigan has argued convincingly that we live
now in an era of 'cool capitalism', which has incorporated disaffected
countercultural appeals to pleasure and autonomy as an appealing
'front' region concealing a more unpleasant, exploitative 'back region'
(McGuigan 2009).[85]

However, given the long history of popular music's embroilment
with progressive politics, it would be hasty and overly pessimistic to
write off popular music's potential as a forum for the exploration of
alternative and oppositional freedoms and pleasures. In Jon Savage's
account of the deep roots of British punk, he notes that the upheavals of
1968 'turned aesthetic style into political gesture. The violent intensity
of the pop that had flooded the world from 1964 was translated into a
public demonstration of the utopian promise: that the world could be
transformed.'[86]

Elsewhere I historicise the fraught positioning of post-punk between residual libertarian, New Left and countercultural ideals of freedom and pleasure and the process of their capture by emerging Thatcherite neoliberalism.[87] Here, I emphasise the significance of a key figurehead of the New Left, who often focused its ideals. The work of Herbert Marcuse is dominantly looked upon as being tied to an era now past. The activist, intellectual and ex-student of Marcuse Angela Davis attributes this situation to the way Marcuse's later writings were so closely bound up with the New Left's ascendancy. She notes the nostalgia evoked in 1960s and 1970s radicals by mention of his name, arguing that such a reaction threatens to relegate Marcuse's insights to a status that is 'meaningful only in the context of our reminiscences' (Davis 2005).[88] However, Marcuse's concern with a qualitative critique of capitalism remains bitingly relevant and thus deserves serious contemporary engagement.[89] Marcuse's work is, with some revision, compatible with a cultural materialist approach to understanding qualitative critiques of capitalism like those of post-punk in terms of freedom and pleasure. Its utopian (Gorz 1989)[90] projections also have a direct historical connection with the moment of post-punk.

How are cultural materialism and Marcuse's work related, and how do they throw light on post-punk's qualitative critique? Both Williams and Marcuse can broadly be described as Marxist humanists; they desired political change based on the recognition that capitalism was not only economically unjust but also ultimately inadequate for a specifically human kind of self-fulfilment. In this, they shared the concerns of the broader libertarian left that shaped post-punk. Williams' recognition that capitalist hegemony reaches the 'fibres of the self'[91] and his acceptance that the biological was a determining factor of social life[92] echo Marcuse's understanding that dominant social systems must work at a biological level to be effective. We are 'libidinally and aggressively' bound to 'the commodity form' (Marcuse 1972).[93]

The flipside of these fairly grim-sounding arguments is that both thinkers built on Marx's theory of human 'species being' and alienation (Marx 1975)[94] to argue that we are simultaneously creative and social creatures (Marcuse 1972).[95] When capitalist social relations predominate, private owners are the main beneficiaries of our collective work. Furthermore, production is largely organised on the basis of the reproduction of capitalism, rather than on a democratically decided fulfilment of social needs and the chance for everyone to put their various capabilities into play.

Thus, we often experience conscious productive activity – one of the main things that makes us human – as something to be got through. Even if we are lucky enough to experience 'job satisfaction', work is still usually an external obligation, a means to the wage that sustains us. As a commodity, it is excessively quantified and calculated, alienating us from full invest- ment in it.[96] Rarely is it a liberating, enjoyable and fully sociable activity. For both Williams and Marcuse, though, as for the New Left more broadly, cultural production occasionally offered a glimpse of how things could be otherwise (Jones 2004).[97]

Here we can see that Williams and Marcuse also owed their arguments to a culturalist inheritance, with its stress on bodily senses and its celebra- tion of culture as transcending capitalist instrumentalism. In Williams' case, this came from the influence of the avowedly culturalist literary critic F.R. Leavis; in Marcuse's, it came from a long line of German aesthetic philosophy.[98] As philosophical materialists and Marxists, though, neither went along with the culturalist mystification of human creativity. Williams negotiated this better than Marcuse, however, with the latter maintaining a lingering mistrust of explicitly politicised cultural production.[99]

If Williams is more advanced than Marcuse on culture as key to political struggles over freedom and pleasure, why draw on Marcuse to look at post-punk? My rationale here has to do with the actual content of Williams' suggestions for a qualitative alternative to capitalism. *Towards 2000*, for example, is fascinatingly suggestive in its acknowledgement of the ecological critique of limitless capitalist growth.[100] It also contains practical suggestions for how new technologies might be used in socialist cultural policy to democratise access to cultural consumption and produc- tion.[101] We could see these as contributions to what Williams termed 'systematic' utopianism: starting to sketch the future practicalities of a different society.[102]

But Williams has less concrete suggestions when it comes to what he refers to as 'heuristic utopias', those whose 'purpose is to form desire' and which are 'imaginative encouragement[s] to feel and relate differently'[103]; in other words those projections which devote greater consideration to issues of freedom and pleasure. In fairness, this reticence comes from Williams' valuable and all too rare concern with 'the problem of how to establish democratic socialism as the political pre-condition for a common culture, rather than with the attempt to identify the specific content of any such culture'.[104] It is a concern that I have attempted to do justice to through my identification of the record label Rough Trade as central to leftist post-punk in its prefiguration of socialist cultural production. Nevertheless, we cannot do without the heuristic utopia; its 'strongest centre', Williams argues, 'is ... the conviction that people can live very differently, as distinct from having different things and from becoming resigned to endless crises and wars'.[105]

It's on this score that Marcuse comes into his own. He argued that 'the emergence of ... new needs and satisfactions [cannot] be envisaged as a mere by-product ... of changed social institutions'. The solution he proposed, to a countercultural audience during the Dialectics of Liberation conference at the Roundhouse in London in 1967, was the necessity of innovating ways of life that prefigured new definitions of freedom and pleasure.[106] Marcuse's rootedness in the movements of the New Left and the counterculture meant he avoided the elitist cultural prescriptivism of some sections of the left that had earlier worried Williams.[107] Although certain elements of the 'new sensibility' Marcuse proposed pre-dated the upsurge in radicalism of the late 1960s, it was this lived moment that provided him with a means of concretising its content.

The point is that heuristic utopias must be popularly rooted in order to carry weight. It may seem unusual, then, that Marcuse's work is drawn upon to frame oppositional freedoms and pleasures in the cultural pro-duction of post-punk, given the historical gap between the late 1960s and the late 1970s and early 1980s. However, post-punk was in many ways an emergent development of the same countercultural movements from which Marcuse drew inspiration and upon which he was hugely influential. Published by large companies in affordable paperback form, his work also circulated significantly: the first edition of *One Dimensional Man* alone sold 300,000 copies (Aronson 2014).[108] Even if post-punks had not read such work, they were most certainly moving in circles with some connection to its ideas. It should be stressed, though, that I don't want to imply that post-punks were simply ventriloquising Marcuse. Marcuse's ideas are helpful because they condense many more general preoccupations of the libertarian left: issues such as sexuality, the human relationship to the natural world and the nature of work.

The historical shift in mood on the left between the late 1960s and the late 1970s and early 1980s may also seem to count against such reasoning; even before the rise of neoliberalism, hopes for radical change had begun to subside in the face of economic crises, preliminary conservative backlashes represented by the governments of Edward Heath in the UK and Richard Nixon in the US and the beginning of the long rolling back of the historical gains of the labour movement. Post-punk was bound up with 'the sense of dread and tension' in Britain at the close of the 1970s with the resurgence of the far right, the election of Margaret Thatcher and the re-escalation of the Cold War.[109] Herbert Pimlott has called this 'structure of feeling' 'crisis music' (Pimlott 2015).[110]

Yet post-punk was also nourished by the residual survival of libertarian left and countercultural structures of feeling. The name of This Heat's rehearsal space seemed to capture the fate of such utopianism: 'Cold Storage'. 'Please', Mark Stewart of the Pop Group pleaded against a clangourous backdrop that portentously descended in pitch, 'don't sell your dreams'. Oliver Loewenstein's severe fanzine *Dangerous Logic*, meanwhile, described itself as 'a grey journal ... with a bit of vigour and hope'.[111]

As well as breaking with punk's 'no future' stance, this attitude stood at odds with the drift of mainstream politics; a drift that continued even after Conservative electoral victory in 1979 seemed superficially to resolve the tension. Noting that the piecemeal management of capitalist crises was becoming an ever-more determinate feature of government policy, distorting or overtaking any manifesto promises, Williams claimed that 'world-weary adaptation', 'sceptical resignation' and 'a willingness to leave matters to ... a strong leader' had come to predominate and that 'the most widely practised form of general thinking about the future, in political programmes and manifestos, carries with it disadvantages which often lead to the abandonment of any real thinking about the future'.[112]

By contrast, the fragile strand of hope detectable in post-punk resonated with the main oppositional response to this 'politics of temporary tactical advantage'. This was the renewal of utopianism 'against the disappointments of current politics ... but also against the incorporated and marketed versions of a libertarian capitalist cornucopia'.[113] Like the libertarian left, post-punk was concerned both with 'systematic utopias' through the building of alternative institutions such as independent labels, and with 'heuristic utopias' through a focus on qualitatively different understandings and practices of freedom and pleasure. The expression of these impulses ran the gamut; they ranged from the precocity of the teenage Pop Group, who saw themselves as 'experimental primitives' [114] decrying the artificiality of urban life,[115] to the lush, playful feminist eroticism of the Raincoats' later work.

CONCLUSION

Because of this, then, post-punk was central to the social and political change of its era, a key component of the 'continuum of resistance and resilience' described in the Introduction to this collection. Yet its direct relationship to the political struggles of the era around freedom and pleasure made it a contradictory phenomenon, as we have seen in the case of new pop.

This is true, too, of its historical legacy. Especially in Britain, post-punk has been incorporated in ways connected fairly directly to the New Labour boom years. When I reflect with hindsight on being swept up in the post-punk revival of the early 2000s as a teenager, there was a definite 'structure of feeling' that fused the predominantly urban, 'arty' and intellectual aura of post-punk to the mania of speculative apartment building which reached its peak on the brink of 2008's global economic crash. In Manchester, the sensibility of local post-punk independent Factory was drawn on in a move that exhumed the city's musical past to advertise the supposedly sophisticated glamour of city-centre living, surrounded by the trappings of a 'post-industrial' creative economy. It was a myth mostly exploited by out-of-town investors and buy-to-let landlords. The most visible and talked-about symbol of this was the building of the luxury Hacienda apartment block on the site of Factory's legendary nightclub, its base adorned with an industrial-chic, die-cut mural depicting key events in the club's story. Lately, a featureless plaza between a new multi-storey carpark and an office block has been named Tony Wilson Place.

Just as much as post-punk has been manipulated as heritage marketing fodder for neoliberal urban regeneration, though, so it is also a resource of hope. Far from being the story of bands that failed, it is proof that radical popular cultural production can come out of moments of political difficulty for the left and still maintain, like the work of Raymond Williams, a guarded optimism and a vision of a very different future.

NOTES

1. D. Wilkinson, *Post-Punk, Politics and Pleasure in Britain* (London, 2016) (Wilkinson 2016).
2. U. Baines of The Fall quoted in Chris Brazier, 'United They Fall', *Melody Maker* 31 December 1977.
3. R. Williams, *Politics and Letters: Interviews With* New Left Review (London, 1979) pp. 163–4 (Williams 1979).

4. A. Milner, *Re-Imagining Cultural Studies: The Promise of Cultural Materialism* (London, 2002), p. 73 (Milner 2002).

5. Examples include queer, mixed-gender bands like Shopping and Downtown Boys who share familiar post-punk preoccupations such as feminism, the politics of the personal and economic independence. The work of Manchester's Lonelady, meanwhile, deliberately avoids explicit political commentary, though there is something clearly oppositional in its romantic investment of utopian possibilities in post-industrial ruins – not to mention its staunchly independent production in affordable, DIY spaces. 'You can't just have middle-class people making music', Lonelady has pointed out in an interview about her second album *Hinterland*. See J. Doran, 'Interiority complex: Exploring Manchester's hinterlands with Lonelady', *Quietus*, 5 February 2015, http://thequietus.com/articles/17173-lonelady-interview-hinterland [accessed 26 July 2016] (Doran 2015).

6. S. Reynolds, *Totally Wired: Post-Punk Interviews and Overviews* (London, 2009), p. 431 (Reynolds 2009).

7. R. Williams, 'Culture is ordinary' [1958], in R. Gable (ed.), *Resources of Hope: Culture, Democracy, Socialism* (London, 1989) (Williams 1989).

8. See Alan Sinfield, *Literature, Politics and Culture in Postwar Britain* 3rd edn (London, 2004), especially chapter 11, 'The rise of left culturism' (Sinfield 2004).

9. D. Dworkin, *Cultural Marxism in Postwar Britain* (Durham, 1997) p. 163 (Dworkin 1997).

10. R. Williams, *Towards 2000* (London, 1983), pp. 145–6 (Williams 1983). ITV's serialisation of *Brideshead Revisited* and the 'nominal' radicalism of postmodernist art came in for particular stick.

11. See, for example, J. Toynbee, *Making Popular Music: Musicians, Creativity and Institutions* (London, 2000), pp. x–xii (Toynbee 2000); K. Negus, *Popular Music In Theory* (Cambridge, 1996), p. 220 (Negus 1996); and *Music Genres and Corporate Cultures* (London, 1999) p. 151 (Negus 1999); D. Hesmondhalgh, 'Post-punk's attempt to democratise the music industry: The success and failure of Rough Trade', in *Popular Music* 16 (3) (1997 Oct), 255–74 (Hesmondhalgh 1997).

12. R. Williams, *Marxism and Literature* (Oxford, 1977), p. 110 (Williams 1977).

13. R. Williams, 'Base and superstructure in Marxist cultural theory' [1973], in *Culture and Materialism* (London, 2005), p. 43 (Williams 2005).

14. Williams, *Marxism and Literature*, pp. 112–114.

15. A. Thrills, 'Spandau Ballet', *NME*, 1 August 1981, pp. 25–7.

16. S. Reynolds, *Rip It Up and Start Again: Postpunk 1978–1984* (London, 2005), p. xxv (Reynolds 2005).

17. S. Reynolds, *Totally Wired: Post-Punk Interviews and Overviews*, p. 431.

18. Williams, 'Base and superstructure in Marxist cultural theory'.
19. A. Sinfield, *Faultlines: Cultural Materialism and the Politics of Dissident Reading* (Berkeley, 1992), p. 9 (Sinfield 1992).
20. A. Milner, *Re-Imagining Cultural Studies*, pp. 104–5.
21. T. Gitlin, 'The Anti-political populism of cultural studies', in M. Ferguson and P. Golding (eds.), *Cultural Studies in Question* (London, 1997), p. 27 (Gitlin 1997).
22. Sinfield, *Literature, Politics and Culture in Postwar Britain*, p. 29.
23. For institutions, see Williams, *Marxism and Literature*, pp. 115–18 and Williams, *Culture* (Glasgow, 1981), pp. 33–56 (Williams 1981).
24. Wilkinson, *Post-Punk, Politics and Pleasure in Britain*, pp. 29–31, 52–6, 63–7.
25. These terms are taken from Williams' discussion of cultural production and the market, *Culture*, pp. 44–52.
26. Williams, *Culture*, p. 52.
27. Toynbee, *Making Popular Music*, p. 1.
28. Toynbee, *Making Popular Music*, p. 2.
29. Reynolds, *Rip It Up and Start Again*, p. 93.
30. T. Eagleton, *The Ideology of the Aesthetic* (Oxford, 1990), p. 11 (Eagleton 1990).
31. F. Mulhern, *Culture/Metaculture* (London, 2000), p. xv (Mulhern 2000).
32. Sinfield, *Literature, Politics and Culture*, p. 46.
33. Mark E. Smith on Dave Fanning's radio show, RTE (Ireland), broadcast 18 October 1980.
34. Steve Sutherland, 'The sane old blues', *Melody Maker*, 1 May 1982.
35. Author interview with Una Baines.
36. Williams, *Culture*, p. 72.
37. Williams, *Marxism and Literature*, pp. 15–17, Milner, *Re-Imagining Cultural Studies*, p. 14.
38. Sinfield, *Literature, Politics and Culture*, p. 323.
39. S. Frith and H. Horne, *Art Into Pop* (London, 1987), pp. 51–2 (Frith and Horne 1987).
40. P. Willis, *Profane Culture* (London, 1978), p. 93 (Willis 1978).
41. Reynolds, *Totally Wired*, p. 410.
42. D. McCullough, 'The nitty gritty on Scritti Politti', *Sounds*, January 1979.
43. K. Gildart, 'From '*Dead End Streets*' to '*Shangri Las*': Negotiating social class and post-war politics with Ray Davies and the Kinks', in The Subcultures Network (eds.), *Youth Culture, Popular Music and the End of 'Consensus'* (London, 2015), pp. 9–34 (p. 14) (Gildart 2015).
44. T. Adorno, 'On the fetish character in music and the regression of listening', in J.M. Bernstein (ed.), *The Culture Industry: Selected Essays on Mass Culture* (London, 1991), pp. 33–5 (Adorno 1991).

45. Mulhern, *Culture/Metaculture*, p. xix.
46. Toynbee, *Making Popular Music*, p. 2.
47. A. Thrills, 'Up Slit creek', *NME*, 8 September 1979.
48. Toynbee, *Making Popular Music*, pp. ix–x.
49. R. Gosling, 'Dream boy', *New Left Review*, 1 (3) (May–June 1960), 30–34 (Gosling 1960).
50. Toynbee, *Making Popular Music*, p. 26.
51. Toynbee, *Making Popular Music*, p. 25.
52. Toynbee, *Making Popular Music*, pp. xi–xii.
53. P. York, *Style Wars* (London, 1980), p. 27 (York 1980).
54. L. Verrico, 'Are you talking to me?', *Dazed and Confused*, December 1998, pp. 56–60 (Verrico 1998).
55. Scritti Politti, '*Rock-A-Boy-Blue*', *Songs to Remember* (Rough Trade, 1982) (Scritti 1982).
56. Quoted in Reynolds, *Rip It Up*, p. 364.
57. Negus, *Music Genres and Corporate Cultures*, p. 178.
58. Sinfield, *Literature, Politics and Culture*, pp. 324–5.
59. Frith and Horne, *Art Into Pop*, p. 180.
60. Sinfield, *Literature, Politics and Culture in Postwar Britain*, p. 325
61. J. Savage, *England's Dreaming: Sex Pistols and Punk Rock* 2nd edn (London, 2005), p. 43 (Savage 2005).
62. T. Parsons and J. Hamblett, Leeds: Mill City', *NME*, 5 August 1978, pp. 7–8 (Parsons and Hamblett 1978).
63. See for example, S. Taylor, 'The popular press or how to roll your own records', *Time Out*, 2 February 1979 (Taylor 1979)_; P. Morley and A. Thrills, 'Independent discs', *NME*, 1 September 1979, p. 23 (Morley and Thrills 1979); C. Burkham, 'Cabaret Voltaire: Prepare to meet your Mecca', *Sounds*, 25 July 1981 (Burkham 1981); Anonymous, 'Scam', *City Fun*, 1 (7) (1979) (Anonymous 1979).
64. T. Gracyk, 'Kids're forming bands: Making meaning in post-punk', in *Punk & Post-Punk* 1 (1) (2011), 73–85 (p. 83) (Gracyk 2011).
65. Williams, *Marxism and Literature*, p. 117.
66. Williams, *Culture*, p. 86.
67. Reynolds, *Totally Wired* p. 408
68. Williams, *Culture*, p. 62.
69. J. Savage, 'Cabaret Voltaire', *Sounds*, 15 April 1978, pp. 16–17 (Savage 1978).
70. 'From the pressing plants to the concert halls, we want some control', *After Hours* fanzine, 1979.
71. O. Lowenstein, 'A Question Of Identity', *Sounds*, 19 August 1978, p. 21 (Lowenstein 1978).
72. Reynolds, *Rip It Up*, p. 212.

73. Reynolds, *Totally Wired*, p. 408.
74. Reynolds, *Rip It Up*, p. 93.
75. Williams, *Culture*, p. 70.
76. Milner, *Re-Imagining Cultural Studies*, p. 73.
77. Eagleton, *The Ideology of the Aesthetic*, p. 13.
78. Sinfield, *Literature, Politics and Culture*, p. 179.
79. Sinfield, *Literature, Politics and Culture*, p. 319.
80. Gosling, 'Dream boy'.
81. Sinfield, *Literature, Politics and Culture*, p. 193.
82. S. Ford, *Hip Priest: the Story of Mark E. Smith and The Fall* (London, 2003), pp. 14–15 (Ford 2003).
83. R. Middleton, *Studying Popular Music* (Milton Keynes, 1990), p. 247 (Middleton 1990).
84. Sinfield, *Literature, Politics and Culture*, p. 202.
85. Jim McGuigan, *Cool Capitalism* (London, 2009), p. 1 (McGuigan 2009).
86. Savage, *England's Dreaming*, p. 27.
87. Wilkinson, *Post-Punk, Politics and Pleasure*, pp. 37–67.
88. A. Davis, 'Preface: Marcuse's legacies', in Douglas Kellner (ed.), *Herbert Marcuse: The New Left and the 1960s* (London, 2005), p. vii (Davis 2005).
89. Davis, 'Preface: Marcuse's legacies', p. xiii.
90. The term is used in the sense of a 'vision of the future on which a civilisation bases its projects, establishes its ideal goals and builds its hopes', following Marcuse's friend and fellow New Left thinker André Gorz – see A. Gorz, *Critique of Economic Reason* (London, 1989) p. 8 (Gorz 1989).
91. Williams, *Marxism and Literature*, p. 212.
92. Williams, *Politics and Letters*, pp. 340–41.
93. H. Marcuse, *An Essay On Liberation* (Harmondsworth, 1972), p. 20 (Marcuse 1972b).
94. K. Marx, *Early Writings* (Harmondsworth, 1975), pp. 327–30 (Marx 1975).
95. Williams, *Marxism and Literature*, p. 212, and Marcuse, *Counterrevolution and Revolt* (Boston, 1972), p. 64 (Marcuse 1972a).
96. Gorz, *Critique of Economic Reason*, p. 22.
97. Williams, 'On reading Marcuse', *Cambridge Review*, 30 May 1969, pp. 366–88 (Williams 1969); P. Jones, *Raymond Williams' Sociology of Culture* (Basingstoke, 2004), p. 64 (Jones 2004).
98. Milner, *Re-Imagining Cultural Studies*, p. 8.
99. Marcuse, *Counterrevolution and Revolt*, p. 106.
100. Williams, *Towards 2000*, p. 18.
101. Williams, *Towards 2000*, pp. 146–7.
102. Williams, *Towards 2000*, p. 13.
103. Williams, *Towards 2000*, p. 14.

104. Milner, *Re-imagining Cultural Studies*, p. 64.
105. Williams, *Towards 2000*, p. 14.
106. H. Marcuse, 'Liberation from the affluent society', transcript of Marcuse's contribution to the Dialectics of Liberation conference, in *Herbert Marcuse: The New Left and the 1960s*, pp. 76–86 (p. 78).
107. R. Williams, 'Culture is ordinary', in *Resources of Hope*, p. 96.
108. R. Aronson, 'Marcuse today', *Boston Review*, 17 November 2014, available online at http://bostonreview.net/books-ideas/ronald-aronson-herbert-marcuse-one-dimensional-man-today [accessed 25 June 2015] (Aronson 2014).
109. Reynolds, *Rip It Up And Start Again*, p. xxv.
110. H. Pimlott, 'Militant entertainment? "Crisis music" and political ephemera in the emergent "structure of feeling", 1976–1983', in The Subcultures Network (eds.), *Fight Back: Punk, Politics and Resistance* (Manchester, 2015), pp. 268–86 (Pimlott 2015).
111. O. Lowenstein, *Dangerous Logic*, no. 1, 1978.
112. Williams, *Towards 2000*, pp. 10–11.
113. Williams, *Towards 2000*, p. 14.
114. Steve Walsh, 'Pop group mania', *NME*, 18 February 1978, p. 19 (Walsh 1978).
115. Max Bell, 'Idealists In distress', *NME*, 30 June 1979, pp. 24–7 (Bell 1979).

REFERENCES

T. Adorno, 'On the Fetish Character in Music and the Regression of Listening', in *The Culture Industry: Selected Essays on Mass Culture*, ed. J.M. Bernstein (London, 1991), pp. 33–5.

Alan Sinfield, *Literature, Politics and Culture in Postwar Britain*, 3rd edn (London, 2004).

Anonymous, 'Scam', *City Fun* 1, 7 (1979).

R. Aronson, 'Marcuse Today', *Boston Review*, 17 November 2014 available online at http://bostonreview.net/books-ideas/ronald-aronson-herbert-marcuse-one-dimensional-man-today [accessed 25 June 2015].

M. Bell, 'Idealists In distress', *NME*, 30 June 1979, pp. 24–7.

C. Burkham, 'Cabaret Voltaire: Prepare to meet your Mecca', *Sounds*, 25 July 1981.

A. Davis, 'Preface: Marcuse's Legacies', in *Herbert Marcuse: The New Left and the 1960s*, ed. Douglas Kellner (London, 2005) p. vii.

J. Doran, 'Interiority complex: Exploring Manchester's hinterlands with Lonelady', *Quietus*, 5 February 2015, http://thequietus.com/articles/17173-lonelady-interview-hinterland [accessed 26 July 2016].

D. Dworkin, *Cultural Marxism in Postwar Britain* (Durham, 1997), p. 163.

T. Eagleton, *The Ideology of the Aesthetic* (Oxford, 1990), p. 11.

S. Ford, *Hip Priest: the Story of Mark E. Smith and The Fall* (London, 2003), pp. 14–15.

S. Frith and H. Horne, *Art Into Pop* (London, 1987), pp. 51–52.

K. Gildart, 'From 'Dead End Streets' to 'Shangri Las': Negotiating Social Class and Post-War Politics with Ray Davies and the Kinks', in *Youth Culture, Popular Music and the End of 'Consensus'*, ed. The Subcultures Network (London, 2015), pp. 9–34 (p14).

T. Gitlin, 'The Anti-political Populism of Cultural Studies', in *Cultural Studies in Question*, ed. M. Ferguson and P. Golding (London, 1997), p. 27.

A. Gorz, *Critique of Economic Reason* (London, 1989), p. 8.

R. Gosling, 'Dream boy', *New Left Review*, 1 (3) (May–June 1960), 30–34.

T. Gracyk, 'Kids're Forming Bands: Making Meaning in Post-Punk', *Punk & Post-Punk*, 1,1 (2011), 73–85 (p. 83).

D. Hesmondhalgh, 'Post-Punk's Attempt to Democratise the Music Industry: The Success and Failure of Rough Trade', *Popular Music*, 16, 3 (1997 Oct), 255–74.

P. Jones, *Raymond Williams' Sociology of Culture* (Basingstoke, 2004), p. 64.

O. Lowenstein, 'A Question Of Identity', *Sounds*, 19 August 1978, p. 21.

H. Marcuse, *Counterrevolution and Revolt* (Boston, 1972a), p. 64.

H. Marcuse, *An Essay On Liberation* (Harmondsworth, 1972b), p. 20.

K. Marx, *Early Writings* (Harmondsworth, 1975), pp. 327–30.

Jim McGuigan, *Cool Capitalism* (London: Pluto, 2009), p. 1.

R. Middleton, *Studying Popular Music* (Milton Keynes, 1990), p. 247.

A. Milner, *Re-Imagining Cultural Studies: The Promise of Cultural Materialism* (London, 2002), p. 73.

P. Morley and A. Thrills, 'Independent discs', *NME*, 1 September 1979, p. 23.

F. Mulhern, *Culture/Metaculture* (London, 2000), p. xv.

K. Negus, *Popular Music In Theory* (Cambridge, 1996), p. 220.

K. Negus, *Music Genres and Corporate Cultures* (London, 1999), p. 151.

T. Parsons and J. Hamblett, Leeds: Mill City', *NME*, 5 August 1978, pp. 7–8.

H. Pimlott, 'Militant entertainment? 'Crisis music and political ephemera in the emergent 'structure of feeling', 1976–1983', in The Subcultures Network (eds.), *Fight Back: Punk, Politics and Resistance* (Manchester, 2015), pp. 268–86.

S. Reynolds, *Rip It Up and Start Again: Postpunk 1978–1984* (London, 2005), p. xxv.

S. Reynolds, *Totally Wired: Post-Punk Interviews and Overviews* (London, 2009), p. 431.

J. Savage, 'Cabaret Voltaire', *Sounds*, 15 April 1978, pp. 16–17.

J. Savage, *England's Dreaming: Sex Pistols and Punk Rock*, 2nd edn (London, 2005) p. 43.

Scritti Politti, 'Rock-A-Boy-Blue', *Songs to Remember* (Rough Trade, 1982).

A. Sinfield, *Faultlines: Cultural Materialism and the Politics of Dissident Reading* (Berkeley, 1992), p. 9.

S. Taylor, 'The popular press or how to roll your own records', *Time Out*, 2 February 1979.

J. Toynbee, *Making Popular Music: Musicians, Creativity and Institutions* (London, 2000), pp. x–xii.

L. Verrico, 'Are you talking to me?', *Dazed and Confused*, December 1998, pp. 56–60

S. Walsh, 'Pop group mania', *NME*, 18 February 1978, p. 19.

R. Williams, *Marxism and Literature* (Oxford, 1977), p. 110.

R. Williams, *Politics and Letters: Interviews With New Left Review* (London, 1979), pp.163–4.

Williams, *Culture* (Glasgow, 1981), pp. 33–56.

R. Williams, *Towards 2000* (London, 1983), pp. 145–6.

R. Williams, 'Culture Is Ordinary [1958]', in *Resources of Hope: Culture, Democracy, Socialism*, ed. R. Gable (London, 1989).

R. Williams, 'Base and Superstructure in Marxist Cultural Theory [1973]', in *Culture and Materialism* (London, 2005), p. 43.

R. Williams, 'On reading Marcuse', *Cambridge Review*, 30 May 1969, pp. 366–88.

P. Willis, *Profane Culture* (London, 1978), p. 93.

D. Wilkinson, *Post-Punk, Politics and Pleasure in Britain* (London, 2016).

P. York, *Style Wars* (London, 1980), p. 27.

David Wilkinson is Lecturer in English at Manchester Metropolitan University, UK. He has worked on the Leverhulme project 'Punk, Politics and British Youth Culture' and is the author of *Post-Punk, Politics and Pleasure in Britain* (2016).

CHAPTER 8

How to Forget (and Remember) 'The Greatest Punk Rock Band in the World': Bad Brains, Hardcore Punk and Black Popular Culture

Tara Martin Lopez and Michael Mills

On 24 June 1979, an unknown punk band opened for British musicians, the Damned, at a small venue in Washington, DC.[1] While the audience was expectantly waiting for the headliners, the frenetic and explosive opening act, Bad Brains, stole the show. One audience member remarked that the show was 'an absolute benchmark'. Punk rock icon, Henry Rollins, went so far as to say, 'Bad Brains blew the Damned with all their makeup and shit right off the stage.'[2]

What was even more remarkable about Bad Brains was that they were all Black musicians in what is commonly perceived as an all-White music genre. Band members Paul Hudson (or HR), Earl Hudson, Gary Miller (or Dr. Know) and Darryl Jenifer made Bad Brains central to the formation of American hardcore punk. Like first-wave punk, hardcore sought to define

T.M. Lopez (✉)
Department of Sociology, Peninsula College, Port Angeles, WA, USA
e-mail: TMartin@pencol.edu

M. Mills
Department of English, Peninsula College, Port Angeles, WA, USA
e-mail: MMills@pencol.edu

© The Author(s) 2017   175
K. Gildart et al. (eds.), *Youth Culture and Social Change*,
Palgrave Studies in the History of Subcultures and Popular Music,
DOI 10.1057/978-1-137-52911-4_8

itself in opposition to mainstream, feel good music, particularly pop, disco and stadium rock, with its perceived intricate musicianship, nine-minute songs, concept albums and bloated drum and guitar solos. Hardcore responded with short, fast, songs, simple chords and beats and biting lyrics that spoke to disaffected youth. The birth of hardcore was also the result of punks' disgust with new wave and the record industry's promotion of an inauthentic version of punk. The same punks harboured a certain degree of distrust for first-wave punk bands who inadvertently or otherwise brought punk to mainstream consciousness. While such bands remained heroes to many for their innovation in sound and attitude, hardcore punks found the Ramones' lyrics lacking in substance and the Sex Pistols' image to be excessively nihilistic.[3] The election of Ronald Reagan in 1980 and the conservative, neoliberal ascendancy throughout the 1980s, also created a sense of political urgency, especially in Washington, DC. Therefore, bands like Bad Brains and Minor Threat made personal and social change central to their message. Consequently, the resulting music and subculture of hardcore thrived in the underground, operating with a 'Do It Yourself' (DIY) mentality, progressive left-wing politics, and attempting to keep itself at arm's length from popular culture and the music industry.[4]

Nevertheless, the images of bands like Minor Threat and Black Flag have emblazoned a specific visage of hardcore punk on collective memory, that of alienated White male youth. Some White punk musicians were the first to perpetuate this idea. When interviewed in 1979, for instance, Johnny Ramone from the Ramones asserted that they were 'playing pure rock & roll with no blues or folk or any of that stuff in it'.[5] That singular and isolated idea stuck, and in 1986 journalist Mykel Board proclaimed that 'punk was the first white music since the 1960s psychedelic stuff'.[6] Charlie Brinkhurst-Cuff critically summarises the overall shape of this hegemonic understanding of history when he writes: 'Like many facets of pop culture, [punk's] historical image has been whitewashed: when you think of punk's history, it's bands like the Clash, the Sex Pistols, and the Ramones that spring to mind.'[7]

Despite the prevalence of this dominant image of punk, among musicians and fans, a powerful undercurrent of memory exists that attests to the undeniably formative influence of Bad Brains. Anthrax guitarist, Scott Ian, is frank when he states, 'The Bad Brains invented hardcore, not Black Flag or Fear. Those bands ruled as well, but they didn't have the density of the Bad Brains.'[8] Obviously, the explosiveness of these upstart punks was not momentary, but for many, Bad Brains had an integral, transformative and long-lasting role in the creation of hardcore punk. Therefore, our aim is to situate Bad Brains in hardcore punk rock history not as an anomaly or a side note, but as an essential force. More importantly, our study will look beyond the late 1970s and early 1980s to the present, and to the memory of Bad Brains and its importance to punks of colour. We will demonstrate that since 2000, a flood of texts, both written and visual, remembering Bad Brains and reclaiming their space in the hardcore punk rock pantheon have appeared. By analysing documentaries, books, zines and interviews, we will argue that these recent excavations represent George Lipsitz's understanding of 'counter-memory'. According to Lipsitz groups like women and African Americans have been ignored in dominant narratives of history. In order to defy such universalising forces that obliterate the traces of subordinate groups' histories, such marginalised groups focus on their localised experiences and engage in a form of remembering that reconstructs history to re-incorporate into collective memory that which was previously obscured. By reassessing common understandings of hardcore punk, new avenues of possibility emerge, especially for punks of colour. As Lipsitz writes, 'socially created divisions appear natural and inevitable unless we can tell stories that illustrate the possibility of overcoming unjust divisions'.[9] Hence, the history of hardcore punk as a White male institution has prevailed in collective memory. By contrast, we will demonstrate that using Bad Brains as a focal point of counter-memory creates possibilities of legacy and belonging within the American hardcore scene for Black punks and other punks of colour.

'BIG TAKEOVER' – THE MARGINALISATION OF THE BLACK EXPERIENCE IN PUNK STUDIES

Maria Wiedlack has observed that 'punk history writing continues the oblivion of representations and politics by people of color'.[10] Such 'oblivion of representations' is especially indicative of the marginalisation of the Black experience generally, and Bad Brains' role in the development of hardcore and punk specifically, which has proliferated throughout scholarly accounts in punk studies.

Such erasures from academic studies appear in sweeping accounts of US social and cultural history. In Jefferson Cowie's recent history of 1970s America, for example, he bemoans how, unlike punk in the UK, punk in the United States 'lacked a conscious infusion of black musical traditions'.[11] Even in accounts which recognise that traditions in Black culture shaped punk rock, mention of Black bands in the scene are conspicuously absent. For instance, although Steven Taylor adamantly rejects the 'absurd notion that punk is purely white music' in his ethnography of punk, his chapter titled 'Hardcore' about the Washington, DC, hardcore scene, makes no mention of Bad Brains.[12] Even more problematic are authors' brief mentions of Bad Brains without addressing broader racialised, gendered and classed inequities that are reflected in punk. Many texts briefly note, or footnote, Bad Brains or include singular photographs of the band. When such authors frame the band as 'four black guys in an all-white world',[13] the texts' trivial treatment of the subject is essentially writing the Black presence out of punk rock. Their existence becomes a novelty or an eclectic addition to an institution assumed to be all-White.[14] Such conspicuous omissions provide the academic foundation upon which more widespread myths of punk as 'White music' have been built.[15]

This chapter challenges such nonchalant dismissals. Not only does Bad Brains' stature in punk refute such assertions, but erroneous claims that rock and punk are exclusively White forms restrict this space of cultural expression from Black musicians and fans. Mainstream collective memory embraced the idea that rock music was a White endeavour, admiring Elvis and the Beatles despite the fact that both acts readily recognised and often cited the debts they owned to Black musicians. As mainstream Whites assumed ownership of rock, many Blacks distanced themselves. Ike Willis, who played guitar and toured with Frank Zappa, notes the most pernicious effects of such racially homogeneous portrayals of rock and punk. Willis reflects:

> In the black community I became even more of an oddball as the years went on because of the fact that the images and the politics being perpetrated on television and radio and commercials and magazines as rock n roll becoming more and more perceived in the black community as a white thing.[16]

Willis echoes the effects of erasing Blacks from punk: rock and punk become inextricably intertwined with Whiteness. Using perceptions of Bad Brains as the starting point of our analysis, the facile depictions of the exclusively White origins of punk quickly reveal themselves to be inaccurate. The more troublesome fact remains that such perceptions serve to perpetuate racialised forms of exclusion in punk today. Therefore, the experiences of Black musicians and fans are central to our analysis, revealing that Black punks have a claim to the development of punk, both historically and in the present day.

While Black influences and the issue of race as a whole were sidelined in accounts of American punk, they were a central focus of research in British punk. In Dick Hebdige's *Subculture: The Meaning of Style*, he argued that reggae and race relations constituted a 'present absence' in punk. According to Hebdige the 'rigid demarcation' that developed between punk and reggae reflected broader divisions and tensions between Black British and White working-class culture.[17] Gilroy further situated the rise of punk in 1970s Britain and asserted that Black dissent, like that of the 1976 Notting Hill Carnival riot, not only coincided with the rise of punk, but such an 'uncompromising statement of black dissent' became 'a source of envy and of inspiration to a fledgling punk sensibility'.[18] Therefore, in contrast to many American accounts of punk, Hebdige and Gilroy implied that the image at the heart of punk identity, that of the rebel, was inspired by Blacks in Britain, which is helpful in reaffirming our focus on the centrality of race relations and Black culture. Nevertheless, their focus on punk and reggae as two distinct entities reaffirms an association of Whiteness with one and Blackness with the other, sidelining those individuals who crossed the resulting imaginary borders. As Elizabeth Stinson concisely observes, such bifurcation, 'hangs on fetishization of the black other and places punk in a production line of whiteness'.[19]

Furthermore, such accounts have also been criticised for ignoring forms of racism that were rooted in punk's origins. Sabin, for instance, argues that British punk's association with Rock Against Racism forever tied the image of punk to left-wing politics, when, in reality, very problematic forms of racism were deeply embedded in its music and subculture.[20] In the United States, one of the most biting criticisms in this same vein came from Daniel Traber. In his work, he accuses Los Angeles punk of critiquing forms of racial and class exclusion, while, in the process, becoming an 'agent' of such oppression and claims that 'its rejection of the dominant culture relies on adopting the stereotypes of inferior, violent, and criminal nonwhites'.[21]

While such accounts have been important lines of criticism in illuminating the limits of punk, the result, nevertheless, can be an essentialised understanding of White and Black popular culture and a lack of awareness of the dynamism of such forms of cultural expression. Hall notes the corrosive effects of such essentialism:

> The essentializing moment is weak because it naturalizes and de-historicizes difference, mistaking what is historical and cultural for what is natural, biological, and genetic. The moment the signifier 'black' is torn from its historical, cultural, and political embedding ... we valorize, by inversion, the very ground of the racism we are trying to deconstruct.[22]

Hall emphasises that there are no intrinsic traits among these groups that create inviolable lines of 'authentic' cultural expression.[23] Gilroy's concept of 'anti-anti-essentialism', provides a force of theoretical equilibrium between the extremes of exceptionalism, which views punk as a force of absolute exclusion, and pluralism, which sees borders as more fluid. Gilroy specifically references Bad Brains in the terrain of this debate.

> The brand of elitism which would, for example, advance the white noise of Washington D.C.'s Rasta thrash punk band the Bad Brains as the last word in black cultural expression is clearly itching to abandon the ground of the black vernacular entirely.[24]

While it is important to not impose limiting definitions of what is and is not Black cultural expression, that understanding must be tempered with an overarching understanding of the historical and contemporary exclusions and inequalities that are particular to Blacks in the United States, UK and Caribbean.

While re-incorporating the Black experience into narratives of punk, the invisibility of women in most of these accounts is also glaringly obvious. McRobbie was one of the first academics to criticise punk studies for its sole focus on men. McRobbie noted that women in subcultures were often seen in the role of girlfriend or groupie, ignoring the creative ways young women developed subcultural identities, oftentimes in domestic rather than public spaces.[25] A concern for a gendered analysis further leads us to unpack other forms of invisibility. Patricia Hill Collins' concept of intersectionality can frame the complexity of marginalisation and privilege Bad Brains experienced as a band. Instead of seeing race, class, gender and sexuality as separate hierarchies, intersectionality urges researchers to see how they all 'mutually construct' one another.[26] Therefore, while we will argue that Bad Brains' exclusion from dominant narratives was highly racialised, it is important that as an all-male band, Bad Brains were able to operate within a highly masculine and sometimes physically violent, male-dominated music scene.

The efforts of academics have culminated in recent research that embraces a more complex understanding of the Black experience in punk and reveals the significance of Bad Brains. One the most notable is Duncombe and Tremblay's *White Riot: Punk and the Politics of Race*, which interrogates hierarchies of race, class, gender and sexuality, while simultaneously highlighting the crucial role Blacks, queers and women played in the development of punk, both as musicians and fans.[27] Scholarly investigations of Bad Brains have also begun to appear. Maskell, for instance, has explored Bad Brains and the concept of memory. She contends that Bad Brains established their own identities as musicians through performances that simultaneously 'forgot' the association of punk with Whiteness and 'reremember[ed] the sociohistorical roots of black rock'n'roll'.[28] Duncombe, Tremblay and Maskell provide essential corrections to the dominant myth of a racially homogenous punk rock, while at the same time, challenging hierarchies intertwined in punk.

This chapter contributes to this literature by examining how Bad Brains were integral to the development of American hardcore punk. Therefore, part one of this chapter examines Bad Brains' influence on hardcore in the United States and their relationship to British punk. While cognisant of the White, heterosexual and male-dominated nature of punk, we frame race, gender and class as social constructs that are powerful in resulting manifestations of solidarity and exclusion, but we reaffirm Bad Brains' guitarist Darryl Jenifer's assertion that punk 'is black expression'.[29] We establish the legacy of Bad Brains in hardcore and set forth how, especially since 2000, books and films have underlined the importance of Bad Brains to a wider audience. We focus on Black punks and how their counter-memory of Bad Brains has allowed them to re-imagine a space for themselves in punk rock. We situate Bad Brains and their status as the 'Greatest Punk Rock Band in the World' in a twenty-first century context.

'BANNED IN DC' – BAD BRAINS IN 1970s WASHINGTON, DC AND BEYOND

Bad Brains' singular genius reflected the distinctive character of Washington, DC at the time. Although other northern metropolitan areas with majority Black populations existed, the numbers in DC far surpassed those of its counterparts. While Gary, Indiana, was 53 per cent Black, and Newark, New Jersey, was 54 per cent Black in 1970, Blacks made up 71 per cent of the population of Washington, DC.[30]

Hopkinson notes that its large population of Blacks earned DC the moniker 'Chocolate City' in the mid-1970s.[31] The 'middle-class flight' in the DC area created 'two different places in the nation's capital', one of a predominantly White, suburban class and another of urban, Black DC residents.[32] Although 92 per cent of Whites in Washington, DC moved to the suburbs, the city also experienced the highest rate of Black suburbanisation in the United States. From 1970 to 1980, the Black population in Washington suburbs increased from 23 per cent to 46 per cent.[33]

Bad Brains emerged from this process of Black suburbanisation. Paul Hudson (HR), Bad Brains' vocalist, and his brother, Earl Hudson, the band's drummer, were raised in District Heights, a primarily Black suburb in Prince George's County. The Hudsons' father had retired from the Air Force by the time the family settled in District Heights, where they lived close to Gary Miller (Dr Know) and Darryl Jenifer, the future Bad Brains' guitarist and bass player. The members of Bad Brains represented a marginal Black middle class that was a particularly distinct feature of the area.[34]

In the mid-1970s, DC was also a hotbed of musical creativity and the heart of the 'go-go' music movement. As a musical genre influenced by Caribbean music, 'go-go' has been compared to hip hop, funk and reggae.[35] Darryl Jenifer described the members' early interest in progressive jazz rock and later interest in punk: 'We wanted to make our music progressive. It was the norm to do the funk and the "go-go". For some reason, I didn't want to be normal!'[36] HR, Earl Hudson, Dr Know and Darryl Jenifer went in a different direction, forming a short-lived jazz-fusion band called 'Mind Power'. Early band member, Sid McCray, is credited with introducing the other members to punk records. With a focus on becoming a punk band, the four musicians formed Bad Brains in 1977.[37]

Most punk music was loud, fast and relatively simple. It was not uncommon for untrained musicians to pick up instruments for the first time and start bands. By comparison, Dr Know, Earl Hudson and Darryl Jenifer were technically accomplished musicians, and HR had an astonishing vocal range. Kory Grow of *Spin* magazine writes, 'Add to that almost-Buddhist, life-is-suffering worldview the fact that Bad Brains could actually play their instruments virtuosically – anathema to the punk spirit of the time – and you had a band operating on a previously unexplored plane.'[38] With these skills they took the attitude and anti-pop sentiment of bands like the Sex Pistols, the Dead Boys and the Damned and honed their own resulting style with faster, tighter, more technically complex songs. They innovated the form further by blending punk and reggae songs into one coherent stage experience. With HR engaging the audience by rolling on the floor, doing backflips and tackling audience members, fans who were drawn to already wild behaviour and music at punk shows knew instantly that they had never seen anything like Bad Brains.[39]

According to Crossley, physical, creative and emotional spaces were central to the evolution of punk.[40] Bad Brains played significant roles in elements of punk space, particularly in two major hardcore scenes: DC and New York, where they lived briefly after being 'banned' by clubs in DC. Maskell argues that this ban was enough to push the band into underground venues: house parties and abandoned buildings, which ultimately resulted in furthering their engaging performance style and attitude due to the lack of a stage to separate the musicians from the audience.[41] Their kinetic stage presence changed the physical experience of punk shows, as evidenced by Henry Rollins' quote, 'that was the start of my life' referring to seeing Bad Brains open for The Damned, when HR pinned Rollins to the ground and sang in his face.[42] Their performances became so infamous by 1982, that journalist Greg Tate stated, 'virtually anybody who cares will tell you that Chocolate City's hardcore scene begins with the Brains'.[43]

As Crossley suggests, emotional space was also an important ingredient for evolving punk scenes. Arguably, Bad Brains had a major impact on the emotional space of the DC and New York scenes. While the band's early live performances seem, at first, to be even more violent than those of first-wave punk bands like the Sex Pistols or the Ramones, upon closer inspection, the band's struggle for positive change, and specifically their emphasis on 'PMA', or 'Positive Mental Attitude', are a logical precursor to one of the largest splinter subcultures within punk: straightedge, which happened to be founded by Ian MacKaye of Minor Threat, one of the young DC punks HR referred to as 'my undergraduates'.[44] Whereas the Sex Pistols' message was 'No Future', DC punk was built on the premise that music could make a difference. As one journalist reflected in the 1980s on the influence of Bad Brains' Rastafarianism: 'The straight-edge punk of early DC mates Minor Threat was the Protestant mirror of the Brains' Rastafarianism and each band articulated a hard ass conviction with more than a touch of the puritan zealot.'[45] 'PMA' eventually began to instill in hardcore a distinctive DIY ethos that shaped the way fans viewed punk. John Joseph from Cro-Mags notes that he was initially drawn to punk because, 'it was about getting fucked up and breaking shit up', but for Joseph, 'Bad Brains were someone who could provide spiritual insight to the music without being preachy'.[46] Maria Wiedlack asserts that this was the crucial component of Bad Brains' significance. According to Wiedlack, Bad Brains 'established the cultural meaning [of] punk rock as a political act'.[47]

Marginalisation within both the White and Black communities constricted Bad Brains' claim to such space. In addition to the association of the term 'punk' with homosexuality in the Black community, Bad Brains also became outcasts because they were associated with 'White' music and subculture. Neither did White audiences fully accept them. At the first show they played, Bad Brains endured racial epithets and threats.[48] HR remembers, 'Because of their stereotypes, sometimes smart alecks would come to the shows and be saying "Aww, get these niggers off the stage. They don't know what the hell they are doing." And they'd throw beer bottles at us and spit on us.'[49] Aaron Thompson suggests that being ostracised from so many social settings made Bad Brains 'doubly punk' because they 'were not traditionally accepted by many African-Americans as sufficiently Black because of their music, style, and image, yet their blackness prevented them from being accepted as fully punk in some circles'.[50] Therefore, marginalisation from both within and outside the punk rock scene limited entry into the fertile ground of freedom and creativity that punk rock could provide.

Bad Brains' struggle for space can also be seen as transcending national boundaries. Gilroy posits that Black British culture cannot be seen in isolation, but the connections among Black British, Black American and African Caribbean cultures must be seen as, 'an intricate web of cultural and political connections [that] bind[s] blacks here [in the UK] to blacks elsewhere. At the same time, they are linked to the social relations in this country'.[51] Therefore, Bad Brains can be seen in this broader geographical and cultural space, which reflects the 'intricate web' Gilroy refers to as 'the black Atlantic'.[52]

Bad Brains' musical trajectory mirrored wider transatlantic currents of punk, but did so in ways that were distinctive in a 'Black Atlantic' context. American punk bands like the Dead Boys and the Ramones were pivotal to the band's transition from jazz-rock to punk. Nevertheless, British punk was a key catalyst. HR said of their time in Mind Power, 'We wanted to innovate… We wanted to be part of something new and different and real. And then I saw the Sex Pistols album, and I said, "BOOM! This is it!"'[53]

British punk also influenced Bad Brains' performances. The anti-racist Rock Against Racism festivals in the UK, for instance, featuring bands like X-Ray Spex and the Clash, inspired HR to use Bad Brains' music and performance as a sonic assault with a social purpose. He wanted 'punk rockers to step out of the embrace of the downtown art scene and take it to the streets'. This concept was realised in September 1979 with their own Rock Against Racism show in the middle of the Valley Green housing project in Washington Highlands, one of the poorest parts of the DC area. Such confident expressions of this PMA or DIY attitude, once again, reveal the profound way that Bad Brains affected the ethos of hardcore. One audience member said about this specific performance: 'The very fact that these shows happened at all changed the memories, and in some small and large ways the lives, of some of the people who witnessed them. A small seed can grow strong in the heart of a young person.'[54]

The band's eventual embrace of Rastafarianism deepened such transnational connections. While it was the Clash that first exposed Bad Brains to reggae, it was attending a Bob Marley concert in 1982 that proved transformative.[55] For Bad Brains, reggae was the anti-racist combination of the musical styles of reggae and punk, 'one that's African and one that's American, the two of them revolutionary'.[56] Despite hardcore fans' negative and/or lukewarm response to Bad Brains' reggae, the band continued to play punk shows and retained a devoted following. A review of Bad Brains' 1982 album in the *Damaged Goods* zine is indicative of the begrudging acceptance punks gave to the band's reggae.

> Their music sounds powerful, coming across better than it does live. The songs are short and to the point leaving little room for self-indulgence. The only real indulgence is in the reggae, which (thankfully) [is] kept short, except for, 'I Love Jah.' The reggae sounds fine, but it comes across as inferior to the rest of the music.[57]

Bad Brains' mark on UK punk is unclear. After Bad Brains' explosive opening for the Damned, they invited Bad Brains to tour with them throughout the UK. That plan did not succeed, because, on arrival at Heathrow, customs searched the band and their crew and found an empty vial of cocaine on one of the techs, and they were then forced to return to the United States.[58]

Bad Brains were eventually able to tour the UK. During an interview with Black American punk, Aaron Thompson, in 2016, he noted that it was his British ex-girlfriend who originally exposed him to Bad Brains' music.[59] British filmmaker and DJ Don Letts was also aware of Bad Brains, but in a distinctly American context. Letts asserts: 'Bad Brains are the Sex Pistols of America. What the Sex Pistols did for the UK scene, Bad Brains undoubtedly did for the American scene.'[60]

In many ways it was Bad Brains' influence that, in part, made hardcore, in the words of Henry Rollins, 'as American as fake wars, apple pies, and baseball'.[61] It was especially the DIY ethos, upon which Bad Brains made such a profound mark, that set hardcore apart and 'reimagined British punk rock'.[62] When Bad Brains left jazz to embrace punk, the band members designed clothes. HR notes, 'That was the thing that was so great about punk when we first discovered it. You made your music, you made your clothes, you created your whole thing.'[63]

In addition to creating sites of independent creativity, Bad Brains and others infused their music with a message that saw punk as a serious conduit of social change. In Bad Brains' song 'Supertouch', this sense of efficacy is tangible. Their development was steeped in a broader socio-political context that was limited by factors such as race and class. Nevertheless, the site of energy and creativity that punk provided allowed Bad Brains to flourish and play a transformative role in American hardcore.

'RIGHT BRIGADE' – THE LEGACY OF BAD BRAINS

While dominant narratives have neglected punks of colour like Bad Brains through a shared assumption that hardcore was inherently a White, middle-class endeavour, from roughly 2000, members of the hardcore scene took a more active role in publicising their own history. This is a history in which Bad Brains existed not as a footnote, but as a foundational element. Lending their voices to a number of books, documentary films, articles and academic works, well-known figures in independent music have forced a wider audience to reconsider generally accepted views of punk.

One of the first thorough accounts to reaffirm the presence of Blacks in the punk rock scene by documenting the importance of Bad Brains' influence emerged in a very punk rock way: through a zine. James Porter and Jake Austen's series of articles about the influence of Blacks in punk, new wave and hardcore emerged in 2002. They note how 'punk rock might have represented another wave of ethnic cleansing in Rock & Roll'. They argued that Blacks did play a transformative role in the development of punk. In particular, they note how Bad Brains was '*perhaps* the most important hardcore band ever'.[64]

Documentaries such as *Bad Brains: A Band in D.C.*, released in 2012, began to echo this same message. In the film, Henry Rollins directly speaks to the issue of memory, while pointing to the significance of Bad Brains. About the album, *Black Dots*, Rollins noted:

> The record was never a record in those days. Had the Bad Brains pressed 1,000 LPs of that tape, that single album would have been determinant in what's known as American hardcore music and American independent music, and it wouldn't have taken until the new century for a documentary on that band to come out.[65]

One of the key histories of the DC hardcore scene, written by Mark Andersen and Mark Jenkins, *Dance of Days: Two Decades of Punk in the Nation's Capital*, also underlines the significance of Bad Brains in the development of American hardcore. In addition to dedicating a significant amount of content to Bad Brains, their music, their performance and their impact on punk, both editions of this book feature the band on their covers. In the 2001 and 2003 editions, three of the most prominent DC punk bands are pictured together: Bad Brains, Fugazi and Bikini Kill. On the cover of the 2009 edition, however, a picture of HR from Bad Brains provides the entire backdrop to the title of the book.

From 2001, with the publication of three editions of *Dance of Days*, each of which prominently feature Bad Brains, three key currents can be observed. Firstly, Andersen and Perkins focus on negative aspects of Bad Brains' experience in punk, detailing the hostile reception they met in the scene for being Black.[66] Secondly, in an overall movement of counter-memory, the timing of the publication of the book in 2001 coincides with the broader current of work to remember Bad Brains' contributions to American hardcore. Finally, the increasing centrality of Bad Brains on the cover art for the various editions of the book, underscores what we will later observe as an intensified movement to reclaim their position in punk.

In a 2013 book of photographs of the early DC punk rock scene by *Washington Post* photographer Lucian Perkins, a picture of Bad Brains is featured on the cover. The book, *Hard Art*, not only represents this push to account for punk rock history, but also by placing a photo of them on the cover, provides a visual representation of counter-memory that re-establishes Bad Brains' importance. The collection of photographs chronicles three shows in 1979 and one in early 1980 and includes photographs of four bands: Trenchmouth, the Slickee Boys, Bad Brains and the Teen Idles. Of its roughly 72 featured photographs, 25 are of Bad Brains, 25 are of the other bands combined and 22 are of audience members.[67]

Increased academic attention to punk, and to Bad Brains in particular, also began to intensify after 2000. One of the most notable works was Duncombe and Tremblay's *White Riot: Punk Rock and the Politics of Race*. The anthology looks beyond facile representations, and sets out to illuminate not only the racialised, classed and gendered limits of punk, but also how punks of colour provided an essential contribution to the scene. Duncombe and Tremblay assert, '[b]lack musical and cultural forms, whether embraced or rejected, have been part of punk since its beginnings'.[68]

The text acknowledges diversity within punk history, while the cover of the book counterposes a picture of HR appearing to sing almost exclusively to a White, female audience member. By contrast, the cover of *Hard Art* shows HR singing to a mixed audience, directly in front of a White youth. Ironically, both are photographs by Lucian Perkins of the same performance. The choice of covers reveal that while the authors of *Dance of Days* are attempting to document a comprehensive and racially and gender inclusive history of hardcore, the editors accomplish this goal, but also problematise the racial dynamics of punk and hardcore.

In 2014, the first history of the band emerged with Prato's self-published, *Punk! Hardcore! Reggae! PMA! Bad Brains!* This account primarily focuses on Bad Brains' history, including interviews with musicians who attest to the band's influence. The fact that the book was self-published attests to the continuing struggle of Bad Brains to fully ascend to the heights of punk rock notoriety. The majority of the musicians interviewed for the book were White males, which inadvertently reaffirms punk's association with Whiteness, even in a text devoted to Black musicians.[69]

Overall, in contrast to the dominant memory of punk, musicians like Ian MacKaye and Henry Rollins, filmmakers like Mandy Stein and authors like Andersen and Prato represent Lipsitz's 'counter-memory' as a new understanding of punk emergence by reclaiming Bad Brains in the twenty-first century.

'I AGAINST I' – COUNTER-MEMORY AND BLACK SPACE IN HARDCORE PUNK

The recent focus on Bad Brains is not just trivia to add to scenesters' punk rock points or fuel for academic scholarship, but it represents a deeper significance as counter-memory for punks of colour. While Black punks' counter-memory brings about an awareness of exclusions and erasures, it also allows them to 'illumine opportunities'[70] of belonging, space and identification with the subculture. Punk, as a site of emotional and creative acceptance continues to be of particular struggle and significance for Blacks. Tasha Fierce observes:

> The idea of punk rock as some kind of beacon of open-mindedness is bullshit. Most white punk rockers like to consider themselves absolved of their privilege simply because they publicly denounce racism and don't attend weekly KKK meetings.[71]

Fierce identifies with punk, but illustrates the contours of experience for those subcultural participants or fans who cross these lines. When she does cross into this predominantly White space, race continues to shape how others see her and her place in the scene. Zinester and punk, Osa Atoe, describes a similar sense of frustration when at different shows, in different cities, she was mistaken for other Black punks. She writes: 'We all don't look alike... Thanks everyone for making me feel completely not at home in my community.'[72]

Therefore, if, as punk and zinester, Yumii Thecato, writes, it is incumbent upon Black punks to 'separate punk from whiteness',[73] the counter-memory of Bad Brains allows for this process to occur, and Whiteness can begin to be decoupled from punk. Their effect on a generation of Black musicians began to appear in the 1980s and 90s. Angelo Moore, the lead singer of Fishbone, reflects:

> Originally, I was a hip-hop kid with a Jheri curl, a green metallic suit from Merry-Go-Round. I had appeared as a dancer in the movie *Breakin'*. When I first heard the Bad Brains, I thought, 'Those White boys are bad!' When I found out they were black, my world just stopped.[74]

Remembering Bad Brains in the history of punk and hardcore has been especially important for Black punks. In the 2010 zine *A terrible, horrible, no good, very bad life # 2,* author Kisha Hope reflects on her own connection to the band:

> The first band I fell in love with was Bad Brains. Bad Brains blew my mind because they played hard, they played fast, and they looked just like me. ... HR is a creepy homophobic jerk and I don't really care for his politics, but those early records seriously changed my life, and I cannot ever deny that.[75]

Hope demonstrates how a claim to Bad Brains allows her to re-remember punk rock in a manner in which she can fully see herself as a part of the subculture.

Tasha Hairston, aka 'Tasha Fierce', who wrote zines about punk as a teenager, is more reticent in her acclaim for Bad Brains. As she developed a punk identity, she knew about Bad Brains, but did not listen to them because she preferred female singers. When listening to male singers, she reflected, 'What are you revolting against?' She explains further: 'Even though, Bad Brains, I know that they're not white dudes, I like having space for women. There are no black women at all.'[76] Hairston reminds us that the counter-memory of Bad Brains must be seen through Patricia Hill Collins' intersectional lens: while Bad Brains creates space for Blacks in punk rock, the band's presence makes the absence of Black women in many punk scenes all the more conspicuous.[77]

Although Black punks of both sexes were substantially fewer in number than their White counterparts, they have always been a part of the scene. While mainstream collective memory may overlook their experiences and contributions, the Black punk community has turned a critical eye to the Whitewashing of punk history since 2000. One of the most notable examples of this is the 2003 documentary, *Afro-Punk.* The documentary follows the lives of four Black punk rockers and includes a multitude of interviews. The film also features performances by acts like Cipher, Tamar Kali and Bad Brains.[78] James Spooner, the director of *Afro-Punk* and organiser of the annual Afro-Punk festival, expresses his own personal struggle with dualities as a 'biracial kid' and a punk: 'That day I was asked to make a choice: punk or black. I'm biracial, black and white; I was born into duality.'[79] In his search to negotiate these dualities, Spooner is also part of a larger movement to reconcile issues of racism and identity. In the process of staking claim to this counter-memory, a space for his own identity emerges: 'In 2001, I picked up a camera and I talked with every black punk in pre-social-network America I could find. I found eighty, and I found myself.'[80]

His documentary follows a similar trajectory of what he calls 'self-validation'.[81] Forty-five minutes into the film, a segment on Bad Brains appears where Black punks emphasise the crucial importance of the band, not only to the development of punk and hardcore, but, more importantly, to creating a sense of belonging for punks of colour. The interviewees express a sense of awe at Bad Brains' talent. EWOLF, says, 'Bad Brains was probably the best punk band to ever exist.' Another interviewee, Ryan Bland, excitedly proclaims, 'It [Bad Brains] was the angriest, most violent punk shit I've ever heard.'[82]

Underlying all of this is an apparent force of counter-memory. Several interviewees express how the presence of Bad Brains in punk made their place in the scene all the more legitimate. Scottie asserts that, 'We're definitely important to it because a lot of us started some of the ground breaking stuff, like we've got Bad Brains... you know.' Djinji Brown notes, '[h]aving the Bad Brains ... That shit made me feel like, yeah, I'm supposed to be here.'[83]

Scottie and Brown powerfully pinpoint a central current of developing a counter-memory of punk rock through the lens of Bad Brains. Lipsitz argues that counter-memory 'focuses on localized experiences with oppression, using them to reframe and refocus dominant narratives purporting to represent universal experience'.[84] These interviews challenge the universalising assumptions of hardcore punk as all White and, instead, reveal a force of counter-memory that refocuses and reimagines punk as something more inclusive.

Spooner's film, *Afro-Punk*, ends by asking AfricanAmerican punks to name bands with Black members. It is both an ironic and a poignant moment in the film, as the interviewees seem momentarily stumped. Watching this, initially a viewer might believe that the dominant narrative is accurate. But then something wonderful happens, and the punks begin to list musicians and bands, finally rattling off a long list, including: Pure Hell, the Dead Kennedys, Fishbone, Burn, No Redeeming Social Value, Suicidal Tendencies, Cro-mags and, tellingly, one of only a small handful of bands that is mentioned more than once, the Bad Brains.

'SALIN' ON' – THE GREATEST PUNK ROCK BAND IN THE
TWENTY-FIRST CENTURY

Almost forty years after Bad Brains made their explosive debut in 1979, much about the world from which they emerged has changed, yet much has remained the same. The DC metro area still ranks as one of the most highly segregated areas in the United States[85] despite the fact that segregation there has decreased somewhat since the 1970s, and Blacks now make up only 49 per cent of the population and Whites 38 per cent.[86] Coates points out that Bad Brains' suburban home of Prince George's County continued to be 'a great enclave of black people'.[87] Although DC has maintained its importance as a centre of vibrant Black culture, collective memory surrounding Bad Brains' importance has continued to evolve.

Yet, despite increased academic and popular interest in the band, Bad Brains remain stranded at the economic margins of hardcore punk. As vociferously as Ian MacKaye and Henry Rollins attest to Bad Brains' genius and influence, MacKaye has a reported approximate net worth of $5 million[88] and Rollins is worth roughly $13 million.[89] Many punk musicians can be found on the same celebrity net worth database: Jello Biafra of the Dead Kennedys and Mike Muir of Suicidal Tendencies, for example, are on the lower end of the spectrum and are of comparable stature to Bad Brains in terms of punk rock history. Yet none of the members of Bad Brains even appear on the database. Earlier this year, the band began crowdsourcing funds for their bandmate, Gary Miller, who suffered a heart attack. The funds were necessary because he did not have medical insurance.[90]

Such stark economic indicators, nevertheless, do not negate the importance of Bad Brains as a catalyst for counter-memory. Bad Brains' role in the development of hardcore punk challenges not only the supposed 'authentic Whiteness' of this music and subculture, but also raises questions of 'authentic' Black cultural expression. As bell hooks reminds us, the process of challenging essentialism:

> allows us to affirm multiple black identities, varied black experience. It also challenges colonial imperialist paradigms of black identity which represent blackness one-dimensionally in ways that reinforce and sustain white supremacy. This discourse created the idea of the 'primitive' and promoted the notion of an 'authentic' experience, seeing as 'natural' those expressions of black life which conformed to a pre-existing pattern or stereotype.[91]

Hooks' observation resonates strongly with how Black punks have used Bad Brains as a prism through which to defy such one-dimensional representations. Furthermore, it underlines the power of Lipsitz's counter-memory to 'draw upon the oppositional cultural practice'[92] of Bad Brains' music to carve out a rightful place for the band in the history of hardcore.

Darryl Jenifer for decades has asserted that punk was 'black expression'.[93] We have argued that in the effort to establish a counter-memory of American hardcore punk from 2000 to 2015, Jenifer's insight has come to fruition for a generation of punks of colour. In May of 2016, the *Washington Post* reported a revival of the hardcore scene in DC. Journalist Chris Richards described this new manifestation as 'pioneered by Bad Brains and popularized by Minor Threat', but with a more inclusive attitude towards punks of colour. Rob Watson, one current hardcore musician, describes how he felt comfortable in the scene when he saw that he was not the only Black person in the room. He also notes, 'now there are all these bands with queer people, women and people of color, and they're making music for people like them'.[94]

Bad Brains' fierce originality, their spasmodic and serene stage presence, their struggle to promote positive social change and their refusal to see musical styles as necessitating racial delineation, have had far-reaching impacts on generations of fans, punks and musicians. As a seminal hardcore band, they are collectively remembered from within the punk subculture, particularly since 2000, in a way that has radiated out with ever higher frequency, aimed not only at punk rock collective memory, but also toward the collective memory of the mainstream. As we approach the fortieth anniversary of the birth of American hardcore, the subculture itself is seizing agency and writing its own history through digital and print publications, radio, television and film. Counter-memory surrounding Bad Brains is only one example of this expanding historical perspective of race in punk.

Bad Brains are far from the only example of people of colour in punk subculture, or even in hardcore, yet they remain one of the most recognisable and influential examples. Ideally, counter-memory surrounding Bad Brains and other punks of colour could destroy the chimera of punk as a White invention and a strictly White, male, middle-class endeavor. Punk as a subculture today still attracts self-identified misfits, rebels and others who are at odds with mainstream life and social expectations. However, the common perception that punk is for one race or another should continue to be challenged not only within punk, but also within mainstream culture.

As Angelo Moore, the lead singer of Black punk band Fishbone powerfully notes: 'No longer do I have to listen when some [people] come up and say, "You're just playing that white boy shit!"' To this he replies: 'Man, listen to some Bad Brains, motherfucker.'[95]

NOTES

1. The title of this chapter refers to the first gig poster for Bad Brains, which billed them as 'the greatest punk rock band in the world'. See D. Jenifer, 'Play like a white boy: Hard dancing in the city of chocolate', in S. Duncombe and M. Tremblay (eds.), *White Riot: Punk Rock and the Politics of Race* (London, 2011), p. 210 (Jenifer 2011).

2. M. Andersen and M. Jenkins, *Dance of Days: Two Decades of Punk in the Nation's Capital* (New York, 2009), pp. 40–41 (Andersen and Jenkins 2009).

3. *American Hardcore: The History of American Punk Rock 1980–86*, directed by Paul Rachman (AHC Productions, 2006) DVD.

4. S. Blush, *American Hardcore: A Tribal History* (Los Angeles, 2001), p. 72 (Blush 2001).

5. T. White, 'The importance of being a Ramone', *Rolling Stone*, 8 February 1979, http://www.rollingstone.com/music/news/the-importance-of-being-a-ramone-19790208?page=5 [accessed 3 March 2017] (White 1979).

6. M. Board, *Maximumrocknroll Magazine*, Issue 34, 1986. Quoted in S. Maskell, 'Performing punk: Bad Brains and the construction of identity', *Journal of Popular Music Studies*, 21(4) (2009), 413 (Maskell 2009).

7. C. Brinkhurst-Cuff, 'Why is the history of punk music so white?: True punk rebellion has always existed in black culture, and continues to exist today', *Dazed*, November 2015, http://www.dazeddigital.com/music/article/28372/1/why-is-the-history-of-punk-music-so-white [accessed 3 March 2017] (Brinkhurst-Cuff 2015).

8. Interview with Scott Ian, quoted in G. Prato, *Punk! Hardcore! Reggae! PMA! Bad Brains!* (Create Space Independent Publishing Platform, 2014), p. 36 (Prato 2014).

9. G. Lipsitz, *Time Passages: Collective Memory and American Popular Culture* (Minneapolis, 2001), p. 212 (Lipsitz 2001).

10. M. K. Wiedlack, '"We're punk as fuck and fuck like punks": Queer–feminist Counter-cultures, Punk Music and the Anti-social Turn in Queer Theory' (Unpublished DPhil. dissertation, Universitat Wien, 2013), p. 208 (Wiedlack 2013).

11. J. Cowie, *Stayin' Alive: The 1970s and the Last Days of the Working Class* (New York, 2010), p. 325 (Cowie 2010). See also: B. Osgerby, '"Chewing out a rhythm on my bubble gum": The teenage aesthetic and genealogies of American punk', in R. Sabin (ed.), *Punk Rock: So What?: The Cultural Legacy of Punk* (London, 2009), pp. 154–69 (Osgerby 2009).

12. S. Taylor, *False Prophet: Fieldnotes from the Punk Underground* (Middletown, 2003), p. 54 (Taylor 2003).

13. Blush, *American Hardcore*, 116.

14. R. Moore, *Sells Like Teen Spirit: Music, Youth Culture, and Social Crisis* (New York, 2010) (Moore 2010).

15. Although referring to British punk, Simonelli refers to punk as 'the white version of Rastafarian ideology', thereby, reaffirming punk as 'White' music. D. Simonelli, 'Anarchy, pop, and violence: Punk rock subculture and the rhetoric of class', *Contemporary British History*, 16(2) (Summer 2002), 121–44 (Simonelli 2002).

16. Ike Willis, Interview by Andy Holliden, 11 November 2009, 'Reclaiming the right to rock collection', Archives of African American Music and Culture, Indiana University Media Collections Online.

17. D. Hebdige, *Subculture: The Meaning of Style* (London, 1979), p. 68 (Hebdige 1979).

18. P. Gilroy, *There Ain't No Black in the Union Jack* (London, 1987), p. 163 (Gilroy 1987).

19. E. Stinson, 'Means of detection: A critical archiving of black feminism and punk performance', *Women & Performance: A Journal of Feminist Theory*, 22 (2–3) (2012), pp. 284–5 (Stinson 2012).

20. R. Sabin, '"I won't let that dago by": Rethinking punk and racism', in Duncombe and Tremblay (eds.), *White Riot*, pp. 57–68.

21. D. Traber, 'L.A.'s 'white minority': Punk and the contradictions of self-marginalization', *Cultural Critique*, 48 (2001), 49 (Traber 2001).

22. S. Hall, 'What is "black" in black popular culture?', in J. Storey (ed.), *Cultural Theory and Popular Culture: A Reader* (Harlow, 2009), p. 380 (Hall 2009).

23. For an exploration of race as a social construct in the United States, see: M. Omi and H. Winant, *Racial Formation in the United States* (New York, 2015) (Omi and Winant 2015).

24. P. Gilroy, *The Black Atlantic: Modernity and Double Consciousness* (Cambridge, 1994), pp. 100–1 (Gilroy 1994).

25. A. McRobbie, *Feminism and Youth Culture: From 'Jackie' to 'Just Seventeen'* (Boston, 1991) (McRobbie 1991).

26. P. Hill Collins, 'It's all in the family: Intersections of gender, race, and nation', *Hypatia*, 13(3) (1998), 62–82 (Hill Collins 1998).

27. Duncombe and Tremblay, *White Riot*.

28. Maskell, 'Performing punk', 411–26.

29. Interview with Darryl Jenifer in Dave Maher, 'Bad Brains interview', *Pitchfork.com*, 29 October 2015, http://pitchfork.com/features/inter view/6663-bad-brains/ [accessed 3 March 2017].

30. D. Massey and N. A. Denton, *American Apartheid: Segregation and the Making of the Underclass* (Cambridge, 1993), p. 45 (Massey 1993).

31. N. Hopkinson, *Go-Go Live: The Musical Life and Death of a Chocolate City* (Durham, 2012) (Hopkinson 2012).

32. Ibid.

33. Massey and Denton, *American Apartheid*, p. 70.

34. G. Tate, 'Hardcore of darkness: Bad Brains', in Duncombe and Tremblay (eds.), *White Riot*, p. 214.

35. Hopkinson, *Go-Go Live*, p. 146.

36. 'Darryl Jenifer of Bad Brains: "I want to be the soldier of my music"', *Ultimate-Guitar.com* (2007): https://www.ultimate-guitar.com/news/ interviews/darryl_jenifer_of_bad_brains_i_want_to_be_the_soldier_of_ my_music.html?no_takeover [accessed 3 March 2017].

37. Andersen and Jenkins, *Dance of Days*, pp. 27–9.

38. K. Grow, 'Hardcore mettle: Bad Brains' strange survival tale', *Spin* (29 November 2012): http://www.spin.com/2012/11/bad-brains-strange-survival-tale/2/ [accessed 3 March 2017] (Grow 2012).

39. Maskell, 'Performing punk', p. 414.

40. N. Crossley, *Networks, Sound, Style, and Subversion: The Punk and Post-Punk Worlds of Manchester, London, Liverpool, and Sheffield, 1975–80* (Manchester, 2015), p. 36 (Crossley 2015).

41. Maskell, 'Performing punk', 415.

42. *Bad Brains: A Band in D.C.*, directed by Mandy Stein and Ben Logan (Plain Jane Productions, 2012).

43. Tate, 'Hardcore of darkness', p. 214.

44. Blush, *American Hardcore*.

45. E. Davis, 'The last apostles', *The Voice*, 10 October 1989, DC Punk Archive/Mark Andersen Collection, Martin Luther King Jr. Memorial Library, Washington, DC.

46. Blush, *American Hardcore*, p. 117.

47. Wiedlack, 'We are punk as fuck', p. 222.

48. Andersen, *Dance of Days*, p. 37.

49. G. Prato, *Punk! Hardcore! Reggae!*, p. 9.

50. T. A. Lee. 'From Bad Brains to afro-punk: An analysis of identity, consciousness, and liberation through punk rock from 1977–2010' (Unpublished MA thesis, Cornell University, 2010), p. 18 (Lee 2010).

51. Gilroy, *There Ain't No Black in the Union Jack*, p. 205.

52. Gilroy, *The Black Atlantic*, p. 7.

53. D. Howland, 'Bad Brains', *Trouser Press Magazine*, 1983.
54. L. Perkins, *Hard Art: DC 1979* (New York, 2013), p. 13 (Perkins 2013).
55. Blush, *American Hardcore*, p. 124.
56. Interview with Bad Brains in *Now What?* No. 0, 1981, Series 1, Box 1, Folder 98, D.C. Punk and Indie Fanzine Collection, Michelle Smith Performing Arts Library, University of Maryland, College Park, MD.
57. 'Review Bad Brains – LP Length Cassette (ROIR)', *Damaged Goods*, 2 (8) (February 1982), Series 2, Box 4, Folder 34. D.C. Punk and Indie Fanzine Collection, Michelle Smith Performing Arts Library, University of Maryland, College Park, MD.
58. Blush, *American Hardcore*, p. 122.
59. Interview with Aaron Thompson by Tara Martin Lopez, 18 April 2016.
60. Interview with Don Letts in *Bad Brains: A Band in DC* Hulu (Web), 29 October 2015.
61. *PUNK: Attitude*, directed by Don Letts (3DD Productions, 2005).
62. L. Bakare, 'From Bad Brains to Cerebral Ballzy: Why hardcore will never die', *The Guardian* (20 November 2014): https://www.theguardian.com/music/2014/nov/20/hardcore-music-hard-fast-us-punk-rock [accessed 3 March 2017] (Bakare 2014).
63. Andersen and Jenkins, *Dance of Days*, p. 34.
64. J. Porter and J. Austen, 'Black punk time, blacks in punk, new wave, and hardcore, 1976–1983', *Roctober*, 32 (2002), 43 (Great Lakes Underground Press Collection, Box 6, Special Collections and Archives, DePaul University, Chicago, IL) (Porter and Austen 2002).
65. Interview with Henry Rollins in *Bad Brains: A Band in D.C.*
66. Andersen and Jenkins, *Dance of Days*, p. 37.
67. Perkins, *Hard Art: DC 1979*; C. Connolly, L. Clague and S. Cheslow, *Banned in D.C.: Photos and Anecdotes from the DC Punk Underground, 79–85* (Washington, 2013) features not only many of Lucian Perkins' photos of Bad Brains, but the title of the book is a direct reference to Bad Brains' 'Banned In D.C.' (Connolly 2013).
68. Duncombe and Tremblay, *White Riot*, p. 206.
69. Prato, *Punk! Hardcore! Reggae!*
70. Lipsitz, *Time Passages*, pp. 212–213.
71. T. Fierce, 'Black invisibility and racism in punk rock', *Bitchcore* 1999, in Duncombe and Tremblay, *White Riot*, p. 283.
72. O. Atoe, 'Shotgun seamstress', 1 August 2006 in *Shotgun Seamstress: Zine Collection, A Zine By and For Black Punks* (Tacoma, 2012), p. 21.
73. Y. Thecato, *Slash They Ass Up: A Black Punk Manifesto* (Chicago, 2013) (Thecato 2013).

74. Interview with Angelo Moore in Michael Gonzalez, 'Afropunk before afropunk', *Ebony* (29 August 2014): http://www.ebony.com/entertainment-culture/afropunk-before-afropunk-232#axzz430seTBES   [accessed   3 March 2017].
75. Quoted in Wiedlack, 'We are punk as fuck', p. 223.
76. Tasha Hairston, interview by Tara Martin Lopez, 13 May 2016.
77. Hill Collins, 'It's all in the family'.
78. *Afro-Punk*, directed by James Spooner (Afro-Punk, 2003).
79. J. Spooner, 'Foreword', in Duncombe and Tremblay, *White Riot*, p. xiii.
80. Ibid, p. xvi.
81. Onome, 'Filmmaker James Spooner goes in-depth with afro-punk: The "rock 'n' roll nigger" experience', *A Gathering of Tribes* (31 October 2006): http://www.tribes.org/web/2006/10/31/filmmaker-james-spoo ner-goes-in-depth-with-afro-punk-the-rock-n-roll-nigger-experience [accessed 3 March 2017].
82. *Afro-Punk*.
83. Ibid.
84. Lipsitz, *Time Passages*, p. 213.
85. J. Logan and B. Stults, *The Persistence of Segregation in the Metropolis: New Findings from the 2010 Census*, 24 March 2011: http://www.s4.brown. edu/us2010/Data/Report/report2.pdf [accessed 3 March 2017] (Logan and Stults 2011).
86. 'Quick facts – District of Columbia', U.S. Census Bureau 2015. https:// www.census.gov/quickfacts/table/PST045215/11 [accessed 3 March 2017].
87. Ta-Nehisi Coates, *Between the World and Me* (New York, 2015), pp. 52–3 (Coates 2015).
88. 'Celebrity net worth: Ian MacKaye net worth', http://www.celebritynet worth.com/richest-celebrities/singers/ian-mackaye-net-worth-2/ [accessed 3 March 2017].
89. 'Celebrity net worth: Henry Rollins net worth', http://www.celebritynet worth.com/richest-celebrities/henry-rollins-net-worth/ [accessed 3 March 2017].
90. M. Cohen, 'Bad Brains raising funds to help support Dr. Know after his near-death illness', *Washington City Paper* (10 March 2016): http://www. washingtoncitypaper.com/blogs/artsdesk/music/2016/03/10/after-nearly-dying-bad-brains-raising-funds-to-help-support-dr-know/ [accessed 3 March 2017] (Cohen 2016).
91. bell hooks, 'Postmodern blackness', in J. Storey (ed.), *Cultural Theory and Popular Culture: A Reader* (Harlow, 2009), p. 392 (hooks 2009).
92. Lipsitz, *Time Passages*, p. 231.
93. Mahr, 'Bad Brains interview.'

94. C. Richards, 'This is hardcore: A new generation is making Washington's punk dialect its own – while It can', *The Washington Post* (12 May 2016): http://www.washingtonpost.com/sf/style/2016/05/12/how-d-c-hardcore-is-being-revitalized-by-a-new-generation-of-bands/ [accessed 3 March 2017] (Richards 2016).
95. Interview with Angelo Moore, *Afro-Punk.*

REFERENCES

M. Andersen and M. Jenkins, *Dance of Days: Two Decades of Punk in the Nation's Capital* (New York, 2009), pp. 40–1.

"Bad Brains: A Band in D.C.," Directed by Mandy Stein and Ben Logan. Plain Jane Productions, 2012.

L. Bakare, 'From Bad Brains to Cerebral Ballzy: Why Hardcore Will Never Die', *The Guardian*, November 20, 2014: https://www.theguardian.com/music/2014/nov/20/hardcore-music-hard-fast-us-punk-rock.

S. Blush, *American Hardcore: A Tribal History* (Los Angeles, 2001), p. 72.

C. Brinkhurst-Cuff, 'Why is the History of Punk Music so White?: True Punk Rebellion has Always Existed in Black Culture, and Continues to Exist Today', *Dazed*, November 2015, http://www.dazeddigital.com/music/article/28372/1/why-is-the-history-of-punk-music-so-white [accessed 3 March 2017].

M. Cohen, 'Bad Brains Raising Funds to Help Support Dr. Know After His Near-Death Illness', *Washington City Paper*, 10 March 2016: http://www.washingtoncitypaper.com/blogs/artsdesk/music/2016/03/10/after-nearly-dying-bad-brains-raising-funds-to-help-support-dr-know/.

C. Connolly, L. Clague, and S. Cheslow, *Banned in D.C.: Photos and Anecdotes from the DC Punk Underground, 79–85* (Washington, 2013).

J. Cowie, *Stayin' Alive: The 1970s and the Last Days of the Working Class* (New York, 2010), p. 325.

N. Crossley, *Networks, Sound, Style, and Subversion: The Punk and Post-Punk Worlds of Manchester, London, Liverpool, and Sheffield, 1975–80* (Manchester, 2015), p. 36.

D. Jenifer in Dave Maher, 'Bad Brains Interview', *Pitchfork.com*, 29 October 2015, http://pitchfork.com/features/interview/6663-bad-brains/.

P. Gilroy, *There Ain't No Black in the Union Jack* (London, 1987), p. 163.

P. Gilroy, *The Black Atlantic: Modernity and Double Consciousness* (Cambridge, 1994), pp. 100–1.

K. Grow, 'Hardcore Mettle: Bad Brains' Strange Survival Tale' *Spin*, November 29, 2012: http://www.spin.com/2012/11/bad-brains-strange-survival-tale/2/.

S. Hall, 'What is "Black" in Black Popular Culture?', in J. Storey (ed) *Cultural Theory and Popular Culture: A Reader* (Harlow, 2009), p. 380.

D. Hebdige, *Subculture: The Meaning of Style* (London, 1979), p. 68.

P. Hill Collins, 'It's All in the Family: Intersections of Gender, Race, and Nation', *Hypatia*, 13, 3 (1998), 62–82.

bell hooks, 'Postmodern Blackness', in J. Storey (ed.), *Cultural Theory and Popular Culture: A Reader* (Harlow, 2009), p. 392.

N. Hopkinson, *Go-Go Live: The Musical Life and Death of a Chocolate City* (Durham, 2012).

D. Jenifer, 'Play Like a White Boy: Hard Dancing in the City of Chocolate', in S. Duncombe and M. Tremblay (eds.), *White Riot: Punk Rock and the Politics of Race* (London, 2011), p. 210.

A. Thompson. 'From Bad Brains to Afro-Punk: An Analysis of Identity, Consciousness, and Liberation Through Punk Rock From 1977–2010' (Unpublished MA Thesis, Cornell University, 2010), p. 18.

G. Lipsitz, *Time Passages: Collective Memory and American Popular Culture* (Minneapolis, 2001), pp. 212–13.

J. Logan and B. Stults, *The Persistence of Segregation in the Metropolis: New Findings from the 2010 Census*, 24 March 2011: http://www.s4.brown.edu/us2010/Data/Report/report2.pdf.

S. Maskell, 'Performing Punk: Bad Brains and the Construction of Identity', *Journal of Popular Music Studies*, 21, 4 (2009), 413.

D. Massey and N. A. Denton, *American Apartheid: Segregation and the Making of the Underclass* (Cambridge, 1993), p. 45.

A. McRobbie, *Feminism and Youth Culture: From 'Jackie' to 'Just Seventeen'* (Boston, 1991).

R. Moore, *Sells Like Teen Spirit: Music, Youth Culture, and Social Crisis* (New York, 2010).

M. Omi and H. Winant, *Racial Formation in the United States* (New York, 2015).

B. Osgerby, '"Chewing Out a Rhythm on My Bubble Gum": The Teenage Aesthetic and Genealogies of American Punk', in R. Sabin (ed) *Punk Rock: So What?: The Cultural Legacy of Punk* (London, 2009), pp. 154–69.

G. Prato, *Punk! Hardcore! Reggae! PMA! Bad Brains!* (Create Space Independent Publishing Platform, 2014), p. 36.

L. Perkins, *Hard Art: DC 1979* (New York, 2013), p. 13.

J. Porter and J. Austen, 'Black Punk Time, Blacks in Punk, New Wave, and Hardcore, 1976–1983', *Roctober*, 32 (2002), 43.

C. Richards, 'This is Hardcore: A New Generation is Making Washington's Punk Dialect Its Own – While It Can', *The Washington Post*, 12 May 2016: http://www.washingtonpost.com/sf/style/2016/05/12/how-d-c-hardcore-is-being-revitalized-by-a-new-generation-of-bands/.

D. Simonelli, 'Anarchy, Pop, and Violence: Punk Rock Subculture and the Rhetoric of Class', *Contemporary British History*, 16, 2 (Summer 2002), 121–44.

E. Stinson, 'Means of Detection: A Critical Archiving of Black Feminism and Punk Performance', *Women & Performance: A Journal of Feminist Theory*, 22, 2–3 (2012) 283–4.

S. Taylor, *False Prophet: Fieldnotes from the Punk Underground* (Middletown, 2003), p. 54.

D. Traber, 'L.A.'s "White Minority": Punk and the Contradictions of Self-Marginalization', *Cultural Critique*, 48 (2001), 49.

Ta-Nehisi Coates, *Between the World and Me* (New York, 2015), pp. 52–3.

Y. Thecato, *Slash They Ass Up: A Black Punk Manifesto* (Chicago, 2013).

M. K. Wiedlack, '"We're Punk as Fuck and Fuck Like Punks": Queer-Feminist Counter-Cultures, Punk Music and the Anti-Social Turn in Queer Theory' (Unpublished DPhil. dissertation, Universitat Wien, 2013), p. 208.

T. White, 'The Importance of Being a Ramone', *Rolling Stone*, February 8, 1979, http://www.rollingstone.com/music/news/the-importance-of-being-a-ramone-19790208?page=5.

Tara Martin Lopez is a professor of sociology at Peninsula College in Port Angeles, WA, USA. She specializes in gender stratification and working class women's activism and recently published *The Winter of Discontent: Myth, Memory, and History* with Liverpool University Press. Martin Lopez has broadened the scope of her research and is currently interested in the role women and people of colour play in subcultures and social movements. In particular, her next project will examine the role of both conservative and progressive Latinx movements in the 2016 Presidential campaign.

Michael Mills is Associate Faculty of English at Peninsula College in Port Angeles, WA, USA, where he is the faculty advisor for *Tidepools* magazine. A writer of short fiction, essays and plays, his work has appeared in *Short Story, Tales from the South, Weird Tales* and other journals and magazines. His research interests include: popular culture, counterculture, creative writing theory and writing pedagogy. A musician, he played in punk rock bands in Eureka, California and Little Rock, Arkansas.

Gangs

'It Wasnae Just Easterhouse': The Politics of Representation in the Glasgow Gang Phenomenon, c. 1965–1975

Angela Bartie and Alistair Fraser

Glasgow has long been a city synonymous with gang violence, with the publication in 1935 of the famous novel set in the Gorbals area of Glasgow, *No Mean City*, 'sealing' its reputation as a city 'terrorised by gangs'.[1] When gangs 'reappeared' in the 1960s, reporters and commentators contrasted the older, criminal interwar 'razor gangs' with a phenomenon perceived as younger, more violent and more likely to involve bystanders in their altercations. The press reported figures pointing to alarming rises in violence, the possession of offensive weapons and crime more generally, many incidents involving more than two people were presented as 'gang' skirmishes, and those involved were denounced as thugs, hooligans and gangsters. Glasgow was, in the words of one journalist, 'exhibited to the world as the most lawless city in Britain where fear-ridden citizens are under constant menace by gangs of young thugs'.[2] The re-emergence of

A. Bartie (✉)
University of Edinburgh, Edinburgh, UK
e-mail: angela.bartie@ed.ac.uk

A. Fraser
University of Glasgow, Glasgow, UK
e-mail: alistair.fraser@glasgow.ac.uk

© The Author(s) 2017   205
K. Gildart et al. (eds.), *Youth Culture and Social Change*,
Palgrave Studies in the History of Subcultures and Popular Music,
DOI 10.1057/978-1-137-52911-4_9

the gang phenomenon onto the public and political agenda was intimately connected with a broader set of fears and anxieties related to post-war youth and social housing.

Whilst the interwar gangs were associated with the slums of inner-city areas like the Gorbals, the gang phenomenon of the 1960s became firmly associated with the new outlying housing estates, built to try to relieve Glasgow's chronic overcrowding and slum conditions, and to provide a fresh start and better living conditions for its citizens. By the mid-1960s, it was the community of Easterhouse – formally opened by Clement Attlee in 1956 and located on the eastern periphery of the city – that was viewed as the worst area for gang violence in Glasgow, quickly becoming the focus of a 'moral panic' about youth, offensive weapons and gang violence.[3] As well as the attention of the media, the police, the local authority in Glasgow and the Scottish Office, this issue also attracted academic attention, as sociologists and other scholars attempted to examine and understand both the causes and possible solutions to the 'reappearance' of a violent subculture associated with an earlier era. In a similar pattern to more recent debates over youth gangs in the UK, a number of competing arguments were presented, rooted in different approaches and epistemological positions. One (in)famous example, James Patrick's *A Glasgow Gang Observed*, drew on explanations rooted in structural disadvantage and psychological trauma.[4] By contrast, a study by Mary Wilson and Gail Armstrong, published as two discrete chapters – 'City Politics and Deviance Amplification' and 'Deviancy and Some Aspects of Housing' – examined the process of social construction involved in the emergence of gangs as a social problem, drawing attention to processes of media amplification of the phenomenon.[5] These contrasting approaches to studying gangs resulted in division and debate, as well as divergent accounts of the appropriate response.

This sequence of events speaks directly to current debates relating to gangs in the UK. In the years following England's 'summer of violent disorder' in 2011, gangs have emerged as a divisive social issue. Echoing the pattern from the 1960s, a range of social actors have become involved, notably police, policy-makers, the media and academic researchers. Scholars have fiercely debated whether gangs exist, and have sought out explanations ranging from the structural to the pathological. On one side, scholars have drawn on the conceptual vocabularies of subcultural theory to argue that local identity and group conflict represent an enduring feature of life in working-class communities across the UK, and as such that territorial 'gangs' are nothing new. On the other, researchers have argued that the subcultural theories of the 1970s are no longer relevant, and that the social and structural shifts brought on by the post-industrial era have resulted in the emergence of new street-based groups for whom the term 'gang' is a meaningful descriptor.[6]

In this chapter, we revisit the politics of representation in the Glasgow gang phenomenon, c. 1965–1975, as a means of drawing attention to the historical antecedents to these recent debates. In so doing we seek to draw attention to the variability in gang research – according to methodological approach, epistemological underpinning and geographical context – and the frequent lack of reflexivity in debate. Like the parable of the blind men and the elephant, where each felt a different part and thought they had discovered its true essence, these debates are too often partial and blinkered. As William B. Sanders argues, 'not only are there different definitions of gangs, but most researchers have defined different types of gang'.[7] Here we re-examine the work of Patrick, Armstrong and Wilson, discussing the valuable distinctions between them, and reflecting on their significance for understanding the gang phenomenon in Glasgow (and elsewhere). We also explore not just what they can tell us about young people's identities, but also about the role of the researchers themselves in shaping and constructing understandings of youth subcultures.

SOME BACKGROUND: YOUTH GANGS AND MORAL PANIC IN 1960s GLASGOW

Gangs in Glasgow have been reported since the 1880s, forming a cyclical source of identity and community, as well as fear and instability, emerging as an object of public and media attention at different historical moments. As Fraser convincingly demonstrates in his recent ethnographic study of youth and gang identity in post-industrial Glasgow, *Urban Legends*, there are marked continuities with previous generations but there are changes too. In certain cases, the same gang names have recurred consistently throughout this period; for example, the Baltic Fleet, from Baltic Street, Dalmarnock, in Glasgow's East End, were first reported in 1916 and remain listed on police intelligence databases to this day.[8] Yet as Fraser argues, drawing on US sociologist John Hagedorn's evocative expression, while gang identities have become 'institutionalised' in certain communities – a hand-me-down identity, passed on from generation to generation – they are nonetheless used and interpreted in different ways by different generations. In this chapter we are focussing on one particular era during which Glasgow's reputation as a 'violent city' became concretised: the late 1960s.

In the 1950s, mass overcrowding and housing shortages in Glasgow resulted in the construction of four housing estates on the outskirts of the city – Easterhouse, Pollok, Castlemilk and Drumchapel – where housing was prioritised above any other amenities.[9] These resulted in populations of 40,000 to 50,000 with little to no shops, schools, churches, recreation facilities and other amenities; a 'desert wi windaes' is how the Scottish comedian Billy Connolly famously described Drumchapel. In 1970, Easterhouse still had 'no public toilets, no public washhouse, no banks, no cinema, no theatre, no public dance hall, no internal transport system, no community centre, no cafes or restaurants and no shopping centre', one pub and very few shops. To access shops selling more than groceries or sundry goods or to claim state benefits of any kind required journeys of at least an hour and a cost of three shillings.[10] In Easterhouse in particular, young families were given priority; resulting, ten years later, in a profusion of young people with few leisure opportunities. In the mid-1960s, it was estimated that around half of the population of Easterhouse was under the age of 21 and, with few resources or amenities, large numbers of young people congregated on street corners and in public spaces.[11] Despite evidence showing that youth gangs remained a larger problem in older housing areas, like Maryhill in the north west of Glasgow, it was the relatively new housing estate of Easterhouse that became firmly connected with concerns about gangs, offensive weapons and violence in the public discourse and in local, Scottish-national and British-national politics.[12] This heightened focus on the area affected the young people involved in 'gangs' as well as residents of the community, and shaped the approaches taken by police and the local authority to those who lived in Easterhouse.

During the mid-1960s, press coverage of youth disorder had given way to a growing focus on and concern about offensive weapons and gang fighting amongst young people in the city. Concurrent with a rise in articles about 'gangs' was a growing concern about new housing, and its failure to provide a fresh start for those who had moved to the new estates.[13] These new housing estates were supposed to have alleviated the kinds of problems – like overcrowding, poverty, crime and fighting – that had been associated with tenements in older parts of the city. Easterhouse began to receive particular attention when, on 10 January 1966, the front page of *The Glasgow Herald* reported that a gang of around 150 Easterhouse youths carrying weapons had been chased by members of a local tenants' organisation formed 'to combat gangs, who have been causing trouble in the area for some six months'.[14] The issue of youth gangs in Glasgow more generally was cemented as a cause for concern after the Chief Constable's Annual Report for 1965 was reported in the press in June 1966: 'The year 1965 brought *new* [our emphasis] difficulties to the Police in the shape of outbreaks of juvenile group disorder'.[15] So, from 1965 to 1966, mounting coverage of youth gangs was increasingly fused with growing concern about the failures of Glasgow's largest overspill housing scheme, Easterhouse, and the two issues were perceived as being inextricably linked. One press article published in March 1966, 'Unrest in the New Housing Estates', argued that the planning of these estates was at the root of the gang problem.[16]

The connection between youth gangs and Easterhouse was further cemented when, on 11 July 1968, in a now legendary episode in Glasgow's history, the popular entertainer Frankie Vaughan visited Easterhouse. Known as 'Mr Moonlight' after his well-known song 'Give me the Moonlight', Vaughan had scored a number of hits in the British charts and, in 1960, had appeared with Marilyn Monroe in the film *Let's Make Love*.[17] Responding to footage he had seen on a recent television programme, BBC's *24 Hours*, Vaughan came to Glasgow and met privately with young people who professed to be the leaders of four local gangs: the Drummy, the Pak, the Rebels and the Toi.[18] After the meeting, Vaughan announced that the four gangs had assured him that they would lay down their weapons in exchange for his promise to help them organise a youth centre of their own.[19] A weapons amnesty ensued, with much public and media attention; despite an appeal to the public to stay away, the *Glasgow Herald* newspaper reported an audience of around 200 spectators, a 'large posse' of photographers and television cameramen, including the National Broadcasting Corporation of America, four ice-cream vans and two fish and chip vans (all there to cater for the audience).[20] Construction began on the resulting youth centre, 'The Easterhouse Project', in 1968. Two disused Nissen army huts were erected with the aid of the Royal Engineers, funded by a combination of Scottish Office, Glasgow Corporation and public donations (many of which came from the proceeds of a concert in the Locarno Ballroom and a variety show held at the Alhambra Theatre in Glasgow).[21] This episode represented the high watermark of public attention to gangs in Glasgow – redirecting pre-existing stereotypes away from older working-class communities, and instead onto Easterhouse (which remains to this day a byword for a range of social problems).

In what follows, we explore the role and significance of place and the politics of representation in the study of youth gangs in Glasgow by looking at two key sociological studies. Though researched at a similar time and published concurrently, Patrick's *A Glasgow Gang Observed* has become an infamous element in the criminological canon while Gail Armstrong and Mary Wilson's research has largely lain dormant among the pages of Ian Taylor and Laurie Taylor's *Politics and Deviance* and Colin Ward's *Vandalism.*[22]

A GLASGOW GANG OBSERVED

In 1973, a pseudonymous researcher, James Patrick, published *A Glasgow Gang Observed* to great public attention.[23] Written explicitly for 'the general reader rather than for the criminologist, the clinical psychologist, or the specialist in the sociology of deviance', the book is based on just under 120 hours of covert participant-observation. This was undertaken between October 1966 and January 1967 with a group Patrick termed the 'Young Team' – a gang of violent young men in their mid-to-late teens – in Maryhill, an old working-class district in northwest Glasgow.[24] Patrick was, at the time, studying for a postgraduate degree in Education, and required a topic for study. In the book, he relays the sequence of coincidences that led to the study's success – principally his relative youth and friendship with the main character in the book, 'Tim Malloy' (pseudonym). Patrick gained entrée through the friendship he struck up with 15-year-old Tim, when Patrick was a teacher at an approved school, and Tim was attending the school for young offenders. The book famously opens with a description of Patrick's attire on his first night with the Young Team:

> I was dressed in a midnight-blue suit, with a twelve-inch middle vent, three-inch flaps over the pockets and a light blue handkerchief with a white polka dot (to match my tie) in the top pocket [...] I had not planned to join a juvenile gang; I had been invited.[25]

Patrick details his careful preparations to help him 'fit in' with the Young Team – allowing his hair to grow long, leaving his nails ragged, and creating a false story as to how he and Tim knew each other. Patrick then goes on to outline how he came to be heading out on a Saturday night in October 1966 to meet Tim and the rest of the Young Team, secretly invited by Tim to 'see whit the score was' in response to Patrick's criticism of boys who got into trouble whilst on weekend leave.[26] In the Preface, Patrick noted that whilst his book was 'unashamedly exploratory', his main aim was to 'present a brief glimpse of the reality which engages Glasgow gang boys, [and, citing David Matza] "to comprehend and to illuminate their view and to interpret the world as it appears to them"'.[27]

The bulk of the book – 17 of the 21 chapters – comprises a descriptive account of the activities of the group. It begins by providing some background on Tim, using not just Patrick's own observations but information gleaned from his file in the approved school, including school and probation reports. We learn that Tim is the youngest of a family of nine, that he was expelled from school at the age of 14, that he got his first criminal conviction at the age of 13 (for theft) and that the charges that resulted in him being sent to an approved school included assault and robbery. We also learn that his three eldest brothers are all in prison, his 16-year-old brother is 'reported to be' on probation and unemployed and that his home is 'situated in a highly delinquent neighbourhood'.[28] Patrick describes this area, Maryhill, as follows:

My own recollections of the neighbourhood are predominantly of black streets lit by pale orange lighting and strewn with broken glass, empty beer cans, half bricks and at times broken down furniture. Where any wooden fences round gardens remain, they are no better than dirty sticks protruding from the ground at all angles. The small patches of grass in front of houses have long since been trampled into mud. And these are the newer pre-war houses I am describing and not the leprous tenements closer to the centre of the city.[29]

Following this 'background', we follow Patrick on his first night with Tim and the boys in a pub near the city centre, followed by a visit to the nearby Granada Dance Hall. In this chapter, Patrick introduces the other boys of the Young Team, shares his discovery that Tim is their 'leader-aff' (leader) and conveys the importance of territory to gang identification and attachment: 'Gangs appeared to me to be based on territory. Boys belonged to the Valley, for example, because they lived in that area.'[30]

In the ensuing chapters, through Patrick's eyes, we see the Young Team playing football, at the pub and parties, hanging out on street-corners and (occasionally) engaging in extreme acts of violence. This includes fighting, stabbing and gang 'battles', a number of which are described in great detail – although much of the violence described is not directly witnessed by Patrick, but recounted to him. Indeed, he notes how important the discussion of these tales and legends about the 'gemmiest boays' were to the Young Team.[31] It was partly the growing pressure to carry and use an offensive weapon and to get more involved in the fighting that ultimately led to Patrick's withdrawal from the group, under the pretense that he was about to start a new job in England.[32]

The last part of the book locates this descriptive account in the extant Scottish, British and American literature on gangs, focusing principally on the fields of sociology and psychology. At heart, Patrick argued that the behaviour of the Young Team must be understood within the context of poor housing, overcrowding, poverty and structural disadvantages experienced by the boys. 'For a hundred years', Patrick wrote, 'Glasgow has suffered from appalling housing conditions. For the same length of time gangs have been known in the city. The inhabitants, I fear, have become inured to both evils, to cramped verminous houses and to brutal, barbarous violence.'[33] Most controversially, however, Patrick noted that he detected pathological tendencies in their acts of violence. In doing so, he allied himself most closely with the work of US sociologist, Lewis Yablonsky, who viewed the gang as 'a pathological entity requiring elimination', and distanced himself from what he termed 'fashionable' accounts within the sociology of deviance.[34] These accounts, originating in the United States in the work of Howard Becker, David Matza and others, were then achieving prominence in the work of the National Deviancy Conference (NDC), and stressed the roles of labelling, stereotyping and social reaction in the construction of crime.[35] These influential conferences, formed by a breakaway group of young sociologists in 1968, ran sporadically between 1968 and 1980 and brought ideas prominent in the American sociology of deviance to the study of crime in the UK.[36] Patrick concluded that, whilst the group of young men he studied were largely representative of other working-class communities in Glasgow, they had no parallel elsewhere in Britain: 'All the available evidence, then, points to the conclusion that there is no English equivalent of the Glasgow gang I have described'.[37] For Patrick, therefore, the American research tradition was more analytically useful.

The book was widely publicised, with serialisation in *The Sunday Times*. As the Glasgow novelist, Archie Hind, noted in his review of the book: 'Extracts have now appeared in a posh paper and no doubt by now its posh readers will have had their weekend shudder as they rubber-neck once again at the behaviour of the lower orders.'[38] Although it was researched and written up in the mid to late 1960s, Patrick had delayed publication until 1973 partly out of 'fear of exacerbating the gang situation in Glasgow which was receiving nationwide attention in 1968 and 1969⊠ (remember, Vaughan had arrived in a blaze of publicity in July 1968).[39] Nonetheless, the book aroused a great deal of controversy at the time, both in the city of Glasgow and in the academic world more generally; indeed, it continues to stimulate debate as to the ethics and politics of covert research.[40] As we have noted, Glasgow had a reputation as a 'violent city' at the time, and for some commentators this book added further fuel to the fire: 'Glasgow: cradle of a violent sub-culture' ran the headline on Geoffrey Wansell's review in *The Times*, whilst Andrew McBarnet for *The Daily Record* commented 'The book is bound to cause a stir: it touches a sensitive area of Glasgow's reputation.'[41] Nearly 20 years later, sociologist Sean Damer criticised *A Glasgow Gang Observed* for its sensationalism, calling it 'a classic of prurient voyeurism cloaked in obscurantist sociological jargon'. He argued that it had 'further amplified the deviant reputation of Glasgow as "Violent City" and did so success-fully precisely because the author was a social scientist' – a group who were 'supposed to be critical of media inspired moral panics'.[42] Interestingly, in an interview for *The Daily Record* in February 1973, the book's central figure, 'Tim', claimed that most of its content 'is right out of the author's imagination'. Although he conceded that he was 'no angel' and that a couple of the violent incidents attributed to him in the book were true, he challenged much of the rest of it, commenting that Patrick 'conned me for a sucker. Most of what he has written just isn't true. All he has done is to try and write another "No Mean City" on the pretence that it's a truthful, serious study.' 'Tim' took particular exception to the claim that he had boasted to Patrick, 'Ma ambition's tae murder someone. That wid be a rerr laugh', retorting 'I never said that. People just don't go around talking like that.'[43] Despite these criticisms, however, the book remains influential and, after many years being out of print, was republished in both 2012 and 2013.[44] It remains possibly the best-known study of Glasgow gangs.

THE MYSTERIOUS CASE OF ARMSTRONG AND WILSON

It was a shared interest in a largely forgotten study of gangs in 1960s Glasgow that brought us together to work on the research project on which this chapter is based. Undertaken by Gail Armstrong and Mary Wilson, two researchers who were then based in the fledgling sociology department at the University of Strathclyde, Glasgow, their study examined youth gangs in Easterhouse between 1968 and 1970. Armstrong had been working as a social worker in Lanarkshire, just outside Glasgow, before she started work as a research assistant in the department, whilst Mary Wilson had just completed a degree in sociology and was starting a postgraduate degree in the subject. They met and discovered shared interests, as well as a shared sense of generational differences with the 'old guard' of sociologists, which ultimately led them to people like Jock Young, Stanley Cohen and the 'critical criminology' of the National Deviancy Conference.

Armstrong and Wilson's articles presented a very different account of gangs to Patrick's better-known study of gangs at the time, and this intrigued us both. Published in 1973, the same year as *A Glasgow Gang Observed*, Armstrong and Wilson's research was based on two separate, though connected, projects – Armstrong conducted what Wilson described as an 'active participant-observation' of the Easterhouse Project (in that everyone knew she was undertaking a study of them, in contrast to Patrick's covert participant observation study), while Wilson examined public and media responses to Easterhouse, the Project and to youth in the area. They attended and presented their findings at the 1970 National Deviancy Conference, held at York University, and produced the two aforementioned chapters.

It was not just the methodology and findings of the research itself that piqued our interest, but the reference to a forthcoming book that had never materialised alongside the apparent disappearance of both researchers after the publication of their research.[45] We combined efforts and, after over a year of detective work, we managed to track down Armstrong and Wilson, both of whom still lived in Glasgow. Crucially, both were very supportive of our research – and much to our excitement had retained a goldmine of original field notes, drafts of papers and transcriptions of interviews conducted with 16 young people then involved in youth gangs in Easterhouse.

Armstrong and Wilson had studied the events in Easterhouse from the perspective of symbolic interactionism and 'deviancy amplification', reporting a discrepancy between press accounts and their own eyewitness accounts of specific incidents.[46] Developed by criminologist Leslie Wilkins, this concept refers to:

> Where the social reaction against the initial deviancy of a group serves to increase this deviance; as a result, social reaction increases even further, the group becomes more deviant, society acts increasingly strongly against it, and a spiral of deviancy amplification occurs.[47]

In short, the issue becomes a self-fulfilling prophecy. Armstrong and Wilson argue convincingly that the reputation of Easterhouse came about less as a result of the gang behaviour itself, but more as a focal point for concerns over lack of amenities and, furthermore, for debates about law and order in the 1968 council elections. With reference to the *Scottish Daily Express* newspaper, Armstrong and Wilson observed that 'the space devoted to "crime reporting" increasingly reflected turns in the debate itself, rather than in actual crime'.[48] Drawing on these ideas, Armstrong and Wilson found the representations of Easterhouse in the press, and in the public discourse more widely, to far outstrip the reality:

> While the existence of gangs in the area could not be denied, they were neither as highly organised nor as widespread as the press indicated ... One boy had posed as a gang-leader in order to get a free plane trip to Blackpool.[49]

In our own work, we have been using oral history interviewing to investigate representations and realities of Easterhouse, and Easterhouse gangs in particular (we hope, ultimately, to do the same with Patrick's research). The study, titled *Narratives of Glasgow*, has the overall aim of interrogating popular stereotypes of Glasgow, particularly those focusing on Glasgow's reputation as a 'violent city', and to analyse gang identities and behaviours, place these in the broader contexts of young peoples' lives, and explore the intersections between representations of gangs in the 'violent city' and lived experience.[50] Thus far, we have explored the original interviews that Armstrong carried out with young people in Easterhouse and have also interviewed a range of individuals with firsthand experiences of the gang phenomenon in sixties Easterhouse, including youth workers, police officers, a social worker and young people who lived in the area.

Our own interviews have included one with Danny McCall [pseudonym], who Armstrong first interviewed in 1969, when he was 18 years old and involved in the Drummy gang (named after Drumlanrig Avenue in Easterhouse). Approaching 60 years old at the time we interviewed him, Danny provided us with the title of this chapter.[51] We started every interview with an open question: 'Can you tell us a bit about Easterhouse?' During the course of his very long and detailed response, he said:

> Me personally I didnae find it as bad as the media made out ... I didnae think it was. Okay we had gangs fights and all the rest of it but at work I had friends from Drumchapel and they had the same scenario in Drumchapel so it wasn't any different, you know, it wasnae any different whatsoever. They had gangs and they fought. Parkhead had gangs, Calton had gangs, the exact same scenario. The difference probably in the town areas was at least they had somewhere to go, we had nothing, absolutely nothing until The Project came, you know. And that certainly helped.

After telling us about how he realised he would need to leave Easterhouse to 'get out of it', Danny said that even after moving away and getting married, 'that didnae mean you moved away frae the gang culture, fight culture, you know, it was, Glasgow was rife with it, it wasnae just Easterhouse'.[52]

Danny's comments suggest a prevalence of gang rivalries across a range of working-class communities and housing estates in the city, yet as Armstrong and Wilson suggest, public attention had very quickly become – and was to remain – concentrated on Easterhouse. In the introduction to their NDC paper 'The History of a Delinquent Area', they wrote:

> The area has been described as a severely delinquent area in terms of gang violence, and has received wide coverage from the press from this angle. It seems that the definition is held by a wide range of people: we have noted that whenever we have seen the topic of youth violence to crop up informally, in public or through the mass media reference to the problem of Easterhouse has usually been made. In terms of the range of reaction, Easterhouse might be considered to have the status of social problem. It has received wide coverage from the national press, from T.V. and

radio, and has been a prominent subject of debate in newspaper letter columns, the City Chambers and in public meetings and lectures. Further, it has attracted social work strategies and has become a research interest to psychologists, sociologists, social workers, urban planners, architects and bodies such as the I.S.T.D. [Institute for the Study and Treatment of Delinquency] and the Scottish Home and Health Department [part of the Scottish Office]. *Other areas in Glasgow seem to have been immune from such a process of reaction over the same period* [our emphasis].[53]

Armstrong and Wilson argued that it was the 'highly visible and extensive practice of peers meeting at the street-corner "hang-out", indulging in what are considered "normal" levels of delinquency, which came to be construed as an extensive network of highly organized and aggressive gangs'.[54] Their fieldwork revealed gaps in understanding between police conceptions of gang fights and the encounters described by the boys. One 'gang boy' interviewed commented:

After I left school there was nothing to do except hang about, you'd just hang about with the same crowd. If anyone got dug-up [usually a *verbal* provocation], you'd all go down; that was classed as a 'gang fight'.

Their interviews also emphasised the 'entertainment value' the boys said they gained from planning large-scale 'battles' with 'gangs' from other areas, mainly as a way of 'letting off steam'.[55] Referring to his own observations of Easterhouse gangs, Graham Noble, first Secretary of the Easterhouse Project, wrote in a piece for *New Society* that he was:

struck by the amount of sheer energy and high dramatic skill which goes into a battle [...] Display counts for a great deal. There is much running about, striking postures, and brandishing weapons [...] Little groups make short charges and then retreat. There is much shouting of slogans incorporating the gang name – 'Toi Rule', 'Drummy Kill', and so on.[56]

Armstrong and Wilson argue that while violence was central to gangs in Easterhouse, this was largely 'symbolic' and 'actual infractions typically occurred as a result of "sounding" and "probing", a function of misunderstanding *between* gangs as well as within them'.[57] In short, they argued that the 'limited interaction between boys from the different neighbourhoods, together with the tone and content of media reportage about the gangs in the areas, set the scene for shared misunderstandings to be generated'.[58]

Unlike Patrick, however, Armstrong and Wilson's research attracted little attention outside academic circles. Though a book was planned, a range of factors conspired to prevent its publication, and thus a full analysis of the period remains missing. Interestingly, both Armstrong and Wilson wrote reviews of *A Glasgow Gang Observed* at the time. For the *British Journal of Criminology*, Wilson wrote:

> One cannot escape the impression that Patrick remained an outsider looking in rather than moving towards a sensitive appreciation of how it feels to be a gang boy, whose subjective world must remain untapped when merely observed within the group.[59]

Armstrong concurred, citing the influence of Matza on Patrick's attempts to 'illuminate the reality' of the Glasgow gang boy, but arguing that Patrick's book had served 'more to obscure than illuminate that reality'. Furthermore, Armstrong continued, 'The gap between how Patrick sees the real world of the gang boy, and the reality experienced by the gang boy himself, would appear to be great':

> There is a failure [by Patrick] to recognise the deviant activity as one facet [...] of the individual's complex but interrelated interactions with the world around him. What emerges is a stereotypical image of the gang boy, a designation which serves not only as a short-hand label indicating the sort of person he *really* is, but also as a prescription for society's treatment of him. Nowhere do we catch a glimpse – however brief – of what gang-membership actually *does mean* in terms of the concrete relationships experienced within a particular sub-cultural setting.[60]

To Armstrong, Patrick had failed to distinguish between myth and reality ('The distinction between data gathered by direct observation, and that acquired by hearsay or anecdote, is blurred'), and had given equal weight in his final analysis to both, ultimately pathologising the behaviour of Tim and the boys throughout the book. For Armstrong, the resulting text therefore divorced the behaviour of the boys from their wider social, economic and political contexts, and Patrick's main proposed response to dealing with gangs – to arrest the 'core' of gang members, in order to break up any given gang – was therefore ineffective. These comments point to the fundamental differences in epistemology between the two studies, differences which find distinct echoes in current debate within UK gang research, and to which we now return.

RESEARCHERS, REFLEXIVITY AND THE POLITICS OF REPRESENTATION

The differences in epistemology between the two studies could not be more striking, and point to the importance of reflexivity in researching these phenomena. Patrick located his study firmly within the oeuvre of gang research (particularly American gang research), while Armstrong and Wilson were fundamentally rooted in social interactionism and deviancy amplification. Neither, however, reflected on the implications of these perspectives on their argument, or on the ethical and methodological implications of these positions for their research. Gang research, perhaps now more than ever, occurs in a context of heightened public debate and awareness. Patrick appears to have recognised the importance of this – delaying publication for some years, addressing the book to the general reader, and including a section on 'treatment and prevention' – but perhaps did not fully appreciate the ways in which his work would be received and responded to. Indeed, a journalist who interviewed Patrick for the *Daily Record* newspaper wrote: 'What James Patrick is most apprehensive about at this stage is the likely treatment his book will receive at the hand of the media [...] He genuinely fears that the serious intention of his research will be missed.'[61] Armstrong and Wilson, for their part, admit that they did little to publicise their research; the book they were working on sadly never came to fruition, so the counter-narrative to *A Glasgow Gang Observed* never saw the light of day. This resulted in an interesting tension in the history and representation of youth gangs in 1960s and 1970s Glasgow. On the one hand, as we have shown, Easterhouse became widely viewed as the 'hotbed' for gang violence in 1960s Glasgow and yet, on the other, it was Patrick's book on gangs in Maryhill that became the most well-known and controversial study of youth gangs in the same era. Armstrong and Wilson had tried in vain to challenge the stereotypes of Easterhouse, to demonstrate how exaggerated the media coverage and public views were and, significantly, to show how the wider public concern and media exaggeration were actually shaping and influencing not just the behaviour of young people in Easterhouse, but official responses to them. For them, the stereotyping of Easterhouse as an area with a terrible reputation for gang violence had very real consequences:

> The reputation created many difficulties, especially for young people living in Easterhouse. For not only did it cause changes on the perceptual level, it brought about real changes in the conditions surrounding them. What began as a myth ended as a *real* social problem.[62]

This manifested itself in a number of ways. In 1966, for example, responding to growing concerns about gang violence in the area, the police introduced what was termed a 'saturation policing' strategy. Policemen who were not from the area were brought in in large numbers to act as a mobile police squad designed to prevent crime by stopping it before it started. Under the heading 'Group Disorders', a public relations handout quoted by Armstrong and Wilson stated:

> Many anonymous phone calls are received from residents in the area that a number of youths are loitering at a particular locus, and they are usually apprehensive about their future conduct. This is dealt with by the plain clothes crew of Echo 10 or the Untouchables.[63]

This controversial squad, nicknamed 'The Untouchables' after the popular television series of the same name, reportedly arrested young men simply for appearing in public in groups of three or more. This resulted in grudges developing against the police and, according to the interviews conducted by Armstrong and Wilson, the attitude 'I got done for breach of the peace for nothing, next time it'll be for something!' quickly spread among boys in the gangs.[64] Wilson argued that the public reputation of Easterhouse also made it less likely that young people with an address in the area would be invited for a job interview, by undertaking an experiment that involved sending fake applications for jobs where the only difference between sets of applications were the names and addresses of the applicant.[65]

Curiously, however, Patrick's study did not result in any stigma for Maryhill, despite *A Glasgow Gang Observed* being the more controversial, well-known and publicised study of Glasgow gangs to emerge about the 1960s. Instead, it appears that Patrick's study shored up the reputation of Glasgow more broadly as a 'violent city', but that by the time of its publication, there was some reluctance to further damage Glasgow's reputation at a time when the economy was experiencing difficulties and Glasgow was trying to attract inward investment. In reference to the serialisation of *A Glasgow Gang Observed*, Andrew McBarnet of *The Glasgow Herald* reported of Patrick:

> Already he is disillusioned by the way a leading Sunday newspaper has handled the publication of extracts from the book. In his own words, he is 'horrified' by the choice of material – almost out of his control – which he considers sensational and unrepresentative.[66]

Armstrong and Wilson argued that the disproportionate focus on gang violence in Easterhouse came about largely a result of wider political concerns about a perceived rise in rates of violence in Glasgow specifically and Scotland more broadly. Initially, this had allowed the left (Labour) and right (Progressive/Tory) in Glasgow to use responses to Easterhouse as a means of publicising how they would tackle the issue, should they be successful in the forthcoming election. But, they argued, once it became apparent that Glasgow was being presented at a national level as a 'city torn by violence', 'both sides stood together to reduce this threat to Glasgow's reputation by denying that things were "this bad"'.[67]

For the current generation of gang researchers, the lesson is to be very conscious of the political context in which research takes place, and to be sensitive to the ways in which research is or might be used – but, nonetheless, to ensure that their research is communicated to the right audiences. Barry Goldson, reflecting on a similar issue, quotes James Sheptycki and Adam Edwards in calling for:

> greater reflexivity among social scientists over the implication of their work in the very social problems they study; social scientists are implicated in the weaponisation of civil society through their representations of the problem and this needs careful management if they are to better control the political manipulation of their work in this and other criminological disputes.[68]

Armstrong and Wilson have since reflected upon how their reading of the situation through the lens of symbolic interactionism and deviancy amplification may have influenced both how they engaged with the data and presented their findings in published form. There is no doubt that there was a 'moral panic' over youth gangs in Glasgow at that time and, as

Armstrong and Wilson's research still persuasively demonstrates, Easterhouse was unfairly highlighted as the main 'problem' area over and above other locales in Glasgow – and this negative stereotyping did impact on both the young people who lived there and the area as a whole. Yet, our reading of Armstrong's interviews in conjunction with our own interviews has revealed everyday violence and threats on a scale we had not originally anticipated. This raises interesting questions about how the conceptual frameworks and approaches to our research that we adopt ultimately shape not just how we view our research subjects, but how this influences its construction and communication to others, whether to academic or wider audiences.

Although Patrick, Armstrong and Wilson approached their subject matter from different perspectives, and with differing levels of effectiveness, their underlying emphasis on the importance of taking seriously the views and experiences of those actually involved in 'gangs' in Glasgow is valuable. Patrick wanted to 'illuminate their reality' whilst Armstrong and Wilson emphasised the necessity of referring 'to the subjective definitions of the situation held by the actors themselves'.[69] Despite the appearance of a major body of academic research exploring gangs in recent years, 'there remains a dearth of research that explores the understandings, experiences and social meanings of "gangs" for children and young people'.[70] Oral history offers a means of exploring subjective identities, and is therefore ideally suited to exploring the meanings associated with gangs, as well as trying to tease out how the politics of representation shapes and influences individual subjectivities in a given time and place. Based on this ongoing research, we argue that representations of gangs give an important insight into not only the phenomenon itself, but also into the broader history and politics of representation in Glasgow. In this sense, the study of gangs offers a unique vantage point from which to analyse the changing fears, mores and values of societies in different times and places, as well as a lens through which to analyse power and social change in different times and places.

FINAL POINTS

Important lessons can be drawn from this period of Glasgow's history, and from both Patrick and Armstrong and Wilson's research with youth gangs in different parts of the city. First, the response to the two studies bears attention. Easterhouse became the byword for gangs in the city despite, as

Patrick, Armstrong and Wilson, and other empirical studies, asserted, the issue having been more pronounced in other areas of the city.[71] The 'moral panic' that arose often reflected fears about the impact of the construction of new peripheral housing estates and the break-up of traditional communities, rather than the behaviour itself. As Armstrong and Wilson observed,

> Despite the dearth of empirical information ... the notion appears to persist [that there is a link between standards of housing and deviance], and certainly regarding the 'Easterhouse problem' there is clear evidence of its prevalence amongst Glasgow's political figures (and others) who were anxious to cite the 'concrete jungle' arguments as explanations of gang violence in the area.[72]

Here, the juvenile 'gang' becomes a focal point for wider concerns and fears during a period of social change, and the availability or otherwise of empirical evidence that contradicts public discourse appears to make little difference. In fact, as Armstrong and Wilson demonstrated, these concerns can actually influence the identities and behaviour of the young people involved, and provide 'proof' that the initial fears were accurate.

Second, while it is clear that the authors arrived at very different conclusions, these differences highlight – at the very least – that there are differences between gangs in different times and places, even where they occur at a similar time in the same city. There were differences between the situation in Easterhouse and that in Maryhill, and it is likely that the groups being studied were different in some ways. For us, this points to the importance of understanding the issue of gangs within a particular local historical context, and of recognising that the history and trajectory of gangs over time are wedded to the particular social, political, cultural and institutional arrangements in – and, as we have seen, within – different cities. Patrick recognised this all too well back in 1973, commenting:

> the gangs of New York appear to differ in kind from those of Boston, Chicago and Los Angeles, and nothing would be gained by incorporating them all in one theory which ignores their essential differences. I believe the same to be true of this country in that the Glasgow gang finds no parallel in Liverpool or London. So theories which were evolved to explain highly specific conditions in England may have precious little relevance to the situation in Glasgow.[73]

In the early twenty-first century, growing academic attention given to the phenomenon of youth gangs in Britain's cities has largely collapsed the unique and distinctive history of gang identities in different cities into a 'UK gang phenomenon'.[74] Our research thus far has revealed a complex landscape in which individual experiences, the local setting and wider concerns about youth violence combine to influence gang identities, behaviours and responses and emphasise the importance of understanding the issue of gangs within a particular local historical context. Even the usage and meaning of that problematic and imprecise term 'gang' can differ across time and place, with young people in 1960s Glasgow preferring the term 'team' to 'gang'. Patrick argued that gangs in Glasgow had 'become institutionalized over the years, forming a violence or conflict subculture within the city'.[75] The value of historical perspectives in understanding youth subcultures like 'gangs' within Glasgow and elsewhere, both in the past and in contemporary society, should not be underestimated.

NOTES

1. A. Davies, 'Glasgow's "reign of terror": Street gangs, racketeering and intimidation in the 1920s and 1930s', *Contemporary British History* 21(4) (2007), 406 (Davies 2007).
2. *Glasgow Herald*, 7 June 1968.
3. A. Bartie, 'Moral panics and Glasgow gangs: Exploring 'the new wave of Glasgow hooliganism', 1965–1970', *Contemporary British History*, 24(3) (2010), 385–408 (Bartie 2010).
4. J. Patrick, *A Glasgow Gang Observed* (London, 1973) (Patrick 1973).
5. G. Armstrong and M. Wilson, 'City politics and deviancy amplification', in I. Taylor and L. Taylor (eds.), *Politics and Deviance: Papers from the National Deviance Conference* (Middlesex, 1973) (Armstrong and Wilson 1973a).
6. See, for example, debates in B. Goldson, *Youth in Crisis? 'Gangs', Territoriality and Violence* (Abingdon, 2011) (Goldson 2011).
7. W. B. Sanders, *Gangbangs and Drive-Bys: Grounded Culture and Juvenile Gang Violence* (New York, 1994), p. 8 (Sanders 1994).
8. Patrick, *A Glasgow Gang*, p. 123; P. Donnelly 'Evaluating gang rehabilitation and violence reduction in Glasgow's East End', Presentation to 18th UKPHA Annual Public Health Forum, Bournemouth International Conference Centre, 24–25 March 2010 (Donnelly 2010).
9. For more on housing, see, for example, M. Glendinning (ed.), *Rebuilding Scotland: The Postwar Vision, 1945–1975* (East Linton, 1995) (Glendinning 1995).

10. G. Noble, 'In defence of Easterhouse', *New Society* 20 (1970), 328 (Noble 1970).
11. Armstrong and Wilson, 'City politics and deviancy amplification', p. 67.
12. For a discussion of this evidence, see Bartie, 'Moral panics and Glasgow gangs', 385–408.
13. These issues are examined in Bartie, 'Moral panics and Glasgow gangs'.
14. *Glasgow Herald*, 10 January 1966.
15. Mitchell Library (Glasgow) Archives and Special Collections (ML-ASC), SR22/40/16, *Report of the Chief Constable of the City of Glasgow for the Year 1965*, p. 7 (Mitchell Library 1965).
16. *Glasgow Herald*, 26 April 1966.
17. For more on Vaughan, see, for example, Denis Gifford's obituary of him in *The Independent*, 17 September 1999.
18. This episode caused some controversy; with claims made that gang fights had been staged. See, for example, *Scottish Daily Express*, 6 June 1968.
19. *Glasgow Herald*, 12 July 1968.
20. *Daily Record,* 12 July 1968. Note: Vaughan was not present but in Bournemouth as part of his tour.
21. For more on the Easterhouse Project, see A. Bartie and A. Fraser, 'The Easterhouse Project: Youth, social justice and the arts in Glasgow, 1968–1970', *Scottish Justice Matters*, 2(1) (2014), 38–9 (Bartie and Fraser 2010).
22. Patrick, *A Glasgow Gang*; G. Armstrong and M. Wilson, 'City politics and deviancy amplification'; G. Armstrong and M. Wilson, 'Delinquency and some aspects of housing', in C. Ward (ed.), *Vandalism* (London, 1973) (Armstrong and Wilson 1973b).
23. It is now widely known that James Patrick was, in fact, Frank Coffield, an education researcher (now retired). See, for example, J. Murray, 'Just suppose this man ran education', *InTuition*, 8 (2012), 8–9 (Murray 2012).
24. Patrick, *A Glasgow Gang*, p. 9.
25. Patrick, *A Glasgow Gang*, p. 13.
26. Patrick, *A Glasgow Gang*, pp. 13–17.
27. Patrick, *A Glasgow Gang*, p. 9.
28. Patrick, *A Glasgow Gang*, pp. 17–26.
29. Patrick, *A Glasgow Gang*, p. 25.
30. Patrick, *A Glasgow Gang*, p. 36.
31. A 'gemmie' is a 'hardman' in local parlance; to be 'gemme' is to demonstrate the ability to both stand up for yourself and to be able to handle yourself; a 'boay' is a local word for boy. Patrick, *A Glasgow Gang*, pp. 27–45.
32. Patrick, *A Glasgow Gang*, pp. 135–9.
33. Patrick, *A Glasgow Gang*, p. 154.

34. Patrick, *A Glasgow Gang*, pp. 178 and 200; L. Yablonsky, *The Violent Gang* (New York, 1962) (Yablonsky 1962).
35. See, for example, H. Becker, *Outsiders* (New York, 1963) (Becker 1963); D. Matza, *Delinquency and Drift* (New York, 1964) (Matza 1964).
36. See S. Winlow, 'The National Deviancy Symposia', in R. Wright (ed), *Criminology* (Oxford, 2014) (Winlow 2014).
37. Patrick, *A Glasgow Gang*, pp. 157 and 164. In 1966, the sociologist David M. Downes had argued in his influential study of youth in the Stepney and Poplar boroughs of London that there was no evidence of US-style gangs: 'observation and information combined point to the absence of delinquent gangs in the East End, except as a thoroughly atypical activity'. D.M. Downes, *The Delinquent Solution: A Study in Subcultural Theory* (London, 1966), p. 198 (Downes 1966).
38. *Glasgow Herald*, 17 February 1973. Archie Hind was the first Assistant Secretary of the Easterhouse Project (1969–70).
39. Patrick, *A Glasgow Gang*, p. 9.
40. See, for example, A. Bryman, *Social Research Methods* (Oxford, 2004) (Bryman 2004); G. Pearson, 'The researcher as hooligan: Where "participant" observation means breaking the law', *International Journal of Social Research Methodology*, 12(3) (2009), 243–55 (Pearson 2009).
41. *The Times*, 16 February 1973; *Daily Record*, 5 February 1973.
42. S. Damer, *Glasgow: Going for a Song* (London, 1990), p. 203 (Damer 1990).
43. *Daily Record*, 14 February 1973.
44. J. Patrick, *A Glasgow Gang Observed* (Castle Douglas, 2013) (Patrick 2013).
45. Armstrong and Wilson had included a note stating 'A more detailed treatment of some of the themes on this paper may be found in G. ARMSTRONG and M. WILSON (George Allen & Unwin, forthcoming). Armstrong and Wilson, 'City politics and deviancy amplification', p. 89.
46. Armstrong and Wilson, 'Delinquency and some aspects of housing', p. 73.
47. Wilkins, cited in J. Young, *The Drugtakers: The Social Meaning of Drug Use* (London, 1973), p. 108 (Young 1973).
48. Armstrong and Wilson, 'City politics and deviancy amplification', p. 74.
49. Armstrong and Wilson, 'City politics and deviancy amplification', p. 62.
50. This project, 'Narratives of Glasgow: Oral histories of youth gangs in Easterhouse, c. 1965–1975', was supported by a British Academy Small Grant (summer 2011). A smaller pilot study, 'Narratives of Glasgow: Oral histories of gangs in 1960s Easterhouse' was conducted by Susan Batchelor, Angela Bartie and Alistair Fraser, and funded by the University of Glasgow Adam Smith Research Foundation Seedcorn Fund (2010).
51. We have written a piece exploring Danny's memories and experiences in relation to the stereotype of the 'hard man' in the 'violent city'. See A. Bartie

and A. Fraser, 'Speaking to the "hard" men: masculinities, violence and youth gangs in Glasgow, c.1965–75', in L. Abrams and E. Ewan, *Nine Centuries of Man: Manhood and Masculinity in Scottish History* (Edinburgh, 2017) (Bartie and Fraser 2017).

52. Interview with Danny McCall, 7 July 2011.

53. Armstrong and Wilson, 'The history of a delinquent area', Paper given at National Deviancy Symposium, University of York, April 1970 (original copy of paper given to us by Gail Armstrong).

54. Armstrong and Wilson, 'Delinquency and some aspects of housing', p. 76.

55. Armstrong and Wilson, 'City politics and deviancy amplification', p. 67.

56. Noble, 'In defence of Easterhouse', 328–9.

57. Armstrong and Wilson, 'City politics and deviancy amplification', p. 62.

58. Armstrong and Wilson, 'City politics and deviancy amplification', p. 81.

59. M. Wilson, '*A Glasgow Gang Observed*' (Book Review), *The British Journal of Criminology*, 13(4) (1973), 411 (Wilson 1973).

60. Armstrong, '*A Glasgow Gang Observed*' (Book Review), 'Sociology further notices' (undated, (circa 1973) photocopy of review given to us by Gail Armstrong).

61. *Glasgow Herald*, 5 February 1973.

62. Armstrong and Wilson, 'City politics and deviancy amplification', p. 88.

63. Armstrong and Wilson, 'City politics and deviancy amplification', p. 79.

64. Armstrong and Wilson, 'City politics and deviancy amplification', pp. 78–80.

65. Armstrong and Wilson, 'The history of a delinquent area'.

66. *Glasgow Herald*, 5 February 1973.

67. Armstrong and Wilson, 'City politics and deviancy amplification', p. 74.

68. Sheptycki and Edwards, cited in B. Goldson, *Youth in Crisis?*, p. 17.

69. Armstrong and Wilson, 'Delinquency and some aspects of housing', p. 75.

70. C. Alexander and B. Goldson cited in A. Fraser, 'Street habitus: Gangs, territorialism and social change in Glasgow', *Journal of Youth Studies*, 16(8) (2013), 971 (Fraser 2013).

71. See, for example, Institute for the Study and Treatment of Delinquency Scottish Branch: Glasgow Working Party, 'The carrying of offensive weapons', *British Journal of Criminology*, 10(3) (1970), 255–69 (Institute for the Study and Treatment of Delinquency Scottish Branch 1970). For a fuller discussion, see Bartie, 'Moral panics and Glasgow gangs', 385–408.

72. Armstrong and Wilson, 'Delinquency and some aspects of housing', pp. 66–7.

73. Patrick, *A Glasgow Gang*, p. 157.

74. For a more detailed discussion, see Fraser, *Urban Legends*.

75. Patrick, *A Glasgow Gang*, p. 154.

REFERENCES

G. Armstrong and M. Wilson, 'City Politics and Deviancy Amplification', in I. Taylor and L. Taylor (eds.), *Politics and Deviance: Papers from the National Deviance Conference* (Middlesex, 1973a).

G. Armstrong and M. Wilson, 'Delinquency and some Aspects of Housing', in C. Ward (ed.), *Vandalism* (London, 1973b).

A. Bartie, 'Moral Panics and Glasgow Gangs: Exploring 'the New Wave of Glasgow Hooliganism', 1965–1970', *Contemporary British History*, 24, 3 (2010), 385–408.

A. Bartie and A. Fraser, 'The Easterhouse Project: Youth, Social Justice and the Arts in Glasgow, 1968–1970', *Scottish Justice Matters*, 2, 1 (2014), 38–9.

A. Bartie and A. Fraser, 'Speaking to the "Hard" Men: masculinities, violence and youth gangs in Glasgow, c.1965–75', in L. Abrams and E. Ewan, *Nine Centuries of Man: Manhood and Masculinity in Scottish History*(Edinburgh, 2017).

H. Becker, *Outsiders* (New York, 1963).

A. Bryman, *Social research methods* (Oxford, 2004).

S. Damer, *Glasgow: Going for a Song* (London, 1990).

A. Davies, 'Glasgow's "Reign of Terror": Street Gangs, Racketeering and Intimidation in the 1920s and 1930s', *Contemporary British History* 21, 4 (2007), 405–27.

P. Donnelly 'Evaluating Gang Rehabilitation and Violence Reduction in Glasgow's East End', Presentation to 18th UKPHA Annual Public Health Forum, Bournemouth International Conference Centre, 24–5 March 2010.

D.M. Downes, *The Delinquent Solution: A Study in Subcultural Theory* (London, 1966).

A. Fraser, 'Street Habitus: Gangs, Territorialism and Social Change in Glasgow', *Journal of Youth Studies*, 16, 8 (2013), 970–85.

M. Glendinning (ed.), *Rebuilding Scotland: The Postwar Vision, 1945–1975* (East Linton, 1995).

B. Goldson, *Youth in Crisis? 'Gangs', Territoriality and Violence* (Abingdon, 2011).

Institute for the Study and Treatment of Delinquency Scottish Branch: Glasgow Working Party, 'The Carrying of Offensive Weapons', *British Journal of Criminology*, 10, 3 (1970), 255–69.

D. Matza, *Delinquency and Drift* (New York, 1964).

J. Murray, 'Just suppose this man ran education', *InTuition*, 8 (2012), 8–9.

G. Noble, 'In Defence of Easterhouse', *New Society* 20 (1970), 328–29.

J. Patrick, *A Glasgow Gang Observed* (London, 1973).

J. Patrick, *A Glasgow Gang Observed* (Castle Douglas, 2013).

G. Pearson, 'The Researcher as Hooligan: Where "Participant" Observation Means Breaking the Law', *International Journal of Social Research Methodology*, 12, 3 (2009), 243–55.

W. B. Sanders, *Gangbangs and Drive-Bys: Grounded Culture and Juvenile Gang Violence* (New York, 1994).

M. Wilson, 'A Glasgow Gang Observed (Book Review), *The British Journal of Criminology*, 13, 4 (1973), 411.

S. Winlow, 'The National Deviancy Symposia', in R. Wright (ed), *Criminology* (Oxford, 2014).

L. Yablonsky, *The Violent Gang* (New York, 1962).

J. Young, *The Drugtakers: The Social Meaning of Drug Use* (London, 1973).

Angela Bartie is a Senior Lecturer in Scottish History at the University of Edinburgh. She is the author of *The Edinburgh Festivals: Culture and Society in Post-war Britain* (2013) and co-editor (with Eleanor Bell) of *The International Writers' Conference Revisited: Edinburgh, 1962* (2012). She has also published on youth gangs in 1960s Glasgow, the policing of youth in post-war Britain, historical pageants, and oral history in Scotland.

Alistair Fraser is currently Senior Lecturer in Criminology and Sociology at the University of Glasgow, where he is also Associate Director of the Scottish Centre for Crime and Justice Research. His research interests focus on youth, crime, and globalisation, with a particular focus on youth gangs in a historical and comparative context. His first book, *Urban Legends: Gang Identity in the Post-Industrial City*, was published by Oxford University Press in 2015.

CHAPTER 10

Gang Girls: Agency, Sexual Identity and Victimisation 'On Road'

Tara Young and Loretta Trickett

Criminological research that explores the participation of women in street-based groups classified as 'gangs' has focussed on gender dynamics, female criminality and victimisation.[1] A key concern running through current academic, and political, debate in the UK is the level of violence, sexual exploitation and abuse experienced by gang-associated young women and girls and the need to tackle it effectively. Recent publications have shown how girls and young women are at heightened risk of abuse by male gang members who use rape as a weapon to keep them in line.[2] With few exceptions, the research on gang-associated girls, in the UK at least, has tended to present the female experience as essentially one of subordination and abuse.

Historically, gang research has tended to be based on the testimony of male gang members; relatively few studies have considered women as participants or given voice to girls by recounting the female experience in their words.[3] Feminist studies have begun to rectify the deficit by

T. Young (✉)
Criminal Justice and Criminology, School of Social Policy, Sociology and Social Research, University of Kent, Canterbury, UK
e-mail: t.l.young@kent.ac.uk

L. Trickett
Criminal Law and Criminology, Nottingham Law School, Nottingham Trent University, Nottingham, UK
e-mail: loretta.trickett@ntu.ac.uk

© The Author(s) 2017
K. Gildart et al. (eds.), *Youth Culture and Social Change*,
Palgrave Studies in the History of Subcultures and Popular Music,
DOI 10.1057/978-1-137-52911-4_10

publishing research that illustrates the harsh social conditions that shape young women's involvement in street-based groups and increases their exposure to violence.[4] For example, Jody Miller's qualitative study examining the links between structural inequality and gender-based violence exposed high rates of physical and sexual abuse against female respondents. In Miller's study, African-American girls were habitually 'getting played' by young men seeking to accrue respect, elevate their status, conceal vulnerabilities and deflect victimisation.[5] Essential to masculine survival in disadvantaged neighbourhoods is the creation of a 'playa' persona. According to Miller, the 'playa' identity is forged upon the bodies of girls and young women whose victimisation is rationalised, normalised and publically tolerated.[6]

Avelardo Valdez's ethnography of Mexican American girls similarly charts the experience of young women situated on the periphery of gangs and reports their risk of victimisation.[7] Like Miller, Valdez's work emphasises the crucial role that social structure plays in the aetiology of violence experienced by girls and young women. Put simply, Valdez, argues that changes in gender roles and sexuality, particularly women's sexual liberation, has altered the dynamic of male-female relationships, placing adolescent girls 'beyond risk'.[8] Girls and young women are, according to Valdez, encouraged (via media advertising and other cultural mediums) to express their sexuality and to exercise agency in relationships with boys and young men. However, these 'social transformations' increase the risk of victimisation and exploitation for girls who hang out with or date gangsters because males in gangs adhere to a street culture that valorises violence.[9] Gangs are, according to Valdez, patriarchal microcosms that endorse male dominance over and control of women's bodies, demand female submissiveness, and punish those who violate gender norms.

Similar abuses of girls and young women have been found in the UK studies.[10] Findings from *Race on the Agenda* research – one of the first policy documents to focus specifically on girls and women 'affected by or associated with gang, group, or serious youth violence' – catalogues the abuse of 'gang-involved' young women and concludes that sexual violence is routinely used as 'a weapon of choice' against them. Furthermore, the abuse of young women 'took place against a backdrop of little support for women where there is confusion about what is acceptable sexual practice and consent.'[11] What the UK studies, and those of Valdez and Miller, point to is the relative powerlessness of women in relation to their male counterparts, and the distinctive social conditions that promote their victimisation. It appears that female victimisation is dependent upon 'who she is', relative to the men she associates with, and the status she occupies thereafter.[12] Thus, girls, by virtue of being in the company of young men seeking to affirm their masculine identity, inadvertently put themselves at risk of sexual abuse unless they are attached to high-profile males who can offer some protection. Young women with no formal attachment to a credible male, and thus devoid of a viable protector, are susceptible to objectification, treated as property and denied their right to refuse to engage in criminal activity or to reject sexual advances made against them. [13]

Some studies have highlighted the extent to which the victimisation of girls is also dependent upon the protective responses, of other, more experienced, women. As noted by Valdez:

> it is the street-wise (i.e. the *cholas*) and those that have strong intimate relationships with members (i.e. wives/girlfriends) who avoid sexual victimisation by monitoring one another's behaviour... Girls who are not part of this protective network... are targeted by the males.[14]

Therefore, a lack of support from 'clued-up', high-status, females can increase the victimisation of naïve young women. Within the patriarchal environment that is the gang, female relationships are confrontational, suspicious and lacking in trust.[15] Such antagonistic and intolerant relationships between girls and young women tend to emerge in 'gang-identified' neighbourhoods where residents are desensitized and culturally blind to violence against women and girls. In Miller's study, routinized verbal and physical assaults against girls and young women who hung around, 'linked' or dated gang members went [largely] unchallenged within the community and contributed to a victim-blaming narrative which positioned women as precipitating their own victimisation. Incidents of abuse and violence against women were internalised, by boys and girls alike, and young women learnt not to intervene on behalf of other women and to be solely responsible for protecting themselves.[16]

A few key points can be gleaned from the research generated by Valdez, Miller and British scholars: firstly, that girls in gangs are susceptible to physical and sexual violence; secondly, that the situational inequalities faced by girls and young women involved with young men in gangs alienates them from each other, and precludes the formation of compassionate relationships between them which increases the risk of victimisation; and, thirdly, the gang environment reduces the ability of girls and young women to effectively exercise power and agency. This chapter sets out to further explore the experience of women involved in gang life. By drawing upon the testimony of gang-associated young people we seek to discover if, and how, young women exercise power, control and achieve sufficiently high status to avoid victimisation in a patriarchal subculture that favours and fosters the agency of young men and situates girls and young women as subordinate and powerless. We argue here that young women are subjected to restrictions when attempting to build a credible [feminine] identity, which puts them at risk of sexual violence. We suggest that some girls are in a no-win situation and end up 'getting played'[17] by both boys and girls in an inequitable, gendered environment. In this chapter we focus on how young women (and some young men) exercise agency in a way that maintains gendered restrictions and, in doing so, increases violence against other young women. We suggest that some young women do attempt to build their feminine identities in ways that actively challenge the status quo but that they do this within a restrictive context.

GIRLS, AGENCY AND SEXUAL IDENTITY

Research on gangs has often underplayed young women's agency and oftentimes failed to concentrate on how women formulate and negotiate their identities 'on-road'.[18] However, some studies have illustrated how the accomplishment of feminine identity requires young women to build 'credible' (sexual) identities to fit in. Indeed, as Messerscmidt notes, 'in the daily life of the youth gang, girls not only participate in the social construction of gender difference but also engage in practices common to boys'.[19] Within the 'on road' context, then, young people formulate their identities from normative discourses around appropriate male and female behaviour. Through social interactions young women, and young men, configure their behaviour and that of others through the notion of 'accountability' to those of the same and of the opposite sex as they build their social and sexual identities. The incidents of sexual labelling and the resistance to such labels, as discussed in this article, involved 'situational accomplishments' of gender within relational settings whereby young men and women who inhabited the same social spaces drew on shared knowledge to judge the behaviours of their peers.[20] At the heart of such interactions is the search for 'respect' and 'status'.[21]

For many young people anxiety about threats to their identity is a key factor in their lives. Indeed, achieving a credible gendered sexual identity is always a work in progress and threats to it must be defended against, contained, minimised or overcome.[22] The gang, as a male domain, provides the space for young men to act out and formulate a credible identity that matches normative standards of masculinity as defined by the culture in which they live.[23]

In this regard research on 'gangs' has illustrated how within the context of 'on road' young men develop aggressive personal identities which present(s) as a form of hyper-masculinity.

The agency of and constraints on young women in relation to this area are less clear. We need to acknowledge that building a credible feminine identity within the social and heavily gendered space of 'on-road' requires young women to fit in to a subculture where female behaviour is scrutinised and sanctioned to a much greater degree than that of males; into a 'social field' that undervalues the agency of girls and young women who struggle for recognition from their male peers.[24] Although not great in sum, there has been some academic discussion on how girls accomplish femininity including their expression of 'bad girl femininity' and female engagement in violence. In a relatively recent debate, Miller and Messerschmidt questioned whether young women's 'gender crossing' within gangs results in the development of a situated identity which escapes the sexualised constraints of dominant femininity yet few (with the exception of the aforementioned) consider how this is achieved without recourse to gender victimisation (nor consider agency as a process).

In the UK, less attention has been paid to female gang identity formation and agency. In the last few years five new publications on the UK gang experience have emerged; all, bar one, focusing on young men.[25] Harding's research stands alone amongst these texts, in exploring how girls and young women construct gender, exercise agency and survive in the 'street casino' that is gang life in the UK. His research also positions girls and young women at the bottom of a 'social field' that privileges men. He argues that girls who associate with 'gang-involved' young men acknowledge their weakened position; they understand the patriarchal codes of the street, accept their subordinate position and associated vulnerabilities and, importantly, realise the competitive struggle they must have with other girls when vying for status in the gang. Thus, in order to move up the social strata – to exercise agency, become 'playas' in their own right, and avoid being labelled a 'sket' – young women strategise and utilise individual competencies to 'position themselves within the field and maximise their advantage'.[26] As skilled manipulators, some girls achieve advantage over other girls (and agency and status) by cleverly reading the social field for opportunities to build street capital by using 'social skills' (e.g. negotiation, entrapment or loyalty skills) and competencies (e.g. fighting) to benefit their male counterparts. Girls who lack credible social skills – e.g. the young and naïve – with few options to assert agency use their sexuality as a means via which to gain entry to the group and align with powerful male members.

Whilst Harding's research contributes to the debate on the role of girls on road, and should be applauded for exploring the construction of female agency, his study follows in the tradition of classical gang research in so far as it offers an essentially androcentric account of young women's existential experience. It is exclusively a male gaze from both the perspective of the researcher and the research subject. In his construction of female agency, Harding's analysis rests, largely, on his interpretation and the narrative of male participants which filters the experience of girls and young women through the script of masculinity ultimately divesting young women of their voice. Harding's assessment of female social skills and individual agency, presented in a chapter entitled 'Playing the Queen: Gender in the gang', makes assumptions from male imaginary; the voices of young women are missing. As a result, his narrative pacifies and disembodies the female, rendering her redundant in her experience; she doesn't exist in it.

Policy research conducted in the UK has sought to give voice to females in gangs. In the main, these efforts have focussed on the nature and scale of sexual violence endured by females associated with gangs.[27] As a body of work they catalogue the harm and abuse experienced by girls and young women associated with gangs, arguing that sexual violence enacted against girls and young women in a gang setting is distinctive, with its own set of characteristics and motivations. The authors contend that girls and young women are routinely coerced or forced to engage in sex acts (sometimes with more than one male) against their will. Oftentimes, young women engage in sexual activities in return for material reward, social status, or protection or fear of physical violence against them.[28] The strategy of engaging in sex in order to be accepted or receive protection is, according to Harding, to credit female sexuality with power it does not have and to misinterpret the position of women within street culture; girls who engage in sexual encounters with gang members believing they will be accepted are fooled by boys who are simply taking advantage. They are '"silly young girls" who may not be fully aware that she's being passed around until later, or aware of how she is viewed and labelled.'[29] Whilst the policy reports do well to draw attention to the heinous acts of sexual abuse perpetrated against girls and young women they offer a limited explanation as to *why* these acts of violence occur against particular girls, and pay little attention the interactive contextual processes that shape and frame the victimisation of girls – beyond indicating that violence, including sexual violence, is a predilection of male gang members and an almost certain experience of females involved with them.

What is required is an account of girls' lives that is grounded in the experience of young women based on their interpretations that can further our knowledge of how women negotiate on road and overcome constraints on individual agency. A fluid conceptualisation of power can help to account for contradictions between, and within, masculine and feminine social identities, including the public and private versions of self which underpin the identities, fears and anxieties discussed. The narrative accounts here revealed that feminine identity involved a social construction and accordingly the girls and young women experienced imbalances and shifts in power. Indeed, these respondents were both potentially powerful and powerless in relation to other young women and men, and their constructions of female identity continually fluctuated between these two polar opposites.

The process of building a credible female sexual identity for these young women took place against the patriarchal space of on-road wherein they were required to engage with a street subculture where female sexual behaviour was scrutinised and sanctioned to a much greater degree than that of males. This scrutinising process drew on normative ideas about appropriate male and female sexual behaviour. The label of 'slut' or 'sket' was not applied to young men as it was for young women, because male promiscuity was usually considered as something to be pursued and celebrated in the construction and maintenance of an acceptable and credible masculine identity, whilst female promiscuity was considered as degrading, as something to be shunned, and was negatively labelled by young men, as well as some young women. These binary ideas about male and female sexuality have a long history; for generations the idea of female sexual promiscuity has been associated with the 'whore' label. What is considered to be honourable behaviour for a female is socially learnt by young women and, yet, ideas about honourable and dishonourable female behaviour are also used by young males when they are attempting to create credible male identities on-road.[30] By examining these ideas and how they inform male and female behaviours we can learn much about male and female interactions within on-road street context. The remainder of this chapter seeks to further our understanding of women's agency by recognising that they choose to exercise agency in ways that do not always challenge the status quo and, in doing so, reduce the agency of other young women. This chapter sets the tone for a subsequent article where we examine testimonies from young women who construct their feminine identities in more directly challenging ways.

THE RESEARCH

The findings presented here are drawn from the testimonies of young men and women involved in research conducted, by one of the authors, as part of a wider exploration of young people's experience of being in, or associating with, gangs. As a body of work they sought to explore the construction of sexuality by gang-involved young people and to explore the nature of relationships between girls and boys on road. In particular, one study sought to explore the gendered, asymmetrical perceptions of sexuality and locate these in an understanding of the power dynamics of those on road. An aspect of this study was to highlight how these power dynamics underpin violence against girls and young women and undermine the projection of female agency.[31]

METHODOLOGY

These studies adopted a qualitative approach as the primary objective was to explore the culture of young people 'on road'. They draw on feminist theory and method. Feminist epistemology, as a methodological approach, takes as its problematic issues that pertain to women; it is a methodology that brings with it the assumption that what constitutes reality in society is unequal and hierarchical and what counts as legitimate knowledge is dependent upon power held both at the level of the individual and the social.[32] Feminist research is a political endeavour concerned to give voice specifically to girls and women who have historically been denied power and the right to produce legitimate knowledge. An important aspect of this methodological approach is the involvement of girls and young women in the research process, as accounts of women's lives need to be gleaned from their perspective not through the filtration of male narratives. There is however in much feminist work also a clear recognition that, in challenging the relationship between the masculine and the feminine; feminism holds out possibilities of changing men's lives for the better too.

Sampling

There was no pre-determined sample frame for the study and so traditional qualitative sampling methods such as convenience, snowball and purposive strategies were utilised to identify young people. The main criterion was to access and include individuals associating with groups known as gangs (these could be youngsters identified by community or statutory agencies as gang-involved or those who self-identified with a street-based group) with expert knowledge (e.g. young people with experience of being 'on road' or family members who have relatives involved in gang-related criminality) of the phenomenon. Contact was made with agencies working with young people in gangs or individuals tangentially associated with them (e.g. girlfriends, siblings). The testimonies presented here are drawn from 38 young men and women aged between 15 and 24. The majority of respondents (26) were female and the majority of respondents (29) interviewed originated from the African Caribbean community.

Data Collection and Analysis

The main method of data collection was the focus group interview. These were semi-structured group interviews that covered a number of topics on young people's perceptions of male and female sexuality, identity and intimate relationships. The group interview, is a certified tool for exploring a topic about which little is known and is particularly useful for exploring youthful attitudes towards sex, violence and aggression.[33] The focus group format also provides an opportunity to observe intra-group dynamics at play within the research setting and get a [limited] sense of how young people interact and express themselves when in a group. This was deemed important since the formation of a credible masculine and feminine identity is formed by micro-social interactions between young people. The focus group setting presented an opportunity for the researcher to observe any consensus of attitude, or dissent, held by the respondents.[34]

Nine single-sexed focus groups were conducted. In the majority of cases the young people attending knew each other as friends or as clients attending a support group. They took place in three inner London boroughs and lasted, typically, between 1 and 1½ hours. The group interview was informed by an interview schedule that covered the following topics: young people's understanding of sex and the impact of youth culture on sexual development, issues around fidelity in relationships and the negotiation of sex, consent in sexual relationships, sexual coercion, and sexual culpability and responsibility. It also included a series of vignettes designed to promote in-depth discussion. These vignettes, which were created from previous research conducted with young people, and drew on some of the experiences they had had or knew about, like party situations where young women had been sexual violated, the sharing of sexually explicit material and intimate partner violence.[35] The interviews were transcribed verbatim and utilised Ritchie and Lewis's 'Framework' method as an analytic tool. Like NVivo, this method enables a thematic and narrative analysis of the data.[36] The data that follows, draws out some of the key themes relating to the formation of a credible agentic self for young women on road what the research exposed is that in the struggle for recognition girls and women are turned into victims. The findings are presented in three sections: Constructing a Credible Identity, Spoiled Identities, and Polluted Bodies.

Constructing a Credible Identity

On the road, young men and women are immersed in a culture that demands the projection of a credible masculine and feminine heterosexual identity. In this context, what boys do with their bodies matters. 'Real men' use their bodies in ways that convey strength and dominance. Dominant male bodies present as tough, heterosexual, sexually active and engage in activities, such as fighting, that command a higher social status over subordinate males and women.[37]

Wanting and seeking out opportunities for sex was viewed as an intrinsic part of being male. Male respondents described how, as youngsters, they felt compelled to be sexually active in order to validate themselves as 'men'. They used words such as 'need', 'urge' and feeling 'horny' to describe their natural propensity for sex, and the general consensus was that men were biologically programmed to seek out opportunities to 'release stuff' when and with whom they could.

> Don't tell me that you don't think about it ten times a day... Oh man, tell me about any teenage boy who ain't ready for sex! (Male, FG3)

Since engaging in intercourse was essential to the construction of a credible heterosexual masculine identity that carried, and accrued, cultural capital, being publicly known as a 'virgin' was not a sustainable ongoing identity. Having sex, or at the very least being thought of as sexually active, was fundamental to the male gender project. To be a virgin, then, was to occupy a subordinate position to those who *were* having sex and who, as sexual performers, could legitimately undermine the individual's claim to an authentic masculine identity. To accrue respect from their peers (and satisfy naturalised urges), young men talked of needing to 'rid themselves' of their virginity as quickly as possible and described how some boys, in order to shed the stigma of inexperience, would have sex with the 'wrong sort of girl' otherwise known as 'bezzels', 'links' or 'skets'.[38]

Being able to perform sexually, that is to have sexual prowess, was pivotal to maintaining a credible masculine identity and garnering respect amongst male peers. Not 'doing it right', lacking in stamina or being unable to perform in accordance to prescribed masculine norms could, if publicly known, have catastrophic consequences.

> [*Laughing*]... If you beat shit [not performing sex to an acceptable standard], [and] everyone knows... that's where your life is; that's where it crumbles. Life is done! You have to hide in your shell for a couple of years and... move out of the country, like change your name and come back as a new person. (Male, FG2)

Two key aspects require stressing here: firstly, the *public* character of sexual identity, and, secondly, the instrumentalism of routine masculinity. Not being up to the job, having a reputation for 'beating shit' and performing poorly could, as dramatically expressed above, have devastating consequences for a young man's reputation. Sexual incompetence can destroy a young man's reputation. Secondly, given the young men were attempting to construct a legitimate heterosexual sexuality, girls and young women could ruin them by exposing their sexual deficiency.

In contrast, girls and young women articulated a very different experience of sexual culture on road. Their asymmetrical experience is built on common assumptions about what it meant to be a credible female. The sexuality of women was not, on the whole, conceived as being innate, nor was it articulated as active or emerging from an authentic centre of desire. Underpinning female responses was the essential *reactivity* of female sexuality. By and large, female respondents subscribed to the biological determinist concept of masculinity expressed above. Male sexuality was assumed to be innate and a natural expression of masculinity; at the very least it was simply a 'given' which girls and young women had to negotiate. They knew the boys were 'on it' all the time and on the look out for sex. That male bodies sought and *did* sex and female bodies were sought and *done to* was expressed in a statements made by female respondents in reference to female (il)legitimacy in the pursuit of sex.

When thinking about female sexuality, rather than referring to a culture of instinct and active pursuit, the young women drew on notions of purity, abstinence and control. A common thought was that females must not openly pursue sex. If a girl or young woman actively sought out sex there was 'something wrong with her'. A recurring theme was that girls and young women should conduct themselves with 'dignity' in sexual matters because 'that's how our society sees it' (Female, FG6). Thus a young woman's sexuality was bounded by cultural norms that emphasizing sex within the strict boundaries of a steady relationship with the right man. Women who failed to follow the prescribed codes of traditional emphasised femininity were not, as one young woman put it, 'good women' but bad ones and 'disrespecting' themselves.

> Good women wait, behave, respect themselves, dress well and not like a 'whore'. Bad girls are those that sleep around, are skets, bitches and ho's. (Female, FG4)

SPOILED IDENTITIES

Both young men and women were aware of the reputational risks of casual sex for girls and women, and sexual reputations had to be managed in a way that did not contravene the normative rules of observing masculine respect and maintaining feminine conviviality. As men's reputation depended, in large part, upon getting sex they sough to, as Reeves-Sandy noted, to 'work a yes out' of a young woman by charming his way into her heart and her pants.[39]

> [I say] '... I know you're not a bad girl, I know you're not a whore. I know you're not a bezzel'. But it's ... 'Come on, you'll do it for me, nice'. [It's like] 'I like you, you know! If you do it like. I won't tell no one'. They [the girls] like a little bit of security, like, to make sure. (Male, FG2)

As the above quotation illustrates wily young men drew on conventional notions of feminine respectability to allay girls of their fear of being labelled as a slag in order to bed her. This speech, one can see, was not a genuine offer to protect the reputation of his target but rather a ruse to get laid. Girls and young women were, to a large extent, aware of the trap set by boys and men. They, all too readily, understood the dichotomous vocabulary of the 'good girl/bad girl' and the reputational penalties, of 'getting played' by the wrong guy and sought to protect themselves from the advances of unscrupulous males. As such, girls used their social skills to decipher the intentions set out in the 'chat up' and navigate the persistent attentions of sexually charged young men. As one young woman noted:

> the difficulty is that they never get tired; you know what I mean! They'll go on and on and on, never finish; [it] never ends. (Female, FG7)

Therefore, young women were required to be adept at working out when to be interested and when to resist in order to 'keep safe.' The social dexterity required to manage the young men came with experience, and some young women were better equipped than others at negotiating the 'chat up' and young men's expectations. Some 'played hard to get' and walked away from men calling and signaling to them in the street but this strategy of ignoring them had limited success since, as one young woman notes:

> A: When you walk off, all they want is to try and come to you, come to you, then.
> Q: What sort of responses do you get when you walk away?
> A: Yeah, they'll like cuss you or they start like swearing, 'Who do you think you are?' ... 'You're ugly, you' .... (Female, FG7)

Given the potential for pursuit from young men and abusive, intimidating confrontations it was not surprising to learn that some girls buckled under the pressure and talked to the guys to avoid a more a more challenging situation. However, it was the 'gullible girls', those who were 'not on point' or 'who did not know how to stand up for themselves' who were caught out and who fell into the trap of having sex [Female, FG5].

Whilst there was some sympathy for inexperienced girls who got caught up in the ruse, implicit in the girl's statements was the idea that young women who hang about with the guys made themselves targets. Street girls contravened the codes of normative femininity since:

> girls are meant to be at home'. That's what goes through the boy's head, yeah, and it's like they're... just mess about, girls..., and then they just give them a name. (Female, FG9)

The expectation is 'good' girls are at home and the 'bad' girls are 'chillin' with the guys outside; and since the girls know the guys are on the look out for sex, the consensus is that their bodies available. The management of sexuality was important and the appropriate response to sexual advances, was key to attaining and maintaining a credible reputation. Young women on road socialising with the boys by drinking and smoking were engaging in a risky social practice that eroded their status as a credible person reducing them to little more than rubbish. As one female respondent noted:

> They just treat them as if they're something off the ground. Pick it up and drop it back [down again]. They just think, 'Oh, you know, she's a girl off the street, she ain't got this, she's got this' [and] pick her up off the street back [and drop her] where she came from. (Female, FG9)

POLLUTED BODIES

Girls are likely to be treated badly if they engage in sex outside of a credible and private relationship but more so if they perform culturally taboo sex acts. There was a unanimous belief that people who 'give brain', or do 'bocat', were 'dirty'.[40] Oral sex did not elevate an individual's sexual identity; far from it. Being publicly known to 'head south' damaged one's reputation, and girls who committed this sex act experienced a greater loss of status than boys.

Young men celebrated receiving oral sex from young women, but male performance of it was vilified.

> Like a man goes down on a girl, that's disgusting!... like you shouldn't be eating those things and any man who did this would lose friends... If somebody done it here, yeah, I will not eat after them like or drink, I will not share, I will not smoke after them. (Male, FG2)

On the whole, young men who engaged in bocat were viewed poorly by their peers and risked being ostracised if they were found out. Again, given the normative heterosexuality of young men, it would be the chatter of girls that divulged this faux pas. Importantly, as the above statement illustrates, the sanctions levied at men were limited to acts that denied them the opportunity to engage socially with friends; it is the act of oral sex that offends (not the person as a whole) and this is punished by the non-sharing of wares and withdrawal of friendship. This was not the case for young women who engaged in fellatio – their bodies were polluted by the doing of the act. They were soiled.

This meant that for young women it is not simply *the act of oral sex but also the person* doing it that is condemned as the following extract shows:

> A: [she's] rubbish.
> A: A sket, a slag.
> A: ... when she walks down the street now, no one don't know her... when she walks down the street and everyone knows she's done that... you're a different person. You get treated differently [with] no respect. ... I could say what I want to you, everyone will. (Young males, FG2)

It is, of course, evident that the male-dominant narrative of heterosexual intercourse that informs both accounts denies the reciprocal giving of pleasure by both males and females as a key objective of heterosexual intercourse. Therefore, men want fellatio but they simply do not, publicly, respect women that do it, and the idea of men engaging in cunnilingus is ridiculed and undermined. Yet it is girls who 'give head' that are branded a 'sket' or a 'bezzel' and, on the whole, disrespected by her male and female peers. The act of oral sex thus *changes* the perception of girls and young women so that, afterwards, *they* are not the same; they are stripped of their subjectivity and viewed purely as object. As the quotation above attests, boys can say, and do, what they want to her since she has polluted herself in the act of sex. Similarly, female peers 'look differently' upon a friend that has engaged in oral sex. As some female respondents suggested, 'something must be wrong with her head' to do that since, in the sexual culture of young people on road, this act is abhorrent and only someone in their 'wrong mind' would do such a thing.

Girls publically known to engage in sex (particularly oral sex) with boys are not, as the testimonies attest, afforded respect, nor are they deemed to have any respect for themselves. Similarly, girls who are 'on it', 'who had sex on the regular' or with more than one boy in a peer group lose the status and support accorded to girls who 'behave properly' and within the confines of respectable femininity; that is to have a reactive sexuality not an active one. And, even though some female respondents showed sympathy for girls who found themselves so labelled, and recognised the significance of being branded a 'sket', they also under-stood the contaminating effects brought to bear on all young women associating with girls with a poor reputation. Thus they sought to distance themselves to avoid the risk of being seen as 'bad girls' as polluted subjects, or objects, as vulnerable and potentially unable to shake off the advances of boys and young men who will look to them for sex. By distancing themselves from the 'other', good girls were actively building a credible feminine identity by contrasting themselves with other girls who were not respected.

Girls who perform oral sex, do it frequently, or with multiple boys are, according to one young man, nothing more than property to be 'passed around' to anyone who wants to 'play'. Like the experiences of girls and young women highlighted in the policy literature, she is deprived of the right to move freely near boys without being pressurised for sex.[41] She is a perpetual target for motivated men who will, as illustrated below, approach (sometimes en masse) her for sex. If she provides this sex her situation, already irredeemable, will only get worse as she has, in effect, been divested of the right to make decisions about her sexual behaviour and of the right to guardianship since within the subculture of the street she is fair game.

> What do I think? I hate girls that do that! But if I want the pleasure and she wants the pleasure and she is . . . I'm not going to care. But girls like that, in general I do not like; I hate them. (Male, FG2).

A: If good girl was to walk past us, one of us would move to her for it. If a bad girl was to move, like to walk past us, then everyone would move [onto her]; everyone would go... Gang bang! (Male, FG2)

Despite using the term 'gang bang' which is generally associated with coercion and force, both young men and young women frequently down-played the level of violence stating that girls were not forced to do group sex it but engaged of their own free will. They argued that girls make a *choice* to engage in collective sex.

A few of the guys line up and she will give them a 'blow job'. The girl's always willing. The guys don't force girls to do anything as that ain't acceptable. No one likes that kind of thing, forcing. Line-ups are common. Loads of chicks do it. Don't know why as it ain't respectful but I guess they might think it's great 'cause of who the guy is; i.e. well known, respected, yeah, and partly because he's bad. ... They don't treat them with respect but they wouldn't force them. (Female, FG9)

I've not heard of anyone getting forced to do things like that. But yeah, I do think guys use the girls for sex and blowjobs. Everyone knows that. Girls might think the guy likes her but he's just linking her. They don't get victimised, no. Girls do what they want to do. Yeah, I do think it's gotta do with their self-worth and that'cause I wouldn't just sleep with one man then another, but that's their choice. Those girls and women are always around and still gonna be. (Female, FG5)

As noted earlier, an errant female sexuality results in a social distancing that interferes with the way they are conceived by others. Central to this withdrawal of good opinion is the internalization of views that render girls and young women to blame for their actions. Thus, as illustrated in the quotations above, even in a group setting where the exertion of an active agency is arguably comprised by the presence of multiple sexually charged boys and/or men girls are credited as being willing agents. Ironically, the girls know that sexual coercion is most likely to occur to naïve, deskilled young women who are easy to take advantage of:

That's the path that certain girls choose. They will choose the slaggy path'cause they know they can't fight. So they think, 'I can't fight the boys so let me just do what they want.' They [the boys] will pick the weak ones and the strong ones and they will give you your role(s). (Female, FG5)

Whilst acknowledging that sexual violence (rape) does happen, that gang rape does happen, and that it is wrong, girls, as the following quotations illustrate, are seen to be willing or to have brought it on themselves.

> Well, I've heard people .... People have been forced to do dirty stuff and do dirty things with boys and stuff. They've been forced to do it and since they've been forced they carry on. It's like they do it and then after they like it and they carry on doing it to other boys. Then you've got other boys and girls calling them dirty names and that. When I'm in my area they call me 'stushy' and I won't do things. I think I don't care what you call me I'm not doing dirty jobs for no one. ... Even though people haven't asked me to do things like that because they know they can't I wouldn't go straight away and do stuff like that. (Female, 15)

> No question about it, gang rape or group sex or whatever, that is wrong, no question about it whatsoever. However, I think ... like a lot of girls actually put themselves in that situation. I'm not saying that they deserve what's coming for them, but a lot of girls do actually put themselves into that situation. (Female, FG6)

In an environment where female sexuality is about restraint and control, some girls are perceived as willing participants or blamed for not taking the proper precautions to protect themselves. Constructing a narrative about how some girls (i.e. the skets) have made informed choices or 'have deserved it', helps other girls and young women believe that they are in control of their own lives and can protect themselves from the risks that boys and men pose. As one young woman notes:

> It's kind of like an insult to us [ex women] gang members, saying that the girls in the gangs now are the victims and stuff. When I was involved, yes, I was vulnerable because of my age [15] but I knew what I was doing. I was no victim and I stood my own .... Girls now linked with gangs are used for holding things and the sex thing is just girls in that area having sex with guys; they ain't particularly gang girls. It is like saying all us women involved in gangs are used for sex; that's not true! ... I've known girls to have threesomes [and] give head to man one after the other just 'cause they are gang members. Why do they do this? They obviously think it's OK or maybe morals have changed and values. Who am I to judge them? If this is what they do, that's their choice. (Female, FG4)

In the young women's narratives there is, then, an unresolved tension between agency and responsibility. Given the overt nature of male sexual identity, protecting oneself was deemed to be relatively 'easy' despite the difficulties in evading unwanted attention. Bad boys with, or in pursuit of, a reputation did little to hide their intentions. As such, the consensus shared amongst the young women was that if a young woman enters their social space then she accepts the consequences.

DISCUSSION

This chapter set out to explore how young women construct a credible identity, exercise power and stave off victimisation in patriarchal sub-culture that favours young men and constructs girls as subordinate. It sought to do this by drawing on the testimony of young women's interpretations of how girls negotiate 'on road' and attempt to overcome constraints on their individual identity. The data presented here concur with existing research that suggests gang culture is a microcosm of wider societal values and argues that the creation of a credible identity is inextricably linked to sexuality and the maintenance of normative standards of masculinity and femininity.[42] The behaviour of young men and women 'on-road' can be explained by the accepted 'double standard' on the sexuality of men and women, which is pre-valent in wider society, based on a patriarchal cultural code which is approved of and practised as a means of controlling female sexuality. The honour–shame complex that informs this code suggests that a woman's value lies in her chasteness and that she must control her sexuality; these ideas have a long cultural history.

Young men within on-road contexts have power over women both through their potential for physical violence and because of the power afforded them by the patriarchal honour codes that approve of sexual promiscuity for men but disapprove of it for women. This double standard provides the potential to stigmatize others, and the process of labelling others negatively serves personal functions for those that do so by redu-cing personal anxiety, building self-esteem and increasing one's own sub-jective sense of well-being.[43] Labelling some young women as 'skets' was part of the process of young men 'on-road' affirming their masculine identities as heterosexual males who were always on the 'look-out' for sex whilst also attempting to keep the 'double-standards' and their own male identities protected from scrutiny.

The preceding paragraph outlines both the group interest and self-interest of young men in labelling some young women. For whilst 'gang research' has indicated that the street tends to be a patriarchal space, it is partly this fact that underpins the fragility of the hard and heterosexual gendered identities of its male inhabitants and feelings of anxiety about not being seen as 'man enough'. Young men within street contexts are at risk of 'losing face' in front of both their male peers and young women if their sexual identities come under scrutiny.

As this chapter has demonstrated, however, there are also undoubtedly benefits for some young women in labelling other young women as 'skets' in order to distance themselves from them and present themselves as credible females. As the accomplishment of a credible on-road masculine or feminine identity is always a work in progress, always transient, it could at any time, be exposed as a charade. We can theorise the nature of this dilemma fuelled by unease about identity by drawing on Gidden's ideas about the contingent nature of risk:

> Living with a calculative attitude to the open possibilities of action, positive and negative, which, as individuals and globally we are confronted with in a continuous way. [44]

Jock Young refers to an actuarial stance where people are wary and preoccupied with damage limitation, which is important when considering reputations. The question now, he suggests, is 'what likelihood there is of your rules being broken and that unit of risk is your chance of victimisation'.[45] This preoccupation with damage limitation and anxieties about one's rules and norms being questioned leads us to a consideration of Goffman's notion of the 'Umwelt'. Goffman understood the Umwelt to be a core of accomplished normality with which individuals and groups surround themselves. Young points to how the Umwelt has two dimensions: the 'ore' in which one feels secure and the area in which one is aware; and, secondly, 'the area of apprehension', which shrinks and expands in relation to one's surroundings. The nature of the Umwelt varies by social category, class and age, it is gendered and racialised.[46] Young refers to another sign of Umwelt, that of 'apprehension whilst keeping a lookout for indications of prey and the possibility of predation'.[47] By applying these ideas we can see that young men and women need to neutralise threats to their gendered identities in order to protect and retain control over their 'ore' the core of their accomplished normality. They need to guard against humiliation by not losing face, as the possibility of disrespect and ridicule of young men and women is always present, meaning that 'on-road' reputations can be easily damaged; therefore, maintaining the status quo and shielding one's identity and reputation from questions and scrutiny is key, the negative labelling of others helps to shift the attention from oneself and contributes towards the maintenance of the status quo that serves one's own interests.

In contrast to the benefits of the labelling process for the stigmatisers, the stigmatised will often experience status loss and discrimination and a diminution of power once the cultural stereotype is secured. As those labelled become 'stigmatised' and excluded –labellers reason the exclusion based on the original characteristic that led to the stigma, [48] for example, that sexual promiscuity is dishonourable in women. The stigmatization here is done to girls and arguably forms part of their moral career, where they can end up with spoilt social identities that affect self-esteem.

This is not to deny girl's agency or that it is possible to resist stigma or labels. Yet the potential and resources for girls to resist being negatively labelled as a 'slut' within the context of a male-dominant gang where the men back up their patriarchal power with violence is limited. Moreover, there is less potential for young women to publicly label young men,as, due to the sexual double standard, the negative label of 'sket' is less applicable to men.[49] Despite this the young women discussed here did disapprove of such young men and sought to stay away from them.

Additionally, as this research has shown, girls also judge and label other young women by using 'slut/sket' labels and/or shun those so labelled by others as a defence mechanism (i.e. to prevent or deflect such attention from themselves) or for other reasons. All of this indicates that the risk of the 'sket' label is ever-present for young women with gang associations. These limitations do not mean, of course, that such resistance does not happen – yet resistance has been afforded scant attention. It is argued here that far more attention needs to be paid to how young women negotiate and often resist such labels – albeit the women discussed in this chapter resist in ways that perpetuate the status quo of sexually active men and sexually passive women. The notion of young women engaging in sexual activity because they want to – because they 'own' their own 'active' not 'passive' sexuality – is hidden within the binary conceptualisation of heterosexual sex that frames the street encounters discussed.

CONCLUSION

This article has attempted to explain how young women exercise agency and construct a credible feminine identity whilst on-road. We have argued here that, like young men on-road, young women must also build a credible gendered identity. They do this through speech and practices that convey their ideas about what a credible female identity means and also by distancing themselves from what is not credible. In doing so, girls and young women often label the behaviour of other young women as non-credible which, at times, involves discourses of blaming by depicting other young women as either naïve or as making questionable choices around identity.

As previously outlined, our conception of agency suggests that being fully autonomous means having no restrictions on the choices one makes. For young women on-road this is rare as they have to negotiate a credible gendered identity within the context of a patriarchal male-dominated space, framed by the knowledge that normative male sexuality is active whilst women's sexuality (publicly at least) is depicted as passive; consequently women are expected (and required) to self-police and control their sexuality or at least to give the appearance of doing so. Indeed, this provides a prevalent example of how young women exercise agency within a constrained context. Notwithstanding this, there is the possibility that despite such limitations, some young women do construct their gendered identities as sexually active and proactive and in doing so, challenge the gendered sexually active male versus sexually passive female dichotomy that informs the status quo. In a subsequent article we draw on data that helps us explain how and why some young women manage to overcome restrictive normative ideas about what a credible feminine identity should look like by constructing a sexually active female identity.

NOTES

1. See T. Young, 'Girls and gangs: "Shemale" gangsters in the UK', *Youth Justice*, 9 (2009), 224–38 (Young 2009); T. Young, 'In search of the shemale gangster', in B. Goldson (ed.), *Youth in Crisis? Gangs, Territoriality and Violence* (Abingdon, 2011) (Young 2011); J. Pitts, *Reluctant Gangsters: Youth Gangs in Waltham Forest* (Bedford: 2007) (Pitts 2007); M. Chesney-Lind, *The Female Offender: Girls, Women and*

Crime (London, 1997) (Chesney-Lind 1997); K. Joe Laider and J. Hunt, 'Accomplishing femininity among the girls in the gang', *British Journal of Criminology*, 41 (2001), 656–78 (Joe Laider and Hunt 2001); J. Miller, *One of the Guys: Girls, Gangs, and Gender* (New York, 2001) (Miller 2001); J. Miller, 'The strengths and limits of "doing gender" for understanding street crime', *Theoretical Criminology*, 6, 4 (2002), 433–60 (Miller 2002); J. Miller, *Getting Played: African American Girls, Urban Equality, and Gendered Violence* (New York, 2008) (Miller 2008); J. Moore, *Going Down to the Barrio: Homeboys and Homegirls in Change* (Philadelphia, 1991) (Moore 1991).

2. See, for example, Pitts' *Reluctant Gangsters* and C. Firmin, *Female Voice in Violence Project: A Study into the Impact of Serious Youth and Gang Violence on Women and Girls* (London, 2010) (Firmin 2010). The authors of this chapter recognise that the concept 'gang' is problematic and acknowledge tensions in the debate around the definition. We direct readers to other sources – such as S. Hallsworth and T. Young, 'Street collectives and group delinquency: social disorganisation, subcultures and beyond', in E. McLaughlin and T. Newburn (eds.), *The Sage Handbook of Criminological Theory* (London, 2010) – that address this conceptual conundrum and critically evaluate what is meant by this term since we are unable to fully consider, and give due credit to, the varied positions here (Hallsworth and Young 2010). For the purposes of this piece it is important to stipulate that the term 'gang' is being used as an umbrella to describe street-based groups or 'street collectives'.

3. Young, 'Girls and gangs', 224–38

4. A. Campbell, *The Girls in the Gang: A Report from New York City* (Oxford, 1984); Moore, *Going Down to the Barrio*; Miller, 'The strengths and limits of "doing gender"', 433–60 (Campbell 1984).

5. Miller, *Getting Played*.

6. See also L. Trickett, 'Birds and sluts: Views on young women from boys in the gang', *International Review of Victimology*, 22 (1) (2015), 25–44 (Trickett 2015).

7. A. Valdez, *Mexican American Girls and Gang Violence: Beyond Risk* (New York, 2007) (Valdez 2007).

8. Ibid, p. 2.

9. Ibid, p. 111

10. Pitts, *Reluctant Gangsters*; Firmin, *Female Voice in Violence Project*; C. Firmin, *'This is It: This is My Life': Female Voice in Violence Final Report: On the Impact of Serious Youth Violence and Criminal Gangs on Women and Girls across the Country* (London, 2011) (Firmin 2011); H. Beckett, I. Brodie, F. Factor, M. Melrose, J. Pearce, J. Pitts, L. Shuker, and C. Warrington, *'It's wrong . . . . but you get used to it': A Qualitative Study of Gang-associated Sexual Violence*

Towards, and Exploitation of, Young People in England (London, 2013) (Beckett et al. 2013); Centre for Social Justice, *Girls and Gangs* (London, 2014) (Centre for Social Justice 2014).

11. Firmin, *Female Voice in Violence Project*, p. 13.
12. C. A. MacKinnon, *Toward a Feminist Theory of the State* (Massachusetts, 1989) (MacKinnon 1989).
13. H. Beckett, I. Brodie, F. Factor, M. Melrose, J. Pearce, J. Pitts, L. Shuker, and C. Warrington, *Research into Gang-associated Sexual Exploitation and Sexual Violence* (Luton, 2012) (Beckett et al. 2012).
14. Valdez, *Mexican American Girls and Gang Violence*, p. 121.
15. Firmin, *Female Voice in Violence Project*.
16. Miller, *Getting Played*.
17. Ibid.
18. Following Hallsworth and Young's 'Street collectives and group delinquency', the term 'on road' is used rather than the gang. This is because we consider it to be a more facilitative concept with which to understand the complexity and fluidity of urban street life. The generic term 'gang' is replete with racial and stereotypical representations of the ethnic, urban underclass and, arguably, of limited use for understanding street-based criminality and violence. In contrast, Hallsworth and Young's concept 'on road' allows for a more nuanced interpretation of a subculture that encourages a 'street sovereignty' (Hallsworth and Silverstone, 2009) where young people engage in a world of badness (Gunter, 2010) as it conceives the gang as one component of a complex 'road' culture. To be 'on road' could include being in 'a gang' but it is also an existential way of being in the world for young people in disadvantaged urban neighbourhoods. It is defined as: the 'hood' or the 'ghetto' where young people, worn down by marginalisation and exclusion, struggled to survive in a society they believed did not care or cater for their needs. At its most extreme, the hood – and by extension 'the road' – was a place where young people adopted a 'hood mentality', a fatalistic attitude to life that held 'no dreams, no ambition, no drive; no nothing'. See also S. Hallsworth and D. Silverstone, '"That's life innit": A British perspective on guns, crime and social order', *Criminology and Criminal Justice*, 9 (3) (2009), 359–77 (Hallsworth and Silverstone 2009); A. Gunter, *Growing Up Bad: Black Youth, Road Culture and Badness in an East London Neighbourhood* (London, 2010) (Gunter 2010).
19. J. W. Messerschmidt, *Crime as Structured Action: Gender, Race, Class, and Crime in the Making* (London, 1997), p. 178 (Messerschmidt 1997).
20. Joe-Laider and Hunt, 'Accomplishing femininity among the girls in the gang', 656–78.

21. At the heart of this code is a set of informal rules of behaviour organised around a desperate search for respect that governs social relations (Anderson 1999). E. Anderson, *Code of the Street: Decency, Violence, and the Moral Life of the Inner City* (New York, 1999) (Anderson 1999).

22. See Miller, 'The strengths and limits of "doing gender" for understanding street crime', 433–60, who criticised the work of Messerschmidt in relation to girl's agency and gangs.

23. J. W. Messerschmidt, *Masculinities and Crime: Critique and Reconceptualisation of Theory* (Maryland, 1993) (Messerschmidt 1993).

24. S. Harding, *The Street Casino: Survival in Violent Street Gangs* (Bristol, 2014) (Harding 2014).

25. Harding, *The Street Casino*; S. Hallsworth, *The Gangs and Beyond: Interpreting Violent Street Worlds* (Basingstoke, 2013) (Hallsworth 2013); J. Densley, *How Gangs Work: An Ethnography of Youth Violence* (Basingstoke, 2013) (Densley 2013); A. Fraser, *Urban Legends: Gang Identity in the Post-Industrial City* (Oxford, 2015) (Fraser 2015).

26. Harding, *The Street Casino*, p. 223.

27. See Firmin, *Female Voice in Violence Project*; Firmin, *'This is It: This is My Life'*; S. Berelowitz, C. Firmin, G. Edwards, and S. Gulyurtlu, *'I thought I was the only one'*, The Office of the Children's Commissioner's Inquiry into Child Sexual Exploitation in Gangs and Groups (London, 2012) (Berelowitz et al. 2012); Beckett et al., *Research into Gang-associated Sexual Exploitation and Sexual Violence*; Beckett et al., *'It's wrong ... but you get used to it'*; J. J. Pearce and J. Pitts, *Youth Gangs, Sexual Violence and Sexual Exploitation: A scoping exercise for The Office of the Children's Commissioner for England* (Luton, 2012) (Pearce and Pitts 2012).

28. Beckett *et al*, *Research into Gang-associated Sexual Exploitation and Sexual Violence*, p. 8.

29. Harding, *The Street Casino*, p. 239.

30. L. Trickett, 'Birds and sluts', 25–44.

31. Some of the data presented here was collected as part of a collaborative research partnership between Tara Young and Child and Women Abuse Studies Unit.

32. B. Skeggs, 'Situating the production of feminist ethnography', in M. Maynard and J. Purvis (eds.), *Researching Women's Lives From a Feminist Perspective* (London, 1994) (Skeggs 1994).

33. J. T. Bertrand, J. E. Brown and V. M. Ward, 'Techniques for analysing focus group data', *Evaluation Review*, 16, 2 (1992), 198–209 (Bertrand et al. 1992); B. F. Stanton, M. Black, L. Kaljee and I. Ricardo, 'Perceptions of sexual behaviour among urban early adolescents: Translating theory through focus groups', *Journal of Early Adolescence*, 13 (1993), 44–66 (Stanton et al. 1993); J. Norris, P. Nurius and L. A. Dimeff, 'Through her

eyes: Factors affecting women's perception of and resistance to acquaintance sexual aggression threat', *Psychology of Women Quarterly,* 20 (1) (1996), 123–45 (Norris et al. 1996).

34. D. L. Morgan and R. A. Krueger, 'When to use focus groups and why?', in D. L. Morgan (ed.) *Successful Focus Groups: Advancing the State of the Art* (Newbury Park, 1993), pp. 3–19 (Morgan and Krueger 1993).

35. See T. Young, M. Fitzgerald, S. Hallsworth and I. Joseph, *Groups, Gangs and Weapons: A Report for the Youth Justice Board of England and Wales* (London, 2007) (Young et al. 2007).

36. J. Ritchie and J. Lewis, *Qualitative Research Practice* (London, 2003) (Ritchie and Lewis 2003).

37. R. White, *Youth Gangs, Violence and Social Respect: Exploring the Nature of Provocations and Punch-ups* (Sydney, 2003) (White 2003).

38. A 'bezzel' is a woman who engages in fellatio with a man. A 'link' is a girl who is a casual, sexual acquaintance; a 'sket' is a street term for 'slag'.

39. P. Reeves Sandy, *Fraternity Gang Rape: Sex, Brotherhood, and Privilege on Campus* (New York, 1992) (Reeves 1992).

40. 'Bocat' is a euphemism for cunnilingus and 'give brain' is another word for fellatio.

41. Beckett et al, *'It's wrong … but you get used to it'.*

42. Valdez, *Mexican American Girls and Gang Violence;* Miller, *Getting Played.*

43. E. Goffman, *Stigma: Notes on the Management of Spoiled Identity* (Englewood Cliffs, 1963) (Goffman 1963).

44. A. Giddens, *Modernity and Self-Identity: Self and Society in the Late Modern Age* (Cambridge, 1991), p. 28 (Giddens 1991).

45. J. Young, *The Exclusive Society: Social Exclusion, Crime and Difference in Late Modernity* (London, 1999), p. 66 (Young 1999).

46. Ibid, p 72.

47. Ibid, p. 73.

48. E. Goffman, *The Presentation of Self in Everyday Life* (New York, 1959) (Goffman 1959); Goffman, *Stigma.*

49. Such problems are also seen in the prosecution of rape and sexual abuse. See J. Lovett and L. Kelly, *Different Systems, Similar Outcomes?: Tracking Attrition in Reported Rape Cases across Europe* (London, 2009) (Lovett and Kelly 2009).

References

E. Anderson, *Code of the Street: Decency, Violence, and the Moral Life of the Inner City* (New York, 1999).

H. Beckett, I. Brodie, F. Factor, M. Melrose, J. Pearce, J. Pitts, L. Shuker, and C. Warrington, *Research into Gang-associated Sexual Exploitation and Sexual Violence* (Luton, 2012).

H. Beckett, I. Brodie, F. Factor, M. Melrose, J. Pearce, J. Pitts, L. Shuker, and C. Warrington, *'It's wrong... .but you get used to it'*: *A Qualitative Study of Gang-associated Sexual Violence Towards, and Exploitation of, Young People in England* (London, 2013).

S Berelowitz, C. Firmin, G. Edwards, and S. Gulyurtlu, *'I thought I was the only one'*, The Office of the Children's Commissioner's Inquiry into Child Sexual Exploitation in Gangs and Groups (London, 2012).

J. T. Bertrand, J. E. Brown and V. M. Ward, 'Techniques for Analysing Focus Group Data', *Evaluation Review*, 16, 2 (1992), 198–209.

A. Campbell, *The Girls in the* Gang: *A Report from New York City* (Oxford, 1984)

Centre for Social Justice, *Girls and Gangs* (London, 2014).

M. Chesney-Lind, *The Female Offender: Girls, Women and Crime* (London, 1997).

J. Densley, *How Gangs Work: An Ethnography of Youth Violence* (Basingstoke, 2013).

C. Firmin, *Female Voice in Violence Project:* A Study into the Impact of Serious Youth and *Gang Violence on Women and Girls* (London, 2010).

C. Firmin, *'This is It: This is My Life'*: *Female Voice in Violence Final Report: On the Impact of* Serious Youth Violence and *Criminal Gangs on Women and Girls across the Country* (London, 2011).

A. Fraser, *Urban Legends: Gang Identity in the Post-Industrial City* (Oxford, 2015).

A. Giddens, *Modernity and Self-Identity: Self and Society in the Late Modern Age* (Cambridge, 1991), p. 28.

E. Goffman, *The Presentation of Self in Everyday Life* (New York, 1959).

E. Goffman, *Stigma: Notes on the Management of Spoiled Identity* (Englewood Cliffs, 1963).

A. Gunter, *Growing Up Bad: Black Youth, Road Culture and Badness in an East London Neighbourhood* (London, 2010).

S. Hallsworth, *The Gangs and Beyond: Interpreting Violent Street Worlds* (Basingstoke, 2013).

S. Hallsworth and D. Silverstone, '"That's life innit": A British Perspective on Guns, Crime and Social Order', *Criminology and Criminal Justice*, 9, 3 (2009), 359–77.

S. Hallsworth and T. Young, 'Street Collectives and Group Delinquency: Social Disorganisation, Subcultures and Beyond', in E. McLaughlin and T. Newburn (eds.), *The Sage Handbook of Criminological Theory* (London, 2010).

S. Harding, *The Street Casino: Survival in Violent Street Gangs* (Bristol, 2014).

K. Joe-Laider and J. Hunt, 'Accomplishing Femininity Among the Girls in the Gang, *British Journal of Criminology*, 41 (2001), 656–78.

J. Lovett and L. Kelly, *Different Systems, Similar Outcomes?: Tracking Attrition in Reported Rape Cases across Europe* (London, 2009).

C. A. MacKinnon, *Toward a Feminist Theory of the State* (Massachusetts, 1989).

J. W. Messerschmidt, *Masculinities and Crime: Critique and Reconceptualisation of Theory* (Maryland, 1993).

J. W. Messerschmidt, *Crime as Structured Action: Gender, Race, Class, and Crime in the Making* (London, 1997), p. 178.

J. Miller, *One of the Guys: Girls, Gangs, and Gender* (New York, 2001).

J. Miller, 'The Strengths and Limits of "doing gender" for Understanding Street Crime', *Theoretical Criminology*, 6, 4 (2002), 433–60.

J. Miller, *Getting Played: African American Girls, Urban Equality, and Gendered Violence* (New York, 2008).

J. Moore, *Going Down to the Barrio: Homeboys and Homegirls in Change* (Philadelphia, 1991).

D. L. Morgan and R. A. Krueger, 'When to use Focus Groups and Why?', in D. L. Morgan (ed) *Successful focus Groups: Advancing the State of the Art* (Newbury Park, 1993), pp. 3–19.

J. Norris, P. Nurius and L. A. Dimeff, 'Through Her Eyes: Factors Affecting Women's Perception of and Resistance to Acquaintance Sexual Aggression Threat, *Psychology of Women Quarterly*, 20, 1 (1996), 123–45.

J. J. Pearce and J. Pitts, *Youth Gangs, Sexual Violence and Sexual Exploitation: a scoping exercise for The Office of the Children's Commissioner for England* (Luton, 2012).

J. Pitts, *Reluctant Gangsters: Youth Gangs in Waltham Forest* (Bedford, 2007).

P. Reeves Sandy, *Fraternity Gang Rape: Sex, Brotherhood, and Privilege on Campus* (New York, 1992).

J. Ritchie and J. Lewis, *Qualitative Research Practice* (London, 2003).

B. Skeggs, 'Situating the Production of Feminist Ethnography', in M. Maynard and J. Purvis (eds.), *Researching Women's Lives From a Feminist Perspective* (London, 1994).

B. F. Stanton, M. Black, L. Kaljee and I. Ricardo, 'Perceptions of Sexual Behaviour among Urban Early Adolescents: Translating Theory Through Focus Groups', *Journal of Early Adolescence*, 13 (1993), 44–66.

L. Trickett, 'Birds and Sluts: Views on Young Women from Boys in the Gang', *International Review of Victimology*, 22, 1 (2015), 25–44.

A. Valdez, *Mexican American Girls and Gang Violence: Beyond Risk* (New York, 2007).

R. White, *Youth Gangs, Violence and Social Respect: Exploring the Nature of Provocations and Punch-ups* (Sydney, 2003).

J. Young, *The Exclusive Society: Social Exclusion, Crime and Difference in Late Modernity* (London, 1999), p. 66.

T. Young, M. Fitzgerald, S. Hallsworth and I. Joseph, *Groups, Gangs and Weapons: A Report for the Youth Justice Board of England and Wales* (London, 2007).

T. Young, 'Girls and Gangs: "Shemale" Gangsters in the UK', *Youth Justice*, 9 (2009), 224–38.

T. Young, 'In Search of the Shemale Gangster', in B. Goldson (ed), *Youth in Crisis? Gangs, Territoriality and Violence* (Abingdon, 2011).

Tara Young is Lecturer in Criminal Justice and Criminology at the University of Kent's School of Social Policy, Sociology and Social Research (SSPSSR). She has published academic papers on 'gang-related' violence and the experiences of girls and young women in UK gangs.

Loretta Trickett is a Senior Lecturer in Criminal Justice and Criminology. She has a PhD on gendered fear of crime. She has published articles on boys and bullying, men's fear of crime, gang violence, sexual assault and hate crime. Her research interests include gendered crime and victimisation and hate crime.

CHAPTER 11

'Silence is Virtual': Youth Violence, Belonging, Death and Mourning

William 'Lez' Henry and Sireita Mullings-Lawrence

The current debates regarding children and young people's engagement with social media, is centred around the impact, benefit and influences it has as an organiser of their young lives in the virtual world. Facebook, Instagram and Twitter are just some of the platforms that have increasingly become a surrogate space for young people to communicate, especially in cases where real world contact is denied by various constraints.[1] For instance: where a physical/personal appearance at a public event, such as a funeral or gathering, is unwise due to postcode or other rivalries which will place the young person in immediate danger. This has led to the encouraging of educators and parents to monitor young people's usage of the virtual, for potential threats of cyberbullying, facebook depression, sexting[2] and exposure to inappropriate content. These aspects of an online presence are explored by Boyd, who suggests that we consider: 'Why do teenagers flock to these sites? What are they expressing on them? How do these sites fit into their lives? What are they learning from their

W. 'Lez' Henry (✉)
School of Law and Criminology, University of West London, London, UK
e-mail: william.henry@uwl.ac.uk

S. Mullings-Lawrence
School of Applied Social Studies, University of Bedfordshire, Luton, UK
e-mail: sireita.mullings@beds.ac.uk

© The Author(s) 2017   261
K. Gildart et al. (eds.), *Youth Culture and Social Change*,
Palgrave Studies in the History of Subcultures and Popular Music,
DOI 10.1057/978-1-137-52911-4_11

participation? Are these online activities like face-to-face friendships – or are they different or complementary'? In line with Boyd's questions we are keen to gather insight on some of the ways young people engage with the virtual world.[3] In order to get a clear idea of what young people are exposed to, what they are expressing, learning and creating in these spaces, there needs to be a focus on how they articulate their views by way of visual and audio media that are presented in multiple formats across various virtual platforms.

Indeed many who are caught up in these acts of violence, whether as perpetrators or victims, fear reprisals if they physically attend the social gatherings, wakes or funerals of those who have lost their lives. This is because appreciating gang rivalry from their perspective is far more complex than many would imagine; the empirical approach presented here will highlight some of this complexity. It will also make known how the demand for respectability, as a means of demonstrable 'success' in the realms of criminality, manifests as the 'road man' mentality and largely determines the 'safe' and 'unsafe' spaces young people navigate. Therefore, an argument for understanding the ways in which young people share their lives in the public and alternative public arenas, as a conscious choice, will be deployed to make explicit the links between social media and youth crime.

BACKGROUND

The chapter is drawn from empirical work the authors have been involved in with various cohorts of primarily BAME young people, between 12 and 25 years old, for several years in community based settings. The data featured includes the demographics of the young people, in the sense of how they articulate areas of 'danger' and safety', as well as that taken from other sources that offer insight into their young lives. The information gathered from focus groups, participant observations and interviews with youth practitioners, programme leaders and youth participants in these organisations will be featured in this account. These organisations aim to address the complex issues faced by young people, some of which are framed through issues of inclusion and education and target social integration, social mobility, increased confidence and increased life expectancy. However, the effectiveness and impact of the projects is not discussed in detail here, but is drawn upon to give context to the concerns of young people.

The usage of Interviews, focus groups and observations were chosen as being more effective for this piece, as they enabled participants to react and respond to each other through naturally occurring speech, thus yielding a collective and an individual view into their worlds. Doing so gives priority to the views of the young people themselves, who too often complain at being 'silenced' within the wider public arena, which is why many utilise, to the fullest, alternative sites of expression within the virtual world. Unsurprisingly, we noted the manner in which young people interact online occurs in numerous ways,[4] and an observation of a summer photographic workshop as part of the 'Different Endz'[5] project, high-lighted the difficulties faced in any analysis of the virtual threats they experienced or posed to others. The analysis was aided by one particular summer workshop, the main aim of which was to divert a cohort of young people, aged 16–25 who were at risk of gang involvement, due to heightened gang activity within their local community. These young people had online access for 15 minutes during their lunch break, with restrictions placed on the types of websites they could visit. Sites that featured extreme violence and/or pornographic material were blocked as, arguably, they reinforce antisocial and nihilistic behaviours.[6]

MEDIA, POLYTRICKS AND MISREPRESENTATION

Analysing the usage of contemporary forms of social media by young people, to express their innermost concerns, provides insights into their worlds that speak to the complexity of their relationships with the wider communities in which they live and operate.[7] Further, in the context of their position as members of BAME communities within the UK, their usage of social media to address various issues including youth violence, death and mourning, provides a space for a radical rethink on what is largely regarded as an almost apathetic approach to 'black on black' violence. Indeed the seriousness and regularity of violent acts that are attributed to criminal black youth gangs, including various high profile stabbings, attempted murders and murders in a number of locations across the UK, make it necessary for the police service, local authorities and other agencies to establish the best ways forward in this regard. These violent acts often result in very public debates about who is to blame for the actions of these nihilistic black youth, or who is ultimately responsible for dealing with the consequences of their actions. Far too often what is considered 'newsworthy' by the mainstream media merely serves to reinforce certain stereotypes through a form of 'deviancy amplification' that detracts from the real issues.[8] The point is, as Carrabine suggests:

> the mass media now provide us with round the clock news of crisis, disaster and trauma; rising social mobility brings a greater range of experiences, expectations and troubles; technological innovations have brought with them immense global dangers; and since 9/11 'new' forms of terrorism further contribute to the cultural climate of fear.[9]

Such is the manner in which these issues are framed that the black youth presence adds to the febrile atmosphere that feeds the 'cultural climate of fear', because at its core is an investment in the pathological notions of black youth as another thing that needs to be 'fixed' in 'Broken Britain'. This means that the blame for their antisocial behaviour is not regarded as a consequence of living within an inherently racist, classist and sexist society. Rather it is squarely laid at the door of the black community in general and the black family unit in particular, who themselves are criminalised in myriad ways; finding themselves under 'endless pressure' as noted by Pryce.[10] For example, by not taking into account 'the materialist socialisation' of these youth, means that their proneness to 'being victims of crime and especially violent crime' is overlooked.[11] This situation worsened for the black community whose disproportionate representation in the Criminal Justice System is well documented, because 'the 1998 Crime and Disorder Act criminalises children, young people and their parents'.[12] An Act that was introduced by New Labour and further endorsed by ex-prime minister Blair at the Callaghan lecture in Cardiff in 2007, when he confessed that he was 'lurching into total frankness' and stated the need for an:

> intense police focus on the minority of young black Britons behind the gun and knife attacks. The laws on knife and gun gangs needed to be toughened and the ringleaders taken out of circulation.[13]

Blair failed to consider the history of racial oppression that structurally placed the black community at a disadvantage, socially, culturally and politically in the wider public arena, where as suggested by Les Back 'new ethnicities' are in flux and are therefore fluid and not fixed as Blair implies.[14] The suggestion is that intensifying a 'police focus' on the minority within a minority can be counterproductive if the drivers for this behaviour are collapsed into mere criminality, as is often the case in such matters. Indeed the scandal surrounding the Tory MP Oliver Letwin's comments, in a joint memo to then prime minister Thatcher (regarding the riots that took place in various London boroughs in 1985), enable us to understand the racial climate at that time. More importantly, the fact is that he was, and still is, responsible for creating/influencing public policy, is telling when considering how his racist values were central to his political views:

> The root of social malaise is not poor housing, or youth 'alienation', or the lack of a middle class... Riots, criminality and social disintegration are caused solely by individual characters and attitudes. So long as bad moral attitudes remain, all efforts to improve the inner cities will founder.[15]

Moreover, according to Ashton in her study of black male prisoners and how they located their sense of belonging as UK citizens, one youth asked her 'if being a gang leader counted as a formal identity'.[16] This is important to understand because the role the public and alternative public arenas play in moulding and shaping the identities of many of these black youth are the recipients of various forms of inequality that are known but seldom publicly addressed in any meaningful way. Moreover, when such issues are raised, especially in the context of mainstream schooling and how it obscures a positive black historical presence, 'we are accused of political indoctrination and teaching black kids how to hate whites'.[17] Consequently it is the black community as a homogenous mass that is held to account for incidents that, according to Blair, are deemed a consequence of their inability to control their young people. However, Carby suggests that this type of behaviour represents 'the cycle of pathology'; a consequence of black British youth being forcibly socialised into a culture of social practices that do not reflect their lived reality, as 'identifiable others' in the land of their birth.[18] Hence:

> Though the memo in which Mr Letwin made these claims is now some three decades old, there is a clear public interest in exposing the attitudes and values that once guided a still-serving member of the British Cabinet.[19]

It is the 'exposure of these attitudes' that is important here for two main reasons. Firstly, because Letwin speaks of 'black areas' which in truth makes little sense in the context of a UK demographic: secondly, lost in the Letwin debate was Thatcher's written comments stating how 'disturbing' the contents of the memo were, and how there is a need for a heightened police presence in these communities. However, the fact that in the news items Thatcher's 'acceptance' of the language and sentiments of the memo was not interrogated, speaks to how ingrained this worldview of the black community was, and still is, as those who will never belong to Britain. More importantly, this is not new news to the recipients of white racism within the cultural milieu that is the black community, because any sense of belonging is always undermined by some type of sobering experience that is passed on anecdotally from generation to generation. That is why according to one respondent:

> You asked me what does it mean to belong? Well it fucking well ain't dealing with this all the time. I know what they (white people) say about us and some of it's true 'cos I know people who do things. But, you know, most of us don't get involved but I can understand why some do because if their parents went through the same shit as they are now, at school in the streets from everywhere. You're gonna say fuck it I belong with my own and for nuff youts that's the gang.[20]

The fact that these young people are primarily integrated into, and educated about, British culture via the state schooling system's National Curriculum, as well as other agencies of socialisation, must be considered when discussing their supposed 'educational underachievement' and gang affiliation. This lack of consideration results in the emphasis being placed on the black family as a pathological unit rather than the structural inequalities and deficient parenting styles that impact on the life chances of the white working classes in a similar fashion. There is also a denial of the experiences of racism as a psychological factor.[21] in any meaningful way, with regard to the omission of positive forms of self-identification in these young lives, where being black does 'not sit easily with being British'.[22] For instance, debates about a positive black historical presence are too often undermined and discredited in a very public way, as evidenced in the following news item:

> GCSE students are to be taught that some of our nation's earliest inhabitants were Africans who arrived here long before the English. The Mail on Sunday has discovered that the extraordinary rewriting of our island's history – the politically correct work of a Marxist academic – will be offered

to thousands of history students throughout England from September. Its creators claim the course addresses the 'white male-dominated' view of history – but it has outraged some of Britain's most eminent thinkers. Booker and Nobel prize-winning novelist V.S. Naipaul said: 'Once again political correctness is distorting our history and the education of our children.' And historian Sir Roy Strong, author of The Story Of Britain, said: 'This stands history on its head, projecting back on to the past something that isn't true.'[23]

The point is what is arguably lost in this type of media driven 'historical correctness', is the role it plays in further undermining the self-esteem, self-value and self-worth of the very young people who need these positive influences. Moreover, educators and practitioners who work with gang affiliated young people, or those who are impacted by gang culture or youth violence, recognise immediately that these public debates also undermine their credibility in the eyes of these young people. Consequently, this paradoxical argument sits parallel with the current misrepresentation of some black youth, where the hooded top is not read as an innocent youth style or necessity for warmth but has become a symbol of disorder coded with negative perceptions. Unsurprisingly, Prime Minister Cameron once stated 'we the people in suits often see hoodies as aggressive, the uniform of a rebel army of young gangsters'.[24] Similarly, Osgerby makes reference to a series of newspaper articles in both The Sun and the Daily Mirror where headline stories made attempts to demonise black youths as folk devils, stating 'there are slippages between media stereotypes of youth-as-fun and youth-as-trouble'.[25] Similarly, The Runnymede Trust's report (Re)thinking gangs speaks to the problems inherent in the construction of the gang through the image of Black youth and suggests:

> The correlation of gang cultures and criminal activities with young Black boys serves to collectively implicate and criminalise all Black boys and the Black community.[26]

Unsurprisingly then, according to one gang-affiliated young person:

> Can you guarantee me a job if I do my school work? No you can't and I can make more in a week than I'd make working. All that black history stuff you go on about is long and probably aint true anyway.[27] It won't help me hold and my bres hold our corner and protect the Ps.[28]

Jason speaks to the very conscious choices certain young people make when faced with 'that black history stuff', which for them has no bearing or relevance to their future social trajectories. For this reason, in the next section an insight will be provided into how these young people use a notion of belonging that is wrapped up in how they gain, or garner, respectability in their local communities.

REPUTATION, BELONGING AND YOUTH VIOLENCE

For young people who turn to alternative modes of money making, a public or private space is not only a place they 'inhabit but a place they may be called upon to defend', as their 'turf' association is arguably their foremost means of identifying self and other.[29] Crucial to understanding the idea of 'turf' association, such youth make 'an effort to organise hierarchies as a way of gaining some control' over the aspects of their lives they are seen to 'own' and 'control'.[30] Gaining control is one aspect of territorialising their space; it requires the manipulation and organisation of persons, implemented through a hierarchy in which power is disseminated in a top-down fashion. The hierarchy generally consists of family members, friends and peers, and the power is distributed by 'elders'/'shotters', who give instructions and organise the 'business' side that will generate the Ps. They instruct/ command the 'youngers'/ 'tinies'/'soldiers', followed by 'wanabees', 'associates', and fantasy members who choose to align themselves with the group because they are looking for kudos and not gang membership. Pitts accurately sums up the current situation arguing that 'in certain parts of our towns and cities, and among certain social groups, life has become far more dangerous for children and young people'.[31] Efrem noted that gangs are 'stuck in their post codes by the world wide web' and a 'false sense of security' is created as they now also use videos to mark territory.[32] However, the common belief is that the nihilistic behaviour of inner city youth generally perceived as 'minority' groups and 'gang' affiliated, impacts on the movement and public perceptions of all youth who live within the urban landscape, because:

> Gang turf is more than a collection of streets, alleys, stores, and street corners; it is sacred ground that is the site of struggles for identity, power, and status. It is a hallowed space that gives the gang its meaning. It is where members learn group norms and publicly display their group membership

and loyalty, and it acts as a tangible reminder and repository of the gang's history and values.[33]

The young people featured here are aware of the 'gangs' that operate in their area and where some may not know the actual gang members personally, they are knowledgeable of the names and colours that are associated with specific areas. In some cases 'these names reflect the actual postcode that young people have assigned themselves to', as in the case of E9 Balance (East London E9).[34] Where the post code is not embedded in the name, alternative labels are created that become sub sets derived from the areas of origin, such as the south-east London based 'Gypset crew' of Gipsy Hill and 'Bluisham boyz' in Lewisham. Interestingly, in some instances the colours associated with the local 'gangs' are taken from the colour of the dustbins in their area, so for instance in Lewisham the rubbish bins are generally coloured blue; hence blue-borough equals 'bluisham'.[35] In some instances acronyms such as PDC for Poverty Driven Children or Peel Dem Crew become associated with an area in much the same way as the postcode, as one participant expressed for instance, 'when you hear PDC everyone knows they repp Briky [represent Brixton]'.[36]

Unlocking these codes and processes for naming and claiming turf sheds light on the manner in which some young people imagine and narrate themselves as something other than just mindless, nihilistic, gang-affiliated youth. For instance, within these names that in some cases resemble mission statements, there are clear objectives behind them that make known to those who are privy to these codes, exactly what is at stake in peaceful or conflict situations. Spergel notes that 'the symbolic names are more important and enduring for gang function and tradition... inscribed... along with gang names on the walls... as a threat to other gangs' (Spergel 1995).[37] Consequently, they will understand that PDC is in one sense Poverty Driven Children, but PDC can also stand for the Peel Dem Crew. Similarly, Don't Say Nothing (DSN) of Croydon, Shine My Nine (SMN) of Thornton Heath, Spare No One (SN1) of Peckham and South Man Syndicate (SMS) of Stockwell and Brixton, speak to the realisation that the mapping of turf, in this fashion, goes hand in hand with perceived areas of safety and danger. As such these young people now yield an alternative form of empowerment that presents itself in the claiming of place and the resymbolising of locality, which involves the redrawing of their local map and the construction of 'informal' boundaries that are not to be crossed or disrespected. The warnings are no longer limited to the medium of graffiti on a wall or public object, but are evidenced in virtual spaces, as 'strategies of spatial organisation are deeply bound up with the social production of identities'.[38] In other words whilst this ideas of control, representing, respecting and the acquisition of power are being played out, there is the simultaneous production of identities that often reduces young people to violent perpetrators of 'gang crime on road'.[39] Moreover, where their aim is to protect those in their communities, they run the risk of 'victimising others who are not involved' but simply live in the area.[40]

For many black youth an active participation in so called 'gang culture', offers an alternative form of social empowerment through a culture of respectability and belonging that is ultimately self-destructive. Consequently they are often oblivious to the problems associated with this lifestyle, especially when it comes to mapping out a future that is not associated with some form of petty or serious criminality. This is because 'the police or prison doesn't bother us. Our generation just want more things. We're addicted to the hustle'.[41] This attitude speaks to the importance of understanding these formal and informal sites of learning, where the immediate acquisition of 'more things' outweighs the long term benefits of the traditional route to these ends via formal education; that which for them is regarded as 'long'.[42] Unsurprisingly then, the manner in which gang affiliation and other forms of criminal activity serve as an organising principle in what is in effect a culture of abstention, needs to be fully understood. For instance, knowing what you can earn per day (a wage) depending on what your hustle is, to what age-graded sentence you can expect if you get caught with say drugs or a weapon, is crucial. The point is many see the 'streets' as an alternative learning environment and if they are gang-affiliated they will be 'educated' in all things to do with survival on the streets, which includes dealing with living in a racist society. In many ways this speaks to Back's notion of the 'metropolitan paradox' where 'momentary escapes from racism are contiguous with ever more complex forms of racial power and domination', which can be read through the way they posture on the same streets.[43] Moreover, what is important for us to appreciate is that any state reaction to youth crime that does not take into account how these young people view respect through the acquisition of 'more things', becomes problematic, for, as Krinsky states:

Human behaviors acquire their meanings within specific social contexts. Disapproving social reactions to deviant behaviors dictate their significance even for those who engage in them. Therefore, to understand deviance as fully as possible, researchers must explain not only the motives behind particular uncondoned activities, but also, and just as importantly, the fundamental causes of society's responses.[44]

The notion of 'uncondoned activities' becomes central to this argument because the social imbalances that are recognised by many young people as a by-product of living in a racist society, partially explain why many withdraw from various aspects of community life and adopt a 'soldier mentality' whilst operating within 'alternative cognitive landscapes'.[45] For them, exercising distance from the wider community is therefore a very conscious choice, which makes explicit the links between educational underachievement as a consequence of a seeming failure at school, and respectability as a consequence of success in the realms of criminality 'on road'. We therefore need to understand the pull factor of the forces at play that make crime into an appealing career and a pathway, for certain black youth who embrace an anti-school culture, in which a hyper-masculinity that actively encourages embracing the 'road-man mentality' is promoted; literally and virtually.[46] As such a discussion on expressive spaces where they can achieve a sense of belonging is crucial to understanding the school/on road dichotomy because, as was suggested above, they operate within 'alternative cognitive landscapes', where 'on road' success is often coupled with the prevalence of instances of black youth violence. However, as will be explored in the next section, this notion of 'on road' success or even failure, is now being played out in the expressive space that is the virtual, where acts of violence too often translate into the physical world. Unsurprisingly then, within these virtual spaces we witness lamentations as well as reflections of 'life on road' and what it means to be alive, 'I woke up this morning with tears in my eyes, knowing LiL Z is nowhere to be seen. I have to give thanks for what God has done to save me.'[47]

TERRITORIALISM, SILENCE, DEATH AND MOURNING IN THE VIRTUAL

Determining 'failure' or 'success', in the virtual cannot be distanced from the social media sites where these matters are debated, discussed and made visible through young people's online presence.as found in game spaces such as Gangster War, Mafia Wars, Gang War, and Gang Nations. These game spaces feature all forms of extremely graphic violence that is conducted during the acquisition of weapons, drugs, money, mansions and girls/ women. In fact social media has essentially created a new mode of gang activity where public performance and viewership have become just as important as guarding a physical territory. In fact we see an extended or alternative form of territorialism taking place through online convergence, as the Internet as a 'convergence space' is one where gang conflicts amongst young people are intensified and new ones created.[48] Here virtual social worlds are made publicly visible, which often overlap with the real world where many young people do not recognise the embedded histories that are being played out in their day-to-day lives. As a result, contemporary youth who are struggling to find their place in the landscape of Britain often find themselves marginalised, confined to boundaries that ironically result in a shrunken territory. The shrinkage, which is also virtual, happens because of the fear or discomfort that young people experience when travelling 'freely' across London. The result is a form of self-imposed sanction that ends up confining them to the communities in which they live, thereby contributing to forms of 'self-exclusion'.[49] This partially explains why they aim to develop their own sense of security and identity, one where they define their own precepts of inclusion and exclusion, as a form of 'neighbourhood nationalism'.[50] More importantly:

> the long-term implications of being socialised into a culture rooted in networked publics are unknown... teens live in a society whose public life is changing rapidly.[51]

The rapid change that Boyd speaks of is evidenced in the public social media (SoMe) profiles of these young people, through which they express aspects of their young lives.[52] However, what is paramount is that through such profiles, we learn that in addition to the emergence of virtual reputation-building, many are uncomfortable with not being able to freely navigate their neighbouring streets. As a result a form of alternative territorialism, in both real and virtual spaces, has become one of the underlying navigational issues for urban youth. This is because what occurs in the real world is transferred to the virtual and vice versa, which is the current case between groups from Brixton and Peckham. Consequently, this alternate territorialism is a claiming of 'overlapping territories' that in the first instance is borne from the rifts caused by various groups/ gangs representing or 'reppin' an area. This needs consideration because the online acts of violence, far too often exacerbate the existing tensions within and between groups of young people from different communities. For instance, in the case of youths from Peckham and Brixton clashing, the original reasons for the ongoing feuds have become blurred and then remade in ways that make sense in the current moment. Moreover, Brixton and Peckham are not the only boroughs that have 'beef' with each other; Peckham is said to have a history of disputes with 'New Cross, the Old Kent Road and Stockwell'.[53] What is of interest is that these conflicts appear to have no specific point of departure, as such what it means to 'rep' (represent) an area and the mechanisms employed to defend their 'endz' (the areas in which youth live), becomes their key focus. However, as stated above, for many of these young people the history behind these forms of territorialism remains unknown, which means the patterns of behaviour are based on cultural retentions, transferred from generation to generation and taken for granted by each generation of young people. This is evidenced in YCTV2's documentary 'Know Your Endz' which has been written and produced by young people for an audience of their peers. It highlights these postcode rivalries and emphasises the contentions between SW2 and SE15, as well as E8 with NW1. When asked to explain these rivalries, it was suggested:

It's about the street you're from the street your reppin, the street you have grown up in . . . if someone comes into your endz and disrespects your street then you're not going to take it . . . I am not going to let no one disrespect my endz . . . if you disrespect my endz then obviously I am going to come down on you hard . . . if anyone can walk through your area then you have no control of what's happening.[54]

The above reads like a scene from the 1979 American gang movie 'The Warriors'[55] but tellingly speaks to the way in which gangs operate in the real world, or non-virtual space, as discussed extensively elsewhere.[56] Consequently, the way that gangs interact in the virtual has become an increasing area of interest, because the tensions that have emerged as a result of gang rivalry today are transferred and intensified online. For instance, the murders of more than 100 young people through gun and knife crime during 2015, has led some of the young participants in the 'Different Endz' project, to respond to the deaths of friends and family members in the virtual through real concerns over their physical safety. Crucially, whilst working with this cohort, their YouTube and FaceBook profiles curated with images, videos and comments in the form of lamentations, allow access to what these young people are experiencing and expressing. These lamentations shed fresh light on how multiple social media platforms fit into the lives of young people in very interesting ways, as what they gain through such participation is a voice that would normally have been violently silenced. The reason for this is again wrapped up in this notion of 'reppin the endz', because mourning for, or showing sympathy to, the wrong person(s) can have extremely dire consequences that transcend gang rivalries, as innocent family members or friends, are often caught up in the maelstrom.

These concerns were evidenced during the project, whilst searching through the numerous YouTube links that pay tribute to the lives of lost or 'fallen soldiers', from which the young people discovered that they were far from alone in grieving over the deaths of lost ones. Moreover, the participants revealed that many young people living in London, between the ages of 15 to 25, either know or are associated with someone who has died via gun or knife violence. Consequently, YouTube and Facebook are two spaces where notes written to friends and peers who have passed away, have been found to be useful in making sense of their willing or unwilling involvement as innocents, mere associates or gang members. Here, the Internet facilitates young people's use of social media to mourn and engage their peers, through expressions and lamentations that differ from traditional modes of tributes to the dead. In some senses these novel cultural practices amongst young people, form a community of active participants in the emergence of 'digital grave makers' that cater for those who visit sites and spaces for mourning online. Virtual cemeteries and virtual mourning have arisen as a result of our 'electronic culture' and have become a significant part of death and dying rituals amongst young people.[57] There is an increasing field of research that focuses on how death and grief are dealt with on various online platforms and social media, which speaks to 'how the Internet and social media may be changing our ways of grieving and mourning' and our concepts of death and bereavement.[58]

Haley, a young person from the project, brought forward an explanation of the term 'Different Endz' or different ends, to explain how it speaks to 'changes' in the process of grieving and mourning that highlights the importance of the virtual mourning space. She commented on the sanctity and preciousness of life as featured in many of the online tributes (see below), whilst acknowledging the abrupt ending of the lives of the young people she referred to as 'the fallen soldiers'; young people who were personally known to her who have been killed on the street. The significance of discussing the death of 'fallen soldiers', was to encourage the young people to openly discuss their views on gun and knife violence, and reflect on their own lives and life chances in their local communities. Haley's reference and tribute to the 'fallen soldiers' spoke to the way in which memorial tributes of 'fallen soldiers', were not only visited online, but they also offered insight into the sentiments behind the sudden loss of a young life, where somewhat disturbingly:

> Killing each other may not be the way forward as there is no guarantee that your name will make the headlines... so it's really about the number of hits an online profile gets.[59]

The above partially explains the growth of these online networks where mourning is central, as evidenced in the tributes made to 15 year old Zac Olumegbon, affectionately known as Lil Zac from Tulse Hill, south-east London. Zac was said to be a member of the TN1[60] (Trust no one) gang and was stabbed to death by rivals from the GAS (Grind and Stack/ Guns and Shanks) gang outside the Park Campus School he attended in West Norwood, south-east London. Young people identi-fied two R.I.P. video tributes to LiL Zac, produced by Maximum Recordings: one clip filmed on an estate in Tulse Hill, has a total of 73,350 hits with 626 likes and 13 dislikes, whilst the other clip has a total of 114,842 hits, 695 likes and 19 dislikes. Yet whilst the perfor-mers in the video clip make clear that 'TN1 is not a gang but they are family', what emerges from these productions are the manner in which young people choose to express their feelings of hurt, loss and confu-sion as a result of the level of violence that occurs amongst themselves and their peers. However, these hits represent and symbolise the vast increase in the ways young people are able to reach large audiences at a rapid speed, in the relative safety of their homes. Although, despite the 'false sense of security' they gain from marking territory in the virtual, a perhaps unforeseen result of their online presence is an uncanny sense of value for life, as displayed in many of the R.I.P. videos they observed.[61] Tellingly, the R.I.P. videos attributed to another 'fallen soldier', Jozey–Joel Morgan, share exactly the same sentiments. Jozey, a 17-year-old at the time of his death, grew up in Southwark, south-east London and moved to Lambeth during his mid-teens. He was affiliated with the

GAS gang and later died, not through gun or knife crime, but in a car crash. Yet at his funeral, 'gunmen from an unknown rival gang' were reported to have opened fire, killing 21-year-old Ronnie Azezur Khan, a funeral attendee and friend of Jozy.[62]

From the above it is clear that the dangers of attending a funeral of anyone caught up in youth violence are real and explains why social media facilitates grieving and mourning 'publicly', as a viable alternative for these young people. In this way the manner in which they conceptualise death and bereavement, as heavily associated with say for instance gang culture, sheds light on an increase in social media use, where virtual cemeteries have become a symbol of alternative youth expression. Thus with the advent of technology and the enabling of young people to create elaborate online profiles, expressing their feelings and opinions about the harsh realities and consequences of youth crime and violence, through various forms of media, continues to grow. Tributes are therefore made and shared publicly along with the views, feelings, hopes and aspirations from friends of the deceased, which allows us to witness these youthful constructions of self, through these R.I.P. tributes that become both a means of self-promotion as well as a space of autonomous mourning.

CONCLUSION

The chapter has made an argument for understanding how it is that young people share their lives in public and alternative public arenas, as a conscious choice, making explicit the links between social media, gang culture and youth crime. By doing so and actively listening to voices that may be silent, or have been silenced for one reason or other, provides an opportunity to make sense of the situations and difficulties they often find themselves in. It also allows us to witness the shift in how young people respond to their rapidly changing environments, the physical and the virtual, countering the notion that they are generally apathetic to their social situations. Far too often they find themselves legislated for, and done to, but generally they are ignored, not listened to and therefore remain largely unheard in the wider public arena. As such, where young people share their own musings on current affairs, or events that directly impact their lives in some way, shape or form, it is important for us to listen to and understand them in the confines of their expressive spaces.

When these virtual social worlds are made publicly visible, we notice an overlap with the real world, where many young people do not recognise the embedded histories that are being played out in their day-to-day lives. As a result, contemporary youth who are struggling to find their place in the landscape of Britain, often find themselves marginalised and confined to boundaries not of their own making; those that have been passed down generationally which ironically result in them contesting a shrunken territory; their turf. The novel aspect of the shrinkage is it now extends to the virtual, due to the fear or discomfort that young people experience when travelling 'freely' across London, which results in a form of self-imposed sanction that ends up confining them to the communities in which they live, thereby contributing to forms of 'self-exclusion'.[63]

The above partially explains why they aim to develop their own sense of security and identity, one where they define their own precepts of inclusion and exclusion, as a form of 'neighbourhood nationalism'.[64] Consequently, for many young people loyalty is tied to their territory, resulting in an uncanny 'postcode pride', which has a different set of morals based on pride and respect. On one hand the area or postcode is honoured by those who live there, on the other the postcode is used as a means to build a 'reputation', where respect is often earned through intimidation, extreme violence and fear. For this reason, consideration has been given to how young people navigate their neighbourhoods and how exactly it is that they are utilising these platforms as life and death spaces to communicate their positions and emotions. However, virtual reputation building has become a strategy for many young people to navigate their cities with confidence, marking out safe and unsafe spaces both in the real and the virtual worlds.

Moreover, the above enables us to view and experience a new mode of connectivity created by young people, where public performance and increasing viewership, demonstrable by the number of viewings a post has, have become just as important as making known the territorialisation of a physical space. Similarly, through this work we have seen that young people utilise the social media sites to express their emotions, especially when it comes to mourning the 'fallen soldiers', creating a common space amongst them for discussions of loss and condolence. It is therefore clear that, through the idea of turf war, repping the ends and gaining respect, young people organise their own structures, systems and hierarchies as a way of gaining some level of control over their lives. As a result we learn that such spaces have somewhat replaced, and in other instances enhanced, traditional face-to-face friendships or rivalries, as the 'virtual' acts as an autonomous space where young voices can be 'heard'.

Notes

1. J. Pitts, *Reluctant Gangsters: The Changing Face of Youth Crime* (London, 2013), p. 55 (Pitts 2013).
2. K. Duncan, *Sexting 101: Is Your Teen Sex-Texting?* (London, 2010) (Duncan 2010).
3. D. Boyd, *Why Youth Love Social Network Sites: The Role of Networked Publics in Teenage Social Life: Youth Identity and Digital Media* (Cambridge, 2008). Virtual world: an environment that allows people to share and access personal content online (Boyd 2008).
4. See L. Shedletsky, *Cases on Online Discussion and Interaction: Experiences and Outcomes* (Hershey, 2010) (Shedletsky 2010).
5. 'Different Endz' was the title of a youth arts project held at the 198 Contemporary Arts and Learning in 2015. 198CAL is an informal arts education and gallery space in Lambeth, London. The project was funded by Media Box.
6. Computer-technician-applied parental control to prevent young people accessing violent and inappropriate websites.
7. 'Polytricks' or 'partytricks' are Jamaican terms for an awareness of the dangerous games politicians play with ordinary people's lives when supposedly working on behalf of the masses.
8. L. Wilkins, *Social Deviance: Social Policy, Action and Research* (London, 1964) (Wilkins 1964); S. Cohen, *Folk Devils and Moral Panics* (London, 1972) (Cohen 1972).
9. E. Carrabine, *Crime, Culture and the Media* (Cambridge, 2008), p. 55 (Carrabine 2008).
10. W. A. Henry, 'Conceptualisation and effects of social exclusion, racism and discrimination and coping strategies of individuals and families', in C. Hylton and B. Oshien (eds.), *Black Families in Britain as a Site of Struggle* (Manchester, 2010) (Henry 2010); K. Price, *Endless Pressure: A Study of West Indian Life-styles in Bristol* (London, 1979) (Price 1979).
11. For an insight into this perspective of black life, see P. Stanislas, 'The cultural politics of African-Caribbean and West African families in the UK', in Hylton and Oshien (eds.), *Black Families in Britain as a Site of Struggle*.
12. J. Muncie, G. Hughes and E. McLaughlin (eds.), *Youth Justice: Critical Readings* (London, 2002), p. 324 (Muncie et al. 2002).
13. 'Blair blames spate of murders on black culture', *The Guardian* (2007): http://www.theguardian.com [accessed 12 April 2007].

14. L. Back, *New Ethnicities and Urban Culture: Racisms and Multiculture in Young Lives* (London, 1996) (Back 1996).

15. 'Oliver Letwin blamed "bad moral attitudes" for widespread rioting in black areas', *Daily Telegraph*: http://www.telegraph.co.uk [accessed 30 December 2015].

16. S. A. Ashton, 'The Impact of Cultural Heritage Programmes on the Self-concept of Black Male Prisoners in England' Unpublished MPhil Thesis, Cambridge University, 2008, p. 3 (Ashton 2008).

17. G. John, *Taking a Stand* (Manchester, 2006), p. 210 (John 2006).

18. H. V. Carby, *Culture in Babylon: Black Britain and African America* (London, 1999), p. 189 (Carby 1999); W. 'Lez' Henry, *What The Deejay Said: A Critique From The Street!* (London, 1996) ('Lez' 1996).

19. 'Oliver Letwin's racist 1980s views are beyond the pale now', *Independent* http://www.independent.co.uk [accessed 30 December 2016].

20. Jason, Personal Communication (2015), Different Endz, 198 Contemporary Arts and Learning, London.

21. For more on this perspective see A. N. Wilson, 'The political psychology of Black consciousness', in his *The Falsification of Afrikan Consciousness: Eurocentric History, Psychiatry and the Politics of White Supremacy*, New York, 1993) (Wilson 1993).

22. Ashton, 'The Impact of Cultural Heritage Programmes', p. 4. See also W. Henry, 'Projecting the natural: language and citizenship in outernational culture', in J. Besson and K. Fog Olwig (eds.), *Caribbean Narratives Of Belonging: Fields Of Relations, Sites Of Identity* (Oxford, 2005) (Henry 2005).

23. 'GCSE pupils to be taught that the nation's earliest inhabitants were Africans who were in Britain before the English', *Daily Mail*: http://www.dailymail.co.uk [accessed 9 January 2016].

24. a. giddens, *over to you, mr. brown: how labour can win again* (cambridge, 2007), p. 41 (Giddens 2007); p. dorey, 'A new direction or another false dawn? David Cameron and the Crisis of British Conservatism', *British Politics*, 2 (2007), 137–66 (Dorey 2007).

25. B. Osgerby, *Youth Media* (London, 2004), p. 98 (Osgerby 2004).

26. C. Alexander, *(Re)thinking 'Gangs'* (London, 2008), p. 14 (Alexander 2008).

27. See W. A. Henry, 'Shades of consciousness: from Jamaica to the UK', in R. Hall (ed.), *The Melanin Millennium: Skin Color as the 21st-Century International Discourse* (Michigan, 2012) (Henry 2012).

28. Jason, Personal Communication (2015). Ps is another term for money.

29. S. Hallsworth, '"That's life innit": A British perspective on guns, crime and social order, *Criminology and Criminal Justice*, 9 (2009), 359–77 (Hallsworth 2009).

30. D. Massey, J. Allen and S. Pile, *City Worlds (Understanding Cities)* (London, 2000), p. 126 (Massey et al. 2000).
31. Pitts, *Reluctant Gangsters*, p. 170.
32. Efrem, *R.I.P Zac-Full Documentary 1–2* (London, 2012) (Efrem 2012).
33. S. H. Decker and D. C. Pyrooz, *The Handbook of Gangs* (New Jersey, 2015), p. 167 (Decker and Pyrooz 2015).
34. S. Mullings-Lawrence, '"POST CODE WAR": Representations of locality and landscapes of danger, belonging and understanding', *Postcolonial Text 8*: http://postcolonial.org [accessed 19 September 2015].
35. W. Henry, 'Dr Lez Henry on youth crime', *BBC News 24* (2009) (Henry 2009).
36. 'Peel Dem' is a Jamaican take on the African-American term 'peel their cap', meaning shoot them in the head.
37. I. A. Spergel, *The Youth Gang Problem: A Community Approach* (New York, 1995), p. 98 (Spergel 1995).
38. Massey, Allen and Pile, *City Worlds*, p. 127.
39. Henry, *What The Deejay Said*; A. Gunter, *Growing Up Bad? Black Youth, 'Road' Culture and Badness in an East London Neighbourhood* (London, 2010) (Henry 2010).
40. A. Silvestri, M. Oldfield, P. Squires and R. Grimshaw, *Young People, Knives and Guns: A Comprehensive Review, Analysis and Critique of Gun and Knife Crime Strategies* (London, 2009), p. 45 (Silvestri et al. 2009).
41. Rice n Peas Films, *BANG! BANG! In Da Manor* (London, 2007) (Rice n Peas Films 2007).
42. See D. Hobbs, *Lush Life: Constructing Organized Crime in the UK* (Oxford, 2013) (Hobbs 2013).
43. Back, *New Ethnicities and Urban Culture*, p. 250.
44. C. Krinsky (ed.), *The Ashgate Research Companion to Moral Panics* (Farnham, 2013), p. 13 (Krinsky 2013).
45. Pitts, *Reluctant Gangsters*, p. 65.
46. Henry, *What The Deejay Said*.
47. Baby R, Gunna G, Kayoss FT. Shanni, *R.I.P ZAC* (Maximum Recordings, 2011) (Baby et al. 2011).
48. Decker and Pyrooz, *The Handbook of Gangs*, 168.
49. Silvestri et al., *Young People, Knives and Guns*, p. 23.
50. Back, *New Ethnicities and Urban Culture*, p. 47.
51. Boyd, *Why Youth Love Social Network Sites*, p. 22.
52. Online Identities created by young people through avatars, snap chat and Facebook profiles.
53. See Mullings-Lawrence, '"POST CODE WAR"'.
54. YCTV, *Know Your Endz* (London, 2016).
55. W. Hill (dir.), *The Warriors* (1979).

56. Pitts, *Reluctant Gangsters*.
57. J. M. DeGroot, 'Maintaining relational continuity with the deceased on Facebook', *Omega Journal of Death and Dying*, 65 (2015), 195–212 (DeGroot 2015).
58. B. Carroll and K. Landry, 'Logging on and letting out: Using online social networks to grieve and to mourn', *Bulletin of Science Technology and Society*, 30 (2010), 341–49 (Carroll and Landry 2010).
59. Haley, Personal Communication (2015), Different Endz, 198 Contemporary Arts and Learning, London.
60. P. Cheston, 'Gang thugs who knifed A level student 14 times in back face life', *Evening Standard*: http://www.standard.co.uk/ [accessed 17 December 2012].
61. Efrem, *R.I.P Zac-Full Documentary*.
62. P. Peachy, 'Azezur "Ronnie" Khan: Met to face scrutiny over failure to prevent gangland funeral', *The Independent* (2016): http://www.independent.co.uk [accessed 17 October 2015] (Peachy 2016).
63. Silvestri et al., *Young People, Knives and Guns*, p. 23.
64. Back, *New Ethnicities and Urban Culture*, p. 47.

References

C. Alexander, *(Re)thinking 'Gangs'* (London, 2008), p. 14.

S. A. Ashton, 'The Impact of Cultural Heritage Programmes on the Self-concept of Black Male Prisoners in England', Unpublished MPhil Thesis, Cambridge University, 2008, p. 3.

Baby R., Gunna G., Kayoss F. T. Shanni, *R.I.P ZAC* (Maximum Recordings, 2011).

L. Back, *New Ethnicities and Urban Culture: Racisms and Multiculture in Young Lives* (London, 1996).

D. Boyd, *Why Youth Love Social Network Sites: The Role of Networked Publics in Teenage Social Life:* Youth Identity and *Digital Media* (Cambridge, 2008).

H. V. Carby, *Culture in Babylon: Black Britain and African America* (London, 1999), p. 189.

E. Carrabine, *Crime, Culture and the Media* (Cambridge, 2008), p. 55.

B. Carroll and K. Landry, 'Logging On and Letting Out: Using Online Social Networks to Grieve and to Mourn', *Bulletin of Science Technology and Society*, 30 (2010), 341–49.

P. Cheston, 'Gang thugs who knifed A level student 14 times in back face life', *Evening Standard*: http://www.standard.co.uk/ [accessed 17 December 2012].

S. Cohen, *Folk Devils and Moral Panics* (London, 1972).

S. H. Decker and D. C. Pyrooz, *The Handbook of Gangs* (New Jersey, 2015), p. 167.

J. M. DeGroot, 'Maintaining Relational Continuity with the Deceased on Facebook', *Omega Journal of Death and Dying*, 65 (2015), 195–212.

P. Dorey, 'A New Direction or Another False Dawn? David Cameron and the Crisis of British Conservatism', *British Politics*, 2 (2007), 137–66.

K. Duncan, *Sexting 101: Is Your Teen Sex-Texting?* (London, 2010).

Efrem, *R.I.P Zac-Full Documentary 1–2* (London, 2012).

A. Giddens, *Over to you, Mr. Brown: How Labour Can Win Again* (Cambridge, 2007), p. 41.

S. Hallsworth, 'That's life innit': A British Perspective on Guns, Crime and Social Order, *Criminology and Criminal Justice*, 9 (2009), 359–77.

Henry, *What The Deejay Said*; A. Gunter, *Growing Up Bad? Black Youth, 'Road' Culture and Badness in an East London Neighbourhood* (London, 2010).

W. Henry, 'Projecting the Natural: Language and Citizenship in Outernational Culture', in J. Besson and K. Fog Olwig (eds.), *Caribbean Narratives Of Belonging: Fields Of Relations, Sites Of Identity* (Oxford, 2005).

W. Henry, 'Dr Lez Henry on youth crime', *BBC News 24* (2009).

W. A. Henry, 'Conceptualisation and Effects of Social Exclusion, Racism and Discrimination and Coping Strategies of Individuals and Families', in C. Hylton and B. Oshien (eds.), *Black Families in Britain as a Site of Struggle* (Manchester, 2010).

W. A. Henry, 'Shades of consciousness: from Jamaica to the UK', in R. Hall (ed), *The Melanin Millennium: Skin Color as the 21st Century International Discourse* (Michigan, 2012).

D. Hobbs, *Lush Life: Constructing Organized Crime in the UK* (Oxford, 2013).

G. John, *Taking a Stand* (Manchester, 2006), p. 210.

C. Krinsky (ed), *The Ashgate Research Companion to Moral Panics* (Farnham, 2013), p. 13.

W. 'Lez' Henry, *What The Deejay Said: A Critique From The Street!* (London, 1996).

D. Massey, J. Allen and S. Pile, *City Worlds (Understanding Cities)* (London, 2000), p. 126.

J. Muncie, G. Hughes and E. McLaughlin (eds.), *Youth Justice: Critical Readings* (London, 2002), p. 324.

B. Osgerby, *Youth Media* (London, 2004), p. 98.

P. Peachy, 'Azezur "Ronnie" Khan: Met to face scrutiny over failure to prevent gangland funeral', *The Independent*, (2016): http://www.independent.co.uk [accessed 17 October 2015].

J. Pitts, *Reluctant Gangsters: The Changing Face of Youth Crime* (London, 2013), p. 55.

K. Price, *Endless Pressure: A Study of West Indian Life-styles in Bristol* (London, 1979).

Rice n Peas Films, *BANG! BANG! In Da Manor* (London, 2007).

L. Shedletsky, *Cases on Online Discussion and Interaction: Experiences and Outcomes* (Hershey, 2010).

A. Silvestri, M. Oldfield, P. Squires and R. Grimshaw, *Young People, Knives and Guns: A Comprehensive Review, Analysis and Critique of Gun and Knife Crime Strategies* (London, 2009), p. 45.

I. A. Spergel, *The Youth Gang Problem: A Community Approach* (New York, 1995), p. 98.

L. Wilkins, *Social Deviance: Social Policy, Action and Research* (London, 1964).

A. N. Wilson, *The Falsification of Afrikan Consciousness: Eurocentric History, Psychiatry and the Politics of White Supremacy* (New York, 1993).

William 'Lez' Henry is Senior Lecturer in Criminology and Sociology at the School of Law and Criminology, University of West London. He has written widely on the counter-cultures of the African Diaspora, alternative educational arenas, youth crime and violence, race and representation in the media, whiteness, music as politics and continues to deejay under the moniker of Lezlee Lyrix.

Sireita Mullings-Lawrence is Lecturer in the Department of Applied Social Studies at the University of Bedfordshire, Luton, UK. Her work, as a visual sociologist, explores the negotiations, compromises and tensions that exist within youth culture and youth arts spaces. Theoretically, she draws upon post colonial studies, race and representation, youth crime and justice, to understand social exclusion/inclusion, belonging and areas of safety and danger in contemporary city spaces.

INDEX

© The Author(s) 2017
K. Gildart et al. (eds.), *Youth Culture and Social Change*,
Palgrave Studies in the History of Subcultures and Popular Music,
DOI 10.1057/978-1-137-52911-4

Lightning Source UK Ltd.
Milton Keynes UK
UKOW06n2300301017
311900UK00002B/66/P